Maker of Champions

Sylvia Low Tiffany

Published by Sylvia Low Tiffany, 2024.

While every precaution has been taken in the preparation of this book, the publisher assumes no responsibility for errors or omissions, or for damages resulting from the use of the information contained herein.

MAKER OF CHAMPIONS

First edition. November 30, 2024.

Copyright © 2024 Sylvia Low Tiffany.

ISBN: 979-8227275950

Written by Sylvia Low Tiffany.

Table of Contents

Prologue | Reflections by John Ramos 1

Chapter 1 | The early years 5

Chapter 2 | Hector Hatch 19

Chapter 3 | Ern McQuillan 25

Chapter 4 | 1975 – Ramos Boxing Club 35

Chapter 5 | 1976 – Making of champions 43

Chapter 6 | 1977 – International fights 73

Chapter 7 | 1978 – The Commonwealth title fights 103

Chapter 8 | 1979 – Winds of change 147

Chapter 9 | 1980 – End of an era 209

Epilogue | Final words by John Ramos 255

Acknowledgement 263

Bibliography 265

For Margaret (1953 - 2005).

"This is a great account of a compelling slice of Fiji's boxing history, from a significant personality of the Fijian boxing fraternity. Notably, it is also the first book to provide a historical account, of any sort, of boxing in Fiji. It reminded me of all that is possible and frustrating and wonderful about sport in Fiji."

– Greg Madhavan

Prologue
Reflections by John Ramos

In my seventieth year, I found myself reflecting on my life as one does, I suppose at such milestones. I realised that I have been blessed with many great successes as well as disappointments but to have had those memories fills me with a sense of gratitude and a sense of a life lived well.

I was born Mari Muttu in Vunadilo or what is now known as Howell Road in Suva, Fiji on December 16, 1944, to Subramani Nair, a cook, and Patamma, a housewife. I became John Marimuttu when I entered professional boxing in 1966 and later adopted the Ramos name after one of my all-time favourite fighters, Ultiminio "Sugar" Ramos, who I will share more on later.

My father was born in Nadi on June 16, 1916, to Mutamma and Kunji Nair from Kerala, India and my mother was born in Navua on December 31, 1918, to Subamma and Mimaiya Reddy from Andhra Pradesh, India.

My parents were first generation Fiji-born children of indentured labourers who were brought over from India between 1879 and 1916. We were a family of 10 children – five boys and five girls – I was the fourth oldest. My eldest brother Narayan passed away when he was a toddler. His death left my brother Adi as the eldest surviving, followed by my sister Evelyn (Dhannu), myself then my younger sisters and brothers – Sharda (d.2010), Surya, Chandra, Raymond (d.2012), Rohini and Vincent (Vasu).

As a young boy growing up in Vunidilo I never imagined that I would in some small way, contribute to the life of boxing in Fiji or that the club I started, Ramos Boxing Club, would resonate so long and so fondly in the hearts and minds of all Fijians in the years following.

For those born before Fiji's independence, those memories would be present as experienced or as recollections by a father, a brother, an uncle or even a mother, sister, or aunt who watched the fights of Fiji's only Golden Boy, Sakaraia Ve or Wili "Pony" Tarika or any one of the many other colourful fighters that stepped out of Ramos Boxing Club including Setareki

Bolatawa, Isikeli Veitala, Viliame Tabualevu, Anthony Naidu, Kaminieli Vunimasi and Tevita Tui. Bolatawa and Veitala were former amateur champions who later became Fiji Boxing Council middleweight and light-middleweight champions respectively

To get to that level of success in boxing in Fiji requires resourcefulness, commitment, passion and good people around you for support. I was very, very fortunate to have them all in my corner.

The period between 1975 and 1980 could be described as the golden age of boxing for Fiji. It happened at a time when Fiji, with her newly minted independence, searched to carve out her identity as a people. Ramos Boxing Club with its multi-ethnic and multi-cultural blend of colourful and gutsy fighters, gave Fiji a common identity to rally behind. And they did in the thousands as witnessed by the crowds that showed up at the fights where Ramos fighters appeared. All told, this had been possible because of the many people who shared with me their time, friendship, resources as well as their love for boxing.

Ramos Boxing Club also gave back to the community. Through the many exhibition boxing matches and participation at the different church and charity events, I made sure that we showed some social responsibility and respect to the fans by also contributing to their village, church or social development projects whenever we could. We travelled to Vanua Levu and around Viti Levu and held these exhibitions for schools, churches, temples and civil society organisations such as the Suva Crippled Children's School to help them raise much needed funds.

I fondly remember the Hibiscus Festival in August 1977 where we dressed up a flatbed truck, loaded up our boxers in a boxing ring and had them spar along the length of the procession route from the Suva Market to Albert Park. The crowd went wild for the ringside exhibition they saw, and it was gratifying to see and hear their response.

This was our way of saying thank you to the fans who supported us. These events also allowed our champions to take their titles into the communities so that the men, women and children could see their achievements and meet the boxers in person. Ve was always very popular, and he showed the fans respect during these meet-and-greets.

I told these stories to my daughter, Sylvia, when she visited me in Vancouver to celebrate my seventieth birthday on December 16, 2014. It was then that the idea for this book was first raised. I wanted to share my love for boxing and share a few reflections on how the sport can be made great in Fiji once again.

Deep in my heart I know that boxing in Fiji can be returned to its rightful place of interest. We need people who care and are passionate about growing boxing, showing respect for the rules that govern the sport and have the administrative skills required to direct it down the right path.

John Ramos and his granddaughter Cianna Colwell (December 2014, Sylvia Low Tiffany Collection).

Chapter 1
The early years

"Growing up in a family of 10 children had its moments. My father was a public servant who worked as the head chef at the Fiji School of Medicine in Tamavua, Suva, so he was gone very early each day. My mother was the homemaker and the disciplinarian," recalls Ramos.

"Even though we lived frugally, there was never any shortage of food or love amongst us. My parents would always make sure that we had enough to eat and that we did what was expected of us in terms of chores around the house.

"To keep the family going, my father started a vegetable garden up on the hill behind the Howell Road property. He planted a variety of vegetables – pumpkins, long bean, egg plants, spinach, okra, dalo, cassava, breadfruit and a whole lot more. For the boys, our job was to make sure the garden was cleaned and every so often, we'd help our father with preparing the garden beds or fetching whatever our mother wanted to cook for our meals.

"School for me was further up of what was then known as Baniwai Road (now Rewa Street), a two kilometre walk to Samabula Government School which is now called Suva Primary School. I left school after completing class seven to help my father and older brother Adi who were the only breadwinners in our family at the time.

"As I was so young, finding steady non-manual work was hard so I, and a group of my friends got together and managed to get a job as newspaper sellers. I'd wake up at 4am each day and walk/run from Howell Road to Gandhi News Store located at the Stinson's Limited building. If you can recall where that was, you're probably as old as I am. At the time, Stinson's Ltd owned the Prouds franchise which was memorably situated at the Prouds Triangle by the infamous *ivi* (Tahitian chestnut) tree at the junction of Renwick Road and Scott Street. That *ivi* tree, was a popular gathering spot for people in Suva.

"I'd collect about 30 copies of the paper and make my way to the bus stand where I'd wait for the buses to arrive and wave a copy calling out, 'Fiji Times! Fiji Times!' By 7am my copies would be sold out and for my efforts I'd make about five shillings (about 50 cents in the current currency). When that was done, I'd wait around at the bus stand to see if I could get other work.

"My second job came in the form of a Shore Buses Ltd (SBL) driver named Arthur Edwards. Arthur drove the Lami-Suva route. He arrived at the bus stand at about 6am each day. He was a kindly man who told me that if I hung around till 10am I could earn a bit extra by washing and cleaning his bus when he was done with his shift. I'd hang around and at 10am catch a ride with Arthur to the SBL depot in Lami where I'd get on with my cleaning job. After an hour, I'd get another two shillings (20 cents) and be good for the rest of the day.

"My bus cleaning efforts did not go unnoticed, another driver by the name of Manu liked the work I did with Arthur's bus and offered me a third job doing the same for him. My bonus at this job was that I could keep any coins that I found on the floor. Working kept me out of trouble as a teenager. The money I earned, about a pound ($2.50) a week, also helped my father and older brother Adi take care of our family."

SBL at the time was owned by the late Ragunath Singh, a businessman and avid golfer. A former wrestler in his younger days, Mr Singh started his bus operation enterprise with just two buses back in 1947. As the industry became regulated in the 1950s, he along with a few business partners formed SBL in 1958. He later bought out his business partners and became the sole owner, a business that remains with his family until this day (Fiji Development Bank, 2012).

"In 1978, when Ramos Boxing Club was well established, I received a phone call from Mr Singh, who as it turned out, was an avid boxing fan himself. 'John,' he said, 'I'd like to invite you and your wife Margaret to dinner at my place.' I was taken aback and pleasantly surprised by this very kind invitation as Mr Singh had always been someone I had tremendous respect for. I accepted his invitation and over dinner I told him how I worked at his depot cleaning buses in my younger days. He was shocked by my admission.

"'What a story!' he said. 'And look where you are today! You're sitting here, having a meal with me in a much higher position.' It was over this meal that we discussed boxing and cemented a business partnership which saw Mr Singh come on board as a promoter for several international bouts with Mexican boxers from Miami, Florida for Sakaraia Ve and Wili Tarika.

"While I did the newspaper selling, bus washing and other odds and ends to earn a shilling, my older brother Adi was working as a junior clerk at Island Industries, a copra buying subsidiary of what was to become Carpenters Group based at Walu Bay. My bus-washing career soon expanded into a short stint as a mechanic until 1962 when at 17, Adi helped me secure a junior clerk role at Island Industries. Adi was the junior accountant at the time, and I remember being interviewed by a Mr Henry Lestro.

"I must have done well at the interview because I landed my first office job as a junior clerk. Here, I progressively worked my way over the next 20 years to senior costing clerk. It was also here that I met the legendary Hector Hatch, who helped me shape my amateur boxing career.

"In 1959, my older sister Evelyn married a man I considered a giant amongst men, Joseph Mariappa. Joe stood at five feet nine inches tall and weighed in at about 230 pounds. A carpenter by trade, Joe was a body builder as well as a powerlifter. Joe was also Catholic and for a Hindu family, which my family were, this did not cause as much of a stir as I would have thought at the time. I imagine that Joe being the kind-hearted and generous person that he was, always showed concern for those less fortunate than he. This mattered more to my parents than which faith he belonged to," Ramos remembers.

"Joe's father was a chef as well and worked with my father at the Fiji School of Medicine in Tamavua, so we knew his family well at the time.

"After Joe and Evelyn married, Joe moved into our family home in Howell Road, Suva where he set up his gym in the space at the bottom flat of the family house which was being constructed. Amongst the bags of cement, gravel, sand and piles of bricks, Joe set out his free weights and hung up a sandbag for his boxing workouts. Joe trained for hours each day to reach competition level.

"His dedication and passion for these two sports, saw him compete at the national level. His passions also extended to other sports such as boxing, soccer and rugby.

"One day while Joe was doing his daily workout, I decided that I would give the punching bag a go. My 14-year-old scrawny self, decided to wrap my fists with elastic bandage, stepped up to the bag and started throwing punches at it from all angles. I rained punches on the bag as if it was going to attack me. Joe watched me for a few minutes with an amused look on his face until I puffed myself out.

"'Do you want to be a boxer?' he asked. 'Yes,' I said. 'Well, if you want to be a boxer that is not the way to go about it.' He then showed me the correct way to stand, how to place my hands close to my sides and to throw punches properly. I'd have to say his way was so much better. My knuckles didn't feel as if they were going to dislocate with each blow. I kept this going with Joe every afternoon as he did his weights and work out.

"Joe, in seeing my growing enthusiasm for boxing, took me to watch my first ever live boxing match that same year. The fight was for the Fiji lightweight fight between the great champ from Savusavu, Bola Newton, and the challenger, Govind Sami, of Tamavua in Suva.

"The fight was a 15x3 minutes-round held at the open-air York Stadium on Toorak Road, promoted by an uncle of Joe's I remember as a Mr Gopal from Flagstaff who was kind enough to give us ringside tickets to watch these two gladiators.

"York Stadium was a car park owned by Mr Gopal in Spring St, Toorak. The premises cordoned off by a corrugated iron fence and had an open-air seating arrangement inside. He dubbed it York Stadium himself and was a venue where he hosted several boxing promotions in the '50s and '60s.

"Bola was a colourful boxer and quite entertaining to watch. He and Joe knew each other quite well from the time Joe spent working in Taveuni. When I met Bola in Savusavu again in 1977 he said, 'Ramos, keep up the good work that you're doing with boxing.'

"Bola won that fight, over 15 hard-fought rounds, on points. I left that fight, hooked on boxing. I remember looking at the leather and shield-mounted belt that Bola retained. I didn't know then that 17 years later in October 1976, Ve in only his ninth professional fight, would knockout the then title holder, Balwant Singh, in the fourth round for that same belt. As I held that title in my hand, I saw Bola's name engraved on the side shield mounting and thought to myself, 'What a blessing to see this belt now hanging on my living room wall'.

"'Big Joe' as I called him, migrated to England in 1961 with my sister and their two young children, Michael and Margaret, following in 1966. He was such a profound influence in my early days as an amateur boxer, always supportive with his constant words of encouragement. Even later, as an adult when I had my own club, Joe visited our gym in 1977 which was based at the Laucala Bay Hangar (now the Maritime School) in Suva at the time. He met with all my boxers, and he said to me that he never imagined that I would have taken boxing in Fiji to what it was at the time. He offered me his blessing and told my fighters to remain dedicated because they had a good person to lead them. I was very touched by his kind words, and it meant a lot to me.

"Even after he returned to London, Joe would call every now and then to see how I was going, reminding me always to keep my faith in God and to continue to work hard. That was the kind of man he was, and we continued to stay in contact even after I moved to Canada in 1985, so it was devastating to receive that phone call from my sister in the late evening of October 31, 2014, (1 November in London) to be told that he had passed away after a short illness at home at the age 80. A fitting date in keeping with his faith as 1 November is All Saints Day on the Catholic calendar. It was an honour and a privilege to deliver the eulogy at his mass of the resurrection before 200 close family and friends.

"Joe's legacy didn't end with him. His oldest grandson and namesake, Adrian Joseph Mariappa, who played Premier League football (2005-2020) in England and an international for Jamaica (where his mother, Julia is from) having played for Watford, Reading and Crystal Palace football clubs."

Howell Road was a mixed-race community. Right next door to the Nair family home on Howell Road lived the Low family. They had moved into the neighbourhood sometime in 1967. The father Tom, came to Fiji from Canton (now called Guangzhou), China some 20 odd years earlier and worked as a short order cook in a Suva restaurant and the mother Jane, a part-Samoan/Ceylonese woman, worked in a Suva hotel. They had 10 children, of whom Maragaret, the oldest girl caught the eye of a young Mari

Muttu and unbeknownst to both families, began seeing each other quietly not long after the Lows moved in next door.

Inter-racial dating at the time was not common and those who found themselves in such a situation often faced ostracism by one or both families. Coming from a conservative Hindu family, the Nairs had already dealt with welcoming a Catholic-Indian son-in-law but for a Catholic, yet non-Indian girl to marry into their family, would prove to be quite another matter. The Low parents too weren't without their reservations when the relationship became known, fearing the difficulties that their oldest daughter may face marrying into such a conservative family.

Thankfully, the children of both families had gone to or were attending multiracial and multicultural schools at the time and had a more tolerant view of the relationship and it was they who made the adjustments to accommodate their new in-law easier.

Sylvia, their oldest daughter was born on May 10, 1969, and two months later, on July 30, 1969, Mari Muttu and Margaret Low married and started their new life together out of a bottom flat at an uncle's house on Baniwai Road (now called Rewa St).

With baby Sylvia being cared for by Ramos's aunt upstairs, Margaret soon found work as a cashier at a large retailer in Suva, Mari Muttu continued with his clerking job at Island Industries. The new couple had their good and bad days. It was a lot for the young Margaret to adjust to and with a husband who was involved as he was in getting his professional boxing career off the ground, she juggled her new job, raising a child and trying to meet the other demands placed on her as a boxer's wife. There were many rows and disagreements in the early years but somehow, they managed to make it through the brief separations that became a hallmark of their time together.

"Boxing wasn't my only passion growing up. I also played soccer for Green Field and the Sangam soccer clubs in the mid-'60s alongside my ambitions for a professional boxing career. Soccer helped build my stamina as well as strength in my legs which worked well for me whenever I got into the ring," Ramos remembers.

"My dream was to play for Suva and in 1965 the first part of that dream came true when I was selected as a colt to represent Suva in the under-21 side. In 1967, the second part of my dream materialised when I was selected to represent the senior Suva team at the inter-district tournament which was also held in Lautoka. Following that great hoorah, my soccer playing days soon ended because of a recurring injury to my knee from the weekly competitions playing for Sangam.

"I had just turned to professional boxing the year before and my manager at the time, Raman Nair arranged my first professional fight with promoter Raj Kumar at the Kamla Theatre in Sigatoka against a hard-hitting and wild-swinging slugger named Tota Ram, also of Sigatoka. That fight ended in a draw. Sadly, a few years later Raman died in a car accident.

"Also, an inspiration to my boxing ambitions was the exploits of boxing heavyweight and legend, Leweni Waqa who happened to also live in my neighbourhood. The first time I met Leweni was in 1963 when he came to Suva, to live with relatives on Green Street, off Howell Road. He had just returned from Auckland, New Zealand where he fought Americans Bobby Sands, Artie Dixon and Billy Hester. Those were fights that we tuned in on FBC Radio to capture the sound of every punch thrown.

"One evening, me and a group of friends were sitting at Chamu's store on Howell Road having some *kava* (traditional Fijian herbal drink) and a bit of a *talanoa* (chat) when we saw Leweni walk up the street to look for a taxi. One of my friends Viliame said, '*Bula* Champ, *dua na bilo*?' (Hello Champ, have a bowl?). We all hovered around immediately, caught in the spell of his boxing greatness. He politely accepted the offer of some *kava* and spent the next few minutes chatting casually with us before his taxi arrived.

"As he got up to leave, he shook hands with everyone and when it came to my turn, I gripped his huge paw in both of mine and said to him, 'You are my boxing idol and I'm boxing now as an amateur.' He paused for a moment and said, 'Train hard and good luck!' As I look back and see his stocky solid frame topped with ginger hair getting into the taxi, I am reminded of a young Mike Tyson – without ginger hair of course!

"On May 21, 1966, when the legendary Muhammed Ali fought Henry Cooper at the Arsenal Football Stadium in Highbury, London, Waqa fought in the undercard draw against Jimmy Ellis, Ali's sparring partner at the time. Waqa probably had the privilege of being the first Fijian to meet Ali in person.

"Both Ellis and Ali came from Louisville, Kentucky. Whilst he was better known for being Ali's sparring partner, Ellis, who started his professional career as a middleweight in 1961, gradually fought his way up the weight categories to heavyweight by the mid '60s because at 6 feet 1 inches tall, he had difficulty maintaining his weight in the lighter division.

"After a string of wins whilst based in Auckland in 1962, Waqa had only one fight after that in Fiji in 1964 – a rematch against Tongan George Mahoni in Lautoka that July. A fight he won in a first-round knockout.

"I remember British promoter Jack Burns taking Waqa to London in 1965 to train at his gym in Bristol. It was there that Waqa truly established himself as a serious world heavyweight contender in 1965 and 1966 by demolishing opponents Jack Grant in a first-round TKO, Lloyd Walford in a seventh-round KO, Clarence Prince in a fifth-round KO and Johnny Hendrickson in an eighth-round TKO. The only draw on his professional record came from the fight against Giulio Saradi in Italy followed by another win on points against Horst Benedens.

"Waqa was a natural boxer with a good center of gravity and balance in the ring. He could throw power in punches from both hands. He had one of the best left hooks I have ever seen and his exploits in the UK and Europe saw Ring Magazine rate him as number 20 in the world heavyweight division. If I had Waqa as a 20-year-old in the mid '70s along with Ve, Fiji would have had not only a Golden Boy but also a pound-for-pound fighter in Waqa.

"Waqa's winning streak, however, was about to experience a break following a loss on points to Belgian, Lion Ven in Belfast, Northern Ireland in March 1966. The fight against Ellis in the Ali-Cooper undercard in May 1966 was next and our hopes were pinned on Waqa to take out Ali's sparring partner in an entertaining match-up. Our excitement proved to be short-lived as Ellis disposed of Waqa in a first-round KO."

Ellis would go on to become the world heavyweight champion in 1968 following an eight-man tournament of top heavyweight contenders after Ali was stripped off his World Boxing Association (WBA) heavyweight title for refusing to accept the draft to the Vietnam War in 1967.

Waqa would go on to have two more fights in Bristol before running into trouble with the long arm of the law. Outside of the ring, Waqa met with negative influences and on a night out decided to try his left hook on a police officer. That saw him cop a £25 fine and deportation from England.

"Some dates remain etched firmly in my memory and August 29, 1970, is one of those," Ramos continues.

"It was when Leweni fought Filimoni Joe Naliva at the Laucala Bay Hangar in Suva. Promoter/matchmaker Nur Mohammed approached me with 10 days' notice to be on the programme to fight the Fiji number one lightweight contender, Narain Singh of Nadi. To appear in the same programme as my boxing idol was a great privilege and I accepted without hesitation. Narain's scheduled opponent withdrew, and this was my opportunity to make a showing.

"My gym was a makeshift one in the garage next door to where I lived on Baniwai Road. I trained by working that punching bag for 20 minutes to build stamina, shadow-boxed for 15 minutes and skipped for 30 minutes more. I also did morning roadwork every day. I didn't do any sparring because there was no one to spar with.

"In my corner for that fight was my brother-in-law John Low. In that fight, I fought the best I could against Narain. Initially, that fight was scheduled for eight by three-minutes rounds but was scaled back to six by three-minutes rounds by the promoter. I took Narain the full six rounds but lost on points. But that fight was more than that. It was just having achieved my dream of fighting in the same squared circle as my idol, Leweni Waqa. That's why that memory remains with me to this day."

Joseph (Big Joe) Mariappa, second from right (Evelyn Joseph collection circa 1950s).

Margaret Low and John Ramos (circa 1968 – Sylvia Low Tiffany Collection).

John Ramos, seated far right with his Greenfield soccer team (Evelyn Joseph collection, circa 1965).

Nair Family

Standing Back (L-R): Raymond, Surya, Shakuntla (sister-in-law), Adi and John Ramos.

Standing Middle (L-R): Vincent, Rohini and Sharda.

Seated (L-R): Subramani, Patamma with Mohini (niece) and a family friend, Diwan. Evelyn is not in this photo (circa 1967/68, Evelyn Joseph collection).

Fijian heavyweight legend, Leweni Waqa (n.d., John Ramos Collection).

Chapter 2
Hector Hatch

"Starting work at Island Industries in 1962, in an office environment was new for me and took some getting used to. Also working in a more senior role within the same company was Hector Hatch," Ramos recalled of his mentor.

"Hatch was a former Olympian and Fiji amateur welterweight (67kg) champion who, as it happened, was now the boxing trainer at the Suva Youth Centre (now the YMCA) located off Waimanu Road. I joined the SYC and trained under Hector who put me into the weekly amateur competitions at the PWD Gym in Walu Bay on Friday nights. Having a steady income helped pay for gym fees and other incidentals I needed to cater for as an amateur boxer."

The Fiji Amateur Boxing Association (FABA) was established in 1953 and affiliated to the *Association Internationale de Boxe Amateur* (AIBA) or the International Amateur Boxing Association as it's commonly known.

The first international tour of Fiji amateur boxers came in the form of a competition in New Zealand in 1956, the same year that Fiji sent two boxers to the Olympic Games. Those two boxers were Hatch and Thomas Schuster. No Fijian boxer has since represented Fiji at the Olympic Games (FASANOC, 1986).

Schuster boxed in the light-welterweight division at the Melbourne Olympics where he lost his first-round match to Wili Roth of what was West Germany at the time. Roth went on to fight Italian Franco Nenci in the second round and lost. Nenci was the eventual silver medallist for that weight division at the games. Shuster migrated to New Zealand in the 1960s.

Hatch fought Nicolae Linca, the first Olympic boxing champion out of Romania. He lost that first-round fight on a five-nil decision which saw Linca weave, jab and bob his way through to a gold medal in the final against Irishman Frederick Tiedt. That Olympic welterweight final was the most controversial of the games with judges split on a 3-2 decision in favour of Linca, who fought with a severely injured right hand. Because of that battle,

Linca came to symbolise courage and resilience to the Romanian people, propelling him overnight to national hero status.

Hatch served in various administrative capacities for FABA from 1958 until his retirement in 1992. During his time as administrator, some incredible amateur boxing talent emerged, notably bronze medallists at the 1962 Commonwealth Games in Perth, Australia such as Moses Evans in the middleweight division and heavyweight Holgar Johansen. Twenty years later, Tongan Sani Fine would claim gold for Fiji in the light-heavyweight division at the 1982 Commonwealth Games, held in Brisbane, Australia.

Amateur boxing during this time also swelled the professional ranks with outstanding fighters including:

1. Ravuama Roko, the 1963 South Pacific Games middleweight gold medallist who went on to become Fiji's middleweight champion in 1970. The 1963 games was the first time boxing had been added to the regional competition.
2. Basdeo, the 1969 SPG welterweight gold medallist and later South Seas junior welterweight champion in 1978.
3. Alipate Korovou, 1969 SPG middleweight gold medallist and later as Commonwealth middleweight champion in 1978.
4. Wili Tarika, FABA featherweight champion in 1974 and bronze medallist at the 1975 SPG. Under Ramos, he became the Fiji featherweight champion in 1976. Tarika also fought twice, for the Commonwealth super-featherweight title in 1979 and 1980.
5. Sakaraia Ve, 1975 SPG lightweight silver medallist and later Fiji's "Golden Boy" who turned professional with Ramos. He went on to become the South Seas lightweight champion (1976), Fiji lightweight champion (1976), Fiji welterweight champion (1977), South Seas junior welterweight champion (1977), South Seas middleweight champion (1978), and the South Pacific welterweight champion (1979). In 1978, Ve also contended twice for the Commonwealth welterweight title.
6. Timoci Belo, 1975 SPG silver medallist in the light-heavyweight division.
7. Joe Nitiva, 1979 SPG light heavyweight gold medallist.

8. Raiwalui brothers – Vereniki, who won a bronze medal at the 1983 SPG in the bantamweight division and Apete, who won a silver medal at the 1987 SPG in the super-lightweight division.

"It was under Hatch's dedicated administration and leadership that I was able to draw upon and build my pool of professional fighters. I always remember him as the greatest amateur boxing trainer/manager and administrator whose wisdom and passion ensured that amateur boxing would remain ensconced in the national sporting consciousness," Ramos said of his mentor.

"Fiji needs another of the likes of Hatch to resuscitate amateur boxing and restore public confidence in the sport."

In 2005, Hector was presented with the Fiji Olympic Order for his dedication, and involvement first as an athlete and later as an instrumental advocate for the development of amateur boxing.

His award citation read: "His knowledge of boxing and in particular the rules of amateur boxing greatly improved the status of boxing in Fiji and Fiji's standing in the region" (FASANOC, 2016).

"Meeting and getting to know Hector opened my eyes to the realities of competitive amateur boxing. I dedicated my early mornings to road running to build stamina and after work hours training at the SYC. Eventually under Hector's guidance, I was good enough to join in the weekly amateur boxing competition at the PWD Canteen. Those of you who are old enough to remember will know the PWD Canteen as the home of amateur boxing competition in the '60s and '70s," Ramos said.

"I fought in the featherweight division as an amateur for four years in which time I also fought the reigning FABA featherweight champion Solo Brown in 1964. Solo was an extremely crafty fighter. I also fought the FABA lightweight champion I remember only as Peceli of the PWD club in 1965.

"Brown and Peceli both represented Fiji at the SPG games and Brown did the nation proud by walking away with a gold medal, defeating Katoa from Tonga at the 1963 games. For the 1966 games held in Noumea, New Caledonia, I was selected as a reserve for my weight category.

"In 1965, I was selected to represent the SYC by Hector to travel with other boxers from Suva for an amateur competition against boxers in the

West at the Sugar Festival in Churchill Park, Lautoka. I was matched as a featherweight against another boxer, whose name I cannot remember from Nadi in a 3x3-minute round contest which I won on decision.

"The last time I spoke with Hatch was in 1987, when I called from Vancouver to organise a few top-grade amateur boxers from Astoria Boxing Club to visit Fiji on a tour. Amongst George Angelomatis's three boxers that I was arranging for included Manny Sobral, who was the reigning Canadian amateur welterweight champion at the time.

"Sobral represented Canada at the 1988 Olympics and in 1996 became the IBO super-welterweight champion. The other two boxers were a lightweight and a middleweight. This would have been a first for North American amateur boxers to tour and fight in Fiji.

"Arrangements for the tour started out well until the unfortunate turn of political events in Fiji in May that year which put an end to that plan. Hector advised that due to the military coup, it would be best to put that on hold and unfortunately, we never revisited that arrangement further down the road."

Hatch passed away in Lautoka on April 14, 2016, at the age of 80. He will be remembered for his discipline and dedication to amateur boxing in Fiji for close to five decades.

"People like Hector do not come around too often, and it is the likes of him that we need to rebuild the amateur ranks of boxing," Ramos said.

Fiji Team that took part in the 1956 Olympic Games in Melbourne, Australia — (Standing l-r): Hector Hatch (Boxing); Harry Charman (Boxing Team Trainer); Mesulame Rakuro (Athletics); Bill Ragg (General Team Manager). (Front): Tommy Schuster (Boxing). Absent: John Gillmore (Yachting); Nebbie Bentley (Yachting). This photo was taken in front of the Fiji Team quarters in the Olympic Games Village in Heidelberg, Melbourne.

1984 Olympic Games Handbook (FASANOC)

Chapter 3
Ern McQuillan

"After 25 amateur fights, I turned my eye to professional boxing in 1966. This meant that I needed a ring name and at the time, there was a Cuban featherweight by the name of Ultiminio Ramos Zaqueira who became known as Ultiminio 'Sugar' Ramos and later, Sugar Ramos who was causing havoc in the United States," Ramos said of his evolving ring persona.

Ramos was the Cuban featherweight champion in 1960 who fled to Mexico in 1961 when Castro came into power. It was in Mexico that he grew his professional boxing career. Of his 66 fights, he won 55 with 40 by knockouts, losing seven and drawing four. In 1963, he beat the WBC and WBA featherweight champion Davey Moore so badly that Moore died four days later from head injuries sustained during the fight. He lost his world title to Vicente Saldivar in 1964. Ramos was also responsible for another fatality in the ring, that of Jose Blanco in Cuba in 1958 in only his twelfth professional fight.

"Ramos's style and fearlessness appealed to me as a fellow featherweight, and I decided that I would adopt 'Sugar Ramos' as my ring name. In the years to come, I would become known simply as John Ramos," Ramos said. Ramos also shared the name Ultiminio with his son, Jordan when he was born in 1993.

"As a professional, most of my fights were under promoter Raj Kumar Singh of Sigatoka. Singh would also become one of the key promoters for my fighters when I started the Ramos Boxing Club in 1975," Ramos said.

"I remember a promotion Singh had organised in the foothills of Keiyasi in Sigatoka. I was drawn to fight a boxer named Aziz in a six-round bout where the winner got a $30 purse, loser $15 and a draw, $20. We got our $10 bus fare to make the seven-hour bus trip from Suva."

Back in those days, the Suva-Nadi highway was nowhere near what it is today. The winding road laden with gravel the size of miniature boulders, was a painful road to travel. The slow journey also generated a lot of dust and the buses in those days didn't have sliding windows like they have now, instead canvas that was rolled down when it rained or tied up during fine weather. If it was windy during a downpour, you held down that flapping canvas with your hands or you got soaked as the bus sped along. You could be assured that by the end of a long dusty bus ride to the West, you didn't need Brylcreem to hold your hair in place. The dust not only did that but also provided a cheap dye job by turning your hair colour from black to brown.

"When I arrived for the weigh-in at 5pm I was a more than a little tired not only from the travel and dust but also not having had a proper meal since leaving Suva nearly seven hours before," Ramos said.

"All went well with the weigh-in and we headed to the fight venue for the programme start at 7pm. As you can imagine, this was going to be an exceedingly long night. The whole organisation of the programme was very rudimentary.

"When I arrived at the venue, there was no changing room and very little lighting elsewhere at the venue. All they had going was a generator which provided limited lighting to the seating area. For the ring, about a dozen benzene lights were strategically suspended above to provide illumination.

"In a rather comical arrangement, about a similar number of men would descend on the ring apron at the sound of the bell at the end of each round to pump the lamps back into brightness.

"Without a changing room and a place allocated for a warm-up, I had to sit on the hard, dry ground to lace up my boots and make do with a dimly lit space to try to warm up. My fellow boxers were also in the same predicament, but no one complained. That night over a thousand people from the surrounding villages and Sigatoka town turned up to cheer on their best.

"The reason I recount this memory is because my love for boxing had no limitations. I was willing to make the seven-hour bus trip to Sigatoka to fight a six-rounder because I had boxing at heart and Nadroga was also known to produce some great boxers the likes of Iliave Bose, Tevita Kavika, Somi Naidu, Jone Mataitini and Luke Sisiwa who went on to great things in his boxing career. A great town and great people, so there was nothing to complain about.

"That night, everything went off without a hitch and I acknowledge the money and effort Raj put in to pull it altogether. Everyone left that night happy with the programme. This was a time when the Professional Boxing and Wrestling Association of Fiji (PBWAF), which sanctioned the fight, were not so rigid in the application of the standards of boxing."

Ramos continued that while the PBWAF minimised red tape and made certain allowances so that programmes could get underway, it was a different time. A time when passion overrode rules and public safety. This would be unheard of today.

"I had over 16 fights in my professional career which included fighting two Fiji lightweight champions at different times - Balwant Singh of Lautoka, and Somi Naidu of Sigatoka, who held the title at different times - as well as the South Seas lightweight champion Mohammed Rafiq of Nadi. All great fighters at the top of their game at the time," he said.

"In March 1974, I sought to gain greater experience, so I went across to Sydney, Australia for three months leaving behind my wife Margaret and my four-year-old daughter, Sylvia. In my plan I had wanted to start my own boxing gym, but I needed to still learn a few more things and after discussing it with Margaret, I left with her support.

"In Sydney, I stayed with my cousins Mike and Chris, both boys from Belo Street. I asked Chris if he knew of a top boxing gym I could go and train in and he recommended the Newtown Boxing Gym run by Australian boxing legend, Ernie McQuillan."

According to McQuillan's biographer Richard Cashman (2012) McQuillan, a trainee cabinetmaker took up boxing after a trainer, Yank Pearl, spotted him fighting on the street.

"McQuillan lost only two professional bouts out of twenty-two before a bruising twenty-round encounter against George 'KO' Campbell at Leichhardt prompted him to become a trainer instead," Cashman wrote.

"He was a brusque and tough negotiator, who helped his star boxers to secure handsome returns and made a comfortable living for himself."

McQuillan produced more than 60 Australian national, Commonwealth and world-class champions in a career spanning some 56 years including the likes of Tony Mundine Snr, Vic Patrick, Jack Hassan, Bobby Dunlop, and Fiji's own Alipate Korovou, who he took to win the

Commonwealth middleweight title in 1979. Other notable Fijian boxers to have trained in his gym included Semi Bula, Mosese Sorovi, Joe Nitiva and John "Chotka" Krishna.

"With my clearance letter from the PBWAF, Chris and I went to meet the great man. I handed over my letter to him, he read it briefly and barked, 'Get your gear, you start training tomorrow!' and that was that. I turned up at his gym the very next day determined to achieve my objectives which were two-fold: Learn everything I needed to know about how champions were made and secondly, learn what one needed to be a successful gym owner.

"I went through my paces training as a sparring partner to the reigning Commonwealth flyweight champion "Big" Jim West who was scheduled to fight world-ranked Paul Ferreri at the Blacktown RSL Club in west of Sydney on May 16, 1974. I was put on the same card to fight Bobby Green in the junior-welterweight division, a four-rounder that I lost on points, but it did open my eyes to a great many things.

"The fight against Green was tough. Green was the former Queensland amateur junior-welterweight champion, and this fight was the first I fought in this higher weight division. By the end of those four hard-fought and entertaining rounds, the fans showered the ring with coins as a way of showing their appreciation to the boxers.

"The referee of what was to be my last professional fight was the former Commonwealth bantamweight champion, Jimmy Carruthers, the first Australian to win a world title. What an honour and privilege it was to share that space with him."

Carruthers first boxed internationally at the 1948 Olympic Games where he lost in the quarterfinals of the bantamweight division. He turned professional in 1950 and won the Australian championship in his ninth professional fight (Sports, 2000-2016).

In 1952, Carruthers won the world and Commonwealth bantamweight title by defeating South Africa's Vic Toweel (BoxRec, n.d.). This made him the first Australian to be recognised as a world professional championship since Young Griffo in 1890. Carruthers retired undefeated in 1954 and relinquished the crown.

"When I look back at my professional fighting career, I fought some good opponents like Somi Naidu of Nadroga against whom I lost on a close decision following an 8x3-minute rounder at the Suva Civic Centre," Ramos reflected.

"Naidu went on lose against Balwant Singh with whom I also had a colourful fight history. The other person who also comes to mind was the South Seas lightweight champion at the time, Mohammed Rafiq of Nadi. This was also an 8x3-minute rounder in which I prevailed in a second round TKO.

"As I prepared to return home, I spent a fair bit of time picking McQuillan's brilliant mind. I watched and learnt how to properly tape a boxer's hand and how to pep talk and guide your fighter from the corner.

"At the Newtown Gym McQuillan had a sign that read 'Maker of Champions', that's what I wanted for my club. Those three words planted a seed that germinated in my mind for the next year. I had told McQuillan earlier of my plans to be a gym owner like him but to do that I needed to know what one needed to rise to that level. What he told me that day would remain with me for a very, very long time.

"'John,' he said, 'there are only five things you need to know. You must be dedicated to your vision and do what you must, to make it a reality. You will also be required to sacrifice – whether it's family time, personal time, or money – some sacrifice will be required. Find a good venue and set up a proper gym. The facilities are what attract good boxers. Once you have a pool of boxers, take the most promising of the lot and turn him into a champion. When you have a champion, all else will follow and lastly, never allow the promoters to dictate terms to you or your boxers. You set the conditions in the best interest of your fighter, and they will just have to accept it'.

"This was great advice and a lot to take in. I returned home and started setting into motion what I needed to establish the Ramos Boxing Club."

Upon returning to Fiji, Ramos made plans for the club after talking things over with Margaret.

Ern McQuillan Snr with Joe Nitiva (circa
1980s, sourced from Michael McQuillan
Classic Photographs, reproduced under
licence).

John Ramos with his second (name unknown) just before his fight against Robert (Bobby) Green at the Blacktown RSL, NSW Australia (May 16, 1974, John Ramos Collection).

John Ramos (R) in his last professional fight against Robert (Bobby) Green at the Blacktown RSL, NSW Australia (May 16, 1974, John Ramos Collection).

World Featherweight Champion,
Ultiminio (Sugar) Ramos of Cuba (circa
1969, John Ramos Collection).

Chapter 4
1975 – Ramos Boxing Club

In early 1975, Ramos and Margaret bought their first home, a unit in the newly developed Housing Authority estate in Duvula Road, Nadera just outside of the capital Suva. The purchase was timely as the couple prepared for the arrival of their second child later in the year. The expanding brood did not deter Ramos from his plans to start a boxing club.

"I formed the Ramos Boxing Club at my home in Nadera with a few of my mates from work. In starting the club, I had a plan that would provide a platform to grow the amateur ranks of the sport which would in turn feed the professional body. This was the only logical progression to ensure that the sport survived and thrived into the future," Ramos said.

"Our goal was simple: To develop young fighters into champions. Our objective was to ensure that every boxer that walked through the doors of the club would be treated kindly and fairly. This way, everyone is motivated to work hard and if they did, they would get a fair go. In keeping with this simple philosophy, we managed to turn out a few top fighters and champions in a short time.

"On a grander scale, it was my own personal goal to take a Fijian boxer to a major prize fight in boxing – the Commonwealth title and possibly a world title – but to get to that stage, a lot of hard work and sacrifice was needed along the way. My wife Margaret and I were both in full-time employment and with a six-year-old and a new baby on the way, this wasn't going to be easy.

"In the back of mind, I recalled McQuillan's words and steeled myself to prepare for the challenging work ahead. After a few months of scouting for a venue, I managed to secure the Then India Valibar (TIV) Sangam Hall on Belo St in Suva. The club house was conveniently located across from the family home of my cousins, Chris, and Mike's, which allowed me to pop across and get help from my family with anything if I needed.

"The committee looking after the premises offered me a rental of $30 per month with the responsibility for looking after the surrounding lawn. This was the break I needed to get me going and all I needed was a punching bag, skipping ropes, bag gloves, sparring gloves, and other incidental equipment but at this stage, we had no money or sponsor to equip ourselves.

"And so, as you do in Fiji when you need to raise money, you gather your friends, your family, workmates, and neighbours and bring them in for a fun game of *Kati*[1]. We had a great turnout with everyone attending, bringing a prize with them. That first fundraiser helped us collect about $100 and that was good enough to get us started. To maintain ourselves, we held similar gatherings every two weeks, so we could buy equipment and pay our rent.

"Our second daughter, Sandra, was born on July 30, 1975. With two young children to care for and full-time work, I ploughed ahead to get the club organised for the opening. The club opened its doors to the public in August 1975. My vision would finally become reality. Now it was time to put Fiji boxing on the world map.

"*The Fiji Times* was there to record this momentous occasion. I recall the first people to walk in were Tevita Tui and Peni (Ben) Tabua and later Timoci Belo, Penisoni Lagi and a few others including cruiserweight Waqabaca Cama who defected from Sunia Cama's club with two other fighters, Jo Dawai and Anthony Naidu, the former amateur lightweight champion who won the vacant South Pacific lightweight title under my management."

Cama was a good-looking bloke who was entertaining to watch in the ring. His good looks and exploits earned him the moniker 'Fiji's Muhammed Ali'. Cama migrated to San Francisco in 1977.

"It was with a sad and heavy heart that I learnt of Tui's passing in August 2015. He was a founding member of Ramos Boxing Club and a very respectful and an honourable man. It was he who brought the young Ve to the gym at Belo St. He was Ve's sparring partner on many occasions when Ve had to prepare for a fight," Ramos said.

"Tui worked as a welder with the Public Works Department during the day. It was unfortunate that not two years after joining my club, he lost sight in both his eyes. Whether the cause of that was boxing or a prolonged work hazard, I do not know. We all rallied behind him and his family to raise money so that he and his wife could go overseas for specialist treatment. The prognosis was not good, and sadly, he never regained his vision.

"Tui was as tough as they came. He never backed down from an opponent. As a super-middleweight and light-heavyweight boxer, he fought on until the last bell. That was the kind of man he was. He will always be remembered fondly by everyone who knew him."

Up until his death, Tui was a familiar sight in Suva with his white cane and trademark sunglasses, walking through the streets of Suva to collect money for his family.

"Tabua on the other hand was a classy fighter, gutsy, had great ring craft and light on his feet. He stayed with my club for about a year before migrating to Australia in 1976 where he continued his professional boxing career. In Australia, he challenged for the New South Wales light-middleweight title twice against Lou Hurst in 1978 and Phil 'Spider' Davis 1979 but was unsuccessful on both counts. His challenge for the NSW welterweight title against Eddie Buttons the same year, met with the same result," Ramos recalled.

Tui and Tabua were joined a few months later by the likes of Tarika and Ve who had just come through the amateur ranks, fresh from the 1975 South Pacific Games in Guam and looking to turn professional.

"These two young men had tremendous talent but needed to work on a few weak areas which I noticed during sparring and with a few tweaks we started to make gradual progress. Each day the boys got sharper and fitter, their speed and stamina improved to a level that told me they were now ready to turn professional," Ramos said.

When the 1975 South Pacific Games lightweight silver medallist Sakaraia Ve announced his intention to turn professional at age 19 after three years in the amateur ranks, secretary for the PBWAF, Mumtaz Ali welcomed the decision.

"Ve has the ability to become a Fiji champion within a short time. His presence in the lightweight division should make Fiji boxing more active. It's almost dead these days. I think he made the right decision and to turn professional while still young because he has a bright future," Ali said (Rabuka, 1975).

In the first few months of the club's existence, the search for a talent to turn into a champion was in motion. Aside from getting the club started, Ramos also tried his hand at matchmaking. In his first attempt, he paired reigning Fiji and South Seas welterweight champion, 'The Babasiga Terror' Inia Catarogo, against Jo Vucago in a return bout on August 17, 1975.

Former champion Seva Mocesui had fair warning for challenger Vucago: "I warned Vucago in his first fight with Catarogo to stay away from him. He didn't and that's why he failed. He should realise that he is fighting a man with much greater experience. Catarogo is a brilliant mover and Vucago must keep his guard up all the time. The most important thing is not to try and force the fight. He must try and jab and move. If he is to make the move on Monday that he did before, I cannot see him having a chance of winning" (Rabuka, 1975).

Catarogo, a nine-year veteran was not only fearless but a solid puncher as previous opponents Mocesui and Ravuama Roko would attest. The Fiji welterweight champion since dispensing of Mocesui in 1971 in an 11-round disqualification to clinch the title, Catarogo, much like the young Mike Tyson in his prime, liked to take the fight to his opponent from the opening bell.

Vucago it seemed, did not heed Mocesui's caution and lost his second bid for the belt after he was bested two minutes and two seconds into the third round of the scheduled 15-rounder.

Exhilarated by the quick work he made of Vucago, Catarogo issued an open challenge in the ring: "Any more challengers? I'm ready now" (Rabuka, 1975).

The second match Ramos lined up was Catarogo against Jone Radaniva for a headline clash in Labasa on September 13. In that same programme Ramos also matched Tevita Tui against Catarogo's sparring partner, Labasa's Viliame Naibono, for an eight-round return bout after Tui was disqualified in the fifth round in their last encounter in August.

The lack of quality fighters in the welterweight division was also giving Catarogo cause to reassess his fight future in that weight division, telling *The Fiji Times* in an interview he "wanted to challenge Fiji's middleweight champion (Jone Mataitini) for his title immediately. Catarogo left the welterweight class unbeaten and is confident he can regain the belt" (Sport, 1975).

With Ve training at the Ramos club after turning professional, Ramos lined Ve up for his first bout against Ramesh Chand of Navosa in Suva in November 1975. Ve won the six-rounder on points.

Ve's first outing showed that he had the goods to make it in the professional ranks and this brought him to the attention of the then undefeated Fiji lightweight champion, Balwant Singh, of Lautoka. Singh, known for his bluster outside the ring, told *The Fiji Times* that he would teach Ve a lesson when they did meet.

"I have the punching strength which will stop him in the early rounds ... But Ve will have to prove himself first" (Sport, 1975).

Ve's second fight initially was scheduled against John Heritage, the former amateur lightweight champion from Savusavu but was replaced at the last minute by Tevita Varani. Ve won his second professional fight in a fifth-round technical knockout.

Watching ringside, *Fiji Times* reporter Eliki Rabuka had this to say: "Sakaraia Ve is ready to take on lightweight boxing champion Balwant Singh. This is my impression after watching Ve outpunch and outclass the ex-amateur welterweight Tevita Varani of Buca Bay on Saturday ... Varani tried everything but Ve, who gave away seven pounds, had control of the fight and did some damage to (t)his man's nose and head early on" (Rabuka, 1975).

"I picked Varani as a steppingstone for Ve in his only second professional fight as a lightweight. Varani was a hard, solid puncher but he lacked speed and defence which is what Ve exploited to overcome him," Ramos said.

After the Varani fight, Ve laid down the gauntlet to lightweight champion Balwant Singh of Lautoka. In no uncertain terms, Ve made clear to Rabuka that he had his sights on Singh's Fiji lightweight title.

"I think I'm going to give Balwant Singh a good battle. I know I'm ready for him," Ve said.

A non-title contest between Ve and Singh was planned for later in December. Ramos was impressed with the speed of Ve's counterpunching in training.

"Balwant Singh should not underestimate Ve although he is still inexperienced," Ramos said (Sport, 1975).

A few days after that *Fiji Times* report appeared, Singh withdrew from the eight-round contest citing a shoulder injury.

"I have had this shoulder problem for a week. After Friday's training I felt it badly and decided to rest it on Saturday, hoping that it would recover. By Sunday it had not improved so I decided to see my doctor who has advised me not to train or fight for a month," Singh told *The Fiji Times* (Rabuka, 1975).

When the two would finally meet in early 1976, it was going to be epic.

Wili Tarika turned professional in early December after four years as an amateur champion in the bantam and featherweight divisions. His first professional bout was scheduled against Mohammed Yusuf in December, a fight that Tarika won easily (Sports, 1975).

The 1975 South Pacific Games Boxing Team. All except one won medals at the Games. (L-R) Abraham Thomas (Manager-Coach), Lightweight Sakaraia Ve (Silver), Light Heavyweight Timoci Belo (Silver), Light Middleweight Sekonia Ratu (Silver), Featherweight Wili Tarika (Bronze) and Middleweight Salesi Soko (Fiji Times, August 14, 1975).

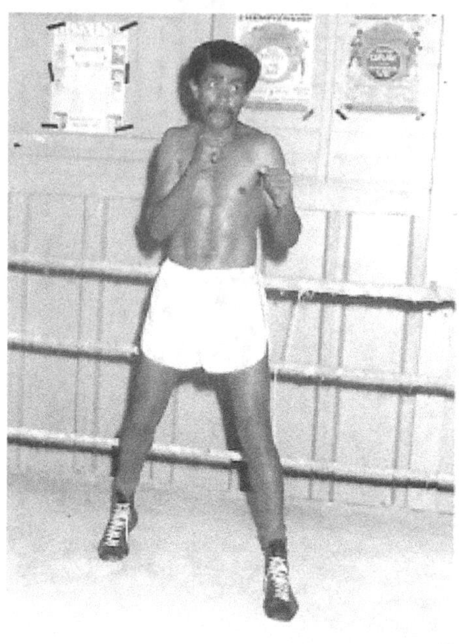

Penisoni Lagi (circa 1978 John
Ramos Collection).

Chapter 5
1976 – Making of champions

"In the back of my mind, I always kept what McQuillan had told me about being careful when selecting opponents for my fighters which I did for Sakaraia Ve and Wili Tarika in the 12 months since the club opened. With each fight and subsequent win, they gained confidence and learnt more about areas they needed to work on. That diligence and patience soon paid off," Ramos said.

JANUARY – STEPPING STONE

In only his third professional fight, Ve beat Daya Nand in a third-round knockout in Lautoka.

"The Lautoka programme promoted by Rennie Mohammed featured three of my boxers – Tevita Tui (vs. Aseri Namua) in the main bout with Peni Tabua (vs. Sekope) and Ve (vs. Daya Nand) in the supporting bouts. Nand was the reigning lightweight champion, Balwant Singh's, sparring partner," Ramos remembers.

In the pre-fight build-up, *Fiji Times* journalist Eroni Volavola suggested that Balwant Singh be ringside to see what his future title challenger (Ve) is capable of.

Volavola observed: "'There is no doubt in the minds of many fight fans that this title fight is only a matter of weeks away with most of their backing on Ve. Ve has proved time and again that, against more professionally experienced opponents that he would be very hard to tackle" (Volavola, 1976).

This was Nand's seventh professional bout and Ve's third, but Ve's preparation for the fight was boosted by the presence of middleweight Waqabaca Cama, who had just come back from New Zealand and was in devastating shape. Ve and Cama's sparring sessions paid off handsomely when Ve went in and took care of Nand in three rounds.

For promoter, Rennie Mohammed the programme was all about finding and promoting new talents particularly in the lower weight classes.

"These boxers, although they are young, are very good so I want them on the programme because they hardly have any fights and that they can show Fiji fight fans what they are missing," Mohammed said.

Nand was Ve's stepping stone to Singh's lightweight title.

FEBRUARY – CHASING SINGH

Lautoka promoter and trainer Brij Sain, who had a long history with Balwant Singh, acknowledged as many fight pundits did, that Ve was the uncrowned lightweight champion of Fiji.

"Sure, Ve is fighting like a champion and has the quality of a title holder," Sain said (Sport, 1976).

Singh, however, maintained that the shoulder injury from late the previous year was still bothering him. Ve countered: "If Singh thinks that he had not recovered from his shoulder injury, I can give him two solid months to prepare himself – and two more months to keep the title before I take it away from him."

Promoter Rennie Mohammed offered Singh a purse of $300 to defend the title – the largest ever paid to any lightweight champion.

Mohammed wasn't the only promoter after Singh for a match-up against Ve. Sigatoka's own "Don King" Raj Kumar Singh was also chasing Singh for a fight for the soon-to be vacant South Seas lightweight title in March.

"I want to make my March 1 promotion in the Suva Town Hall a double title fight. Jone Mataitini will be defending his middleweight championship of Fiji and Singh and Ve for the South Seas lightweight title," Kumar said (Sport, 1976).

At that point, the South Seas title was held substantively by Mohammed Rafiq who had been unable to make the weight limit of 9st 7lbs (60.3kg) for some time. PBWAF secretary Mumtaz Ali advised Rafiq to vacate the title and move up a weight division with an opportunity to challenge in the future should he be able to make the weight again.

Singh's avoidance tactic didn't go very far because not long afterwards the PBWAF also issued him with a six-week ultimatum to defend his title against Ve. The committee's decision to issue the ultimatum followed a letter of complaint by promoter Mohammed over Singh's failure to turn up to the contract signing for the title defence against Ve that was planned for March.

In a statement, the PBWAF said: "Singh must defend his title in six weeks' time. Failing to do so would mean he would be stripped of it. We have not been hard on the lightweight division in the past because it has not been particularly active. Now that the division has become enlivened with contenders to fight for the title, there is no reason why Singh should dodge them, especially so when there is a promoter willing to stage the fight." (Sport, 1976)

Given Singh's reported injury, the next logical contender for the title was Sher Gul of Keiyasi.

Promoter Raj Kumar couldn't wait for Singh, so he went back to Sigatoka to negotiate with Gul to fight Ve for the vacant South Seas title. Outside of Gul, the other lightweight favoured as a contender to fight Ve was 1969 SPG silver medallist Esala Vula.

Vula had only recently turned professional and had only one fight on his record in which he knocked Gul out in the third round of their six-round counter (Sport, 1976).

Two weeks after the PBWAF ultimatum there was still no word from Singh. Kumar managed to bring Gul on board as the contender against Ve for the now-vacant South Seas lightweight championship. The stage was set for a March 1 programme in Suva. Jone Mataitini would also defend his title against former South Seas middleweight champion Inia Catarogo in the main event.

Also scheduled in the programme were Wili Tarika and Peni Tabua in supporting bouts against Mohammed Yusuf and Jo Tawake respectively. Tarika at the time was based with the United Club.

The Mataitini-Catarogo fight was a toe-to-toe entertainer ending on a TKO in the fifth round to Mataitini, who retained his South Seas middleweight title. Catarogo needed stitches to a cut above his left eye which opened in the third round.

In a build-up to the vacant South Seas lightweight title fight, Ve fought Tomu Baca in the Iliavi Bose-Jo Dawai programme promoted by Kumar at the Suva Civic Centre on February 16. Ve easily beat Baca over six rounds.

Eliki Rabuka of *The Fiji Times* wrote after the Baca clash: "Sakaraia Ve should have an easy fight against Sher Gul on March 1 for the vacant South Seas lightweight title. This is my forecast after I saw him in a classic fighting display against the tough Tomu Baca on Monday night's bill. Baca put up a gallant show. Although he took some good punches to the jaw and head, he fought back to surprise the man with two-fisted attacks. But fighting a man like Ve, who is perhaps the best counterpuncher in the division and given the higher grades, Baca needed a better defence" (Rabuka, 1976).

MARCH – SHER GUL AND THE SOUTH SEAS LIGHTWEIGHT TITLE

Ramos had fought Sher Gul at the Civic Centre in Suva in 1970, stopping him in the fifth round. That inside knowledge of Gul's fighting style would prove to be invaluable to Ve's first title fight.

With promoter Singh at the helm, Ve took on Sher Gul in Suva in March for the vacant South Seas lightweight championship.

"This fight was important because it was Ve's opportunity to step up and establish himself as a credible lightweight in the professional ranks," Ramos said.

The fight against Sher Gul lasted five rounds and was one-sided before Ve stopped his opponent and walked away with the South Seas lightweight title.

"Having had a boost in confidence with that first championship title, our next stop was the Fiji lightweight title held by Balwant Singh, who I felt was avoiding Ve ever since the Nand fight in January," Ramos said.

The win gave a more confident Ve a psychological edge over Singh who he again challenged the champion to come out of "hiding".

APRIL – BALWANT SINGH AND THE FIJI LIGHTWEIGHT TITLE

It took Singh a few more weeks before he signed the contract with Kumar to fight Ve. At this point Singh had not defended his title in 13 months (Sport, 1976). The response from the Ramos camp was generous, offering Singh the first right of challenge should he lose as well as an opportunity to fight Ve for the South Seas lightweight title later in the year if Singh proved worthy as a challenger. Ramos was also confident that Ve would stop Singh in the early rounds.

Ve's meteoric rise to South Seas lightweight champion in a record five professional fights brought challengers out of the woodwork, including Sakaraia Qoro, fresh off his draw against French Polynesian lightweight champion Rafael Lecail. Qoro also threw down the gauntlet at Tarika whom he called "green" (Sport, 1976).

As the leading contender for Ve's title at the time, Tarika called out Qoro, offering to forego his purse if Qoro knocked him out.

"He will do a lot of sweating if he wants to do that. I only want to say this to Qoro – he will not be able to win a round, and I could finish his career," Tarika said (Sport, 1976).

The initial Qoro-Tarika fight was eyed as a supporting bout to the Ve-Singh title fight, but Qoro declined the challenge saying that he wasn't consulted to appear on the programme and that he would be lodging a letter of complaint to the PBWAF regarding the matter.

"In fact, I am not afraid to fight Tarika, but I will not be fighting him," Qoro said (Sport, 1976).

To keep every fighter in the club striving to do better, Ramos organised regular intra-club championships at the end of which a trophy for "most improved" would be given to the fighter showing promise since his last appearance (Sport, 1976).

As the April 26 fight against Balwant Singh inched closer, there were concerns that Ve would not be able to make the 9st 9lb weight limit, but Ramos soon quelled those concerns with a precise training plan that included light workouts and sparring with light-heavyweight Tevita Tui as part of his preparations. Reports of Singh's preparations noted that there was no sign of a shoulder injury and rated Singh as being fitter than he was two years ago when he wrested the belt from Somi Naidu (Sport, 1976).

"That fight against Singh would have had to have been Ve's toughest to date. It is never easy when you go up against a champion, something I learnt when I fought him (Singh) at the Suva Civic Centre in 1972," Ramos recalled.

"That fight, an 8x3-minute rounds contest, was to give me a shot at Singh's lightweight title if I won. At the 5pm weigh-in I stood in at 9st 7lbs (60.3kg) and the champ at 9st 4lbs (59kg). Singh refused to get into the ring with me unless I lost 3lbs (1.4kg) by the second weigh-in at 8pm. I was well within the fight weight for the lightweight division, but Singh's camp was determined in their claim that promoter Kumar had promised that I would weigh in at 9st 4lbs.

"All this fuss and all I could think of was that he was scared so I agreed to do a few laps from the Civic Centre to Albert Park and managed to drop 2lbs (0.9kg) by the second weigh-in. As any athlete will tell you, losing weight in a short period is mainly body fluids. I was quite dehydrated by 8pm and felt quite weak. I decided that I would give it a shot anyway. From the first bell, I got in there and landed a few good body shots. Singh, who was shorter by about three inches at 5'6" decided he would go after my kidneys instead, taking foul shots that either the referee didn't see to caution him or just ignored altogether.

"As the fight progressed, I felt my legs getting weaker and by the fourth round I told my corner I couldn't continue. What I learnt from this experience was that Singh was a dirty fighter and crafty with his foul hits.

"With Kumar promoting this fight, Ve now had the opportunity to accomplish what I couldn't against Singh. It was now Ve's turn to wrestle the Fiji lightweight title from Singh once and for all. For that fight, I shared with Ve everything I knew about Singh's style of fighting, his weak spots and how to corner him. I wanted badly for Ve to win this decisively by knockout. 'Go finish this fight for me,' I told him.

"Ve was very quick on his feet and quite smart in how he worked the ring to gain advantage with his punches. Standing the same height as Singh, this would be an even match between a veteran and the apprentice."

The Fiji Times' report of the fight said: "In the first round Ve's superior speed and more accurate punching has Singh in trouble ... Singh attacked with his lefts and wild swinging punches to the side of body ... Ve took most on his guard. In the second, Singh was able to land three good lefts to the body but a volley of punches from Ve had Singh on the defence. In the third, Ve picked his punches to the head and face and hooked the champion with his left. Singh looked a tired man after the third round while Ve looked as though he had not been hit at all. Ve drew blood from Singh's nose in the fourth and connected with accurate short punches to the head, jaw, and face. Singh forced Ve to retreat, scored well with three lefts to the body. Singh came back and stood toe-to-toe with Ve for a while and scored with a right to the side of the head. But Ve, punching with more fire, hit three to the head and a right uppercut to the jaw. Ve won the fifth round easily while Singh fought gamely to keep out of danger as Ve moved in. Singh was forcing the fight in the beginning of the sixth round with body punches, one of which went below the belt" (Rabuka, 1976).

Ramos said that this time the referee did see the "foul shot and stopped the fight, handing the champion a disqualification".

"The decision did not go down well with Singh's fans, but referee Mike Ravula stood firm on his decision. I had never felt so vindicated or so happy in finally seeing this devious fighter meet such an honest end," Ramos said.

"With the disqualification, Ve brought home the Fiji lightweight championship – the same title that I watched Newton and Sami go toe-to-toe for as a 14-year-old boy in Toorak all those years ago. It immediately took place of pride on the living room wall at home in Nadera."

The disqualification was not how Ve envisaged the fight ending, but he admitted that he did feel the low blow. Ve's preference was for a more decisive outcome rather than a disqualification. Singh's fans were outraged at the decision storming the ring in protest. Sensing unfinished business, Ve offered Singh a return bout (Sport, 1976).

JUNE TO SEPTEMBER – WILI TARIKA COMES ONBOARD

That loss would have been difficult for Singh. Promoter Kumar scheduled a return bout for Lawaqa Park in Sigatoka for October. With six months to prepare, Ramos knew Ve still needed to build his speed and stamina to defend his title.

"In the meantime, I arranged two fights for him – the first against Ramesh Chand in June and the second against Joe Vucago in August. Both fighters were taken out in the fourth round. These two fights cemented his position as champion in the 135lb division," Ramos said.

Ve's youth, punching speed, timing jabs and good right-hand counterpunch saw his opponents outclassed and outboxed each time either by knockout or technical knockout. As time progressed, Ve learnt quickly and got better with each opponent put before him. He knew how to use the ring well; he was a trainer's dream.

"I had to be careful in how I selected fighters to box against him," Ramos said. "The idea was to get him to top-level competition by building not only his skill but his confidence as a fighter."

The time was also right to start thinking of overseas opponents for Ve, so negotiations began for former Tahitian-born 1972 French Olympian Maurice Apeang, who was also the Tahitian lightweight champion, to meet Ve.

The planned meeting for July was postponed when Apeang broke his thumb in the contest against fellow Frenchman Gilbert Orsaldo in May. Apeang endured the pain to outpoint Orsaldo (Sport, 1976).

"The fight against veteran welterweight Vucago who was also the No.2-ranked contender for the Fiji welterweight title, was drawn to gauge if Ve was ready to take on the might of Fiji welterweight champion Inia Catarogo down the line," Ramos said.

"The match against Vucago was the first time that Ve would also be fighting in his hometown of Levuka, so there was a lot at stake other than just securing a hometown victory."

While working to find boxers in the higher weight divisions for Ve, Ramos had to also keep in mind that the Fiji and South Seas lightweight champion still had to defend his titles if he wanted to remain champion, so the return title bout against Singh for October was finalised with promoter Raj Kumar Singh in July (Sport, 1976).

By this time Tarika had moved across from the United Club to join Ramos Boxing Club. On that same fight card, Tarika lined up against Esala Vula in the main support bout.

"Vula had his sights on Ve's lightweight title since turning professional, but I had other plans as I thought he would be a better contender for Tarika for the vacant featherweight title to be scheduled for another programme down the line," Ramos said.

Vula was unbeaten as an amateur in the lightweight division. But Vula wasn't the only SPG medallist after Ve. SPG gold medallist (1969) Basdeo also made it known that he was interested in meeting Ve if he (Ve) ever made the welterweight division (Sport, 1976).

OCTOBER TO DECEMBER – DAYA NAND AND THE FIJI FEATHERWEIGHT TITLE

After the Vucago match, Ve was back into training for Singh.

"I kept a close eye on his diet and his training schedule because I knew that Singh would be returning with his arsenal of dirty tricks bar none," Ramos said.

Of course, the usual pre-match verbiage started with Singh calling it an early fight, predicting a fourth-round knockout of Ve. Ve agreed with Singh that it would be a premature end, but for Singh, when they met on October 2.

"It just so happened that my friend, Johnny Lewis, one of Australia's greatest boxing trainers, was in Fiji as well at the time and he helped out in the corner for the Ve-Singh rematch in Sigatoka," Ramos said.

In 2006, Lewis was inducted into the Australian Boxing Hall of Fame and awarded the Medal of the Order of Australia. World champions that he's trained include Jeff Fenech, Kostya Tszyu, Jeff Harding, Gary St Clair, and Virgil Hill.

Ve fought Singh in a smart fight. His jabbing speed and counterpunches were lightning fast and this time he had a more comprehensive win – a fourth-round knockout to retain the Fiji lightweight title.

From the start Ve threw straight jabs to the former champ's head. Singh was caught off-guard and could not collect himself in enough time to even parry a half-decent response. Ve's superiority was stamped from the beginning with repeated jabs to the head – repeatedly.

Singh came back in the second round but a hard right to the head put the challenger on the canvas for the first time. After an eight count, he came back with a shot to Ve's kidney which thankfully referee Mumtaz Ali saw and cautioned him. Ve responded with an explosive right to Singh's head that put him down for the second time in that round. Luckily for Singh, he was saved by the bell.

In the third and fourth rounds Singh reeled from Ve's solid combinations. He went down for the third and last time in the middle of the fourth round.

The fight ended how Ve wanted it, decisively. There was no doubt in anyone's mind that the boy from Lovoni deserved to hold the Fiji lightweight championship title. Lewis was impressed by Ve and rated him as someone with a bright future. Lewis even offered to help him get fights in Australia (Sport, 1976).

In Ve's next fight, he took out Ramesh Chand in a second-round knockout. It was their third match-up since Ve turned professional in 1975 with Ve winning two by knockout and one on points.

At age 20, Ve was now the dominant force in the lightweight category for Fiji and the South Pacific, and he was running out of local contenders in that category.

"The limited number of fighters in the lightweight division, which Ve had dispatched of quickly in the first 12 months, prompted me to start looking at the next two weight divisions – the junior-welterweight and welterweight categories – for his next crop of opponents," Ramos said.

"It occurred to me then also that there was a need for bridging weight classes for the feather and lightweight as well as welter and middleweight categories in Fiji, so I decided to write to the PBWAF to create the junior-lightweight and junior-welterweight divisions. I even had people lined up to donate the belts for these two new weight classes."

The top contender for the vacant South Seas junior-welterweight title at the time was a veteran of the ring, 1969 SPG gold medallist, Basdeo. Basdeo was a hard hitter and a craftsman in the ring. His opponents will tell you of his punishing combinations and his hard head. He is not someone you could easily put down on the canvas.

"As a matchmaker, the prospects of pitching an up-and-coming champion from the lighter division against a heavier veteran such as Basdeo would be considered reckless but no guts, no glory, right?" Ramos said.

"After negotiations with Basdeo's trainer/manager and boxing promoter Brij Sain, we agreed to a 10x3-minute rounds, non-title, super-lightweight contest in November which was the next progressive category for Ve.

"Sain was a great guy with a long-associated history with boxing in Fiji. Sain also trained one of my idols, the former Fiji heavyweight champion Leweni Waqa.

"Basdeo was formidable in his amateur career and had fight experience locally and internationally. He was someone to be respected and not taken lightly. As a former Fiji amateur champion, I always had respect for Basdeo's skills and experience and knew that Ve would have a decent challenge on his hands.

"This fight would become one of the most widely anticipated matchups in Fiji boxing because Basdeo, a much-loved son of Lautoka, had a strong following in his own right. To overcome him, Ve would have to be clever and not engage with him in a toe-to-toe contest but use the ring wisely and outbox him over the distance. This match-up was to gauge if Basdeo was a suitable contender for the lightweight title challenge against Ve in the future."

The Ve-Basdeo fight was to feature as a supporting bout to the Jone Mataitini-Nemani Waka contest for the vacant Fiji middleweight title and the Wili Tarika vs Daya Nand contest for the vacant Fiji featherweight title scheduled for October 23.

If Tarika won the title, it would have been the first time in 20 years that a holder had come from the Southern division. The last southerner to hold the title was S.P. Singh (Sport, 1976).

Ve already had had ten professional fights, winning three on points and seven by knockout.

At age 32, Basdeo was considered past his prime against an up-and-coming champion 12 years his junior. But the veteran was undeterred, despite a long layoff.

"I am very sure of my boy retaining his title against Basdeo and there is no doubt in my mind that he will win this fight again with flying colours," Ramos said at the time (Volavola, 1976).

Basdeo passed away in Lautoka on August 30, 2020, at the age of 76. Ramos described him as a warrior, with an undefeatable spirit in the ring, the mere mention of whom brought a signalled caution to any challenger.

"There will never be another like him in this lifetime," Ramos said.

Ve had won the Fiji lightweight title in his fifth fight and the South Seas lightweight title in his sixth. His star had risen faster and brighter than any other Fijian boxer before him.

Ve and Tarika's career trajectories were helped by the fact that Ramos had a strict policy about tobacco smoking and alcohol consumption for his club. Ramos viewed the consumption of the two as performance inhibitors and a conduit to indiscipline. All fighters who were serious about their professional or amateur careers were required to abide by this policy. One such example was prominent light-heavyweight Sefanaia Vakacegu, who joined Ramos's club the year it formed but left in early 1976 because he couldn't meet these requirements. After a six-month lay-off he rejoined the club in October after Ramos agreed to give him a second chance. Ramos gave Vakacegu a four-week grace period to prove his dedication before being considered for fights (Sport, 1976).

At the weigh-in for the Mataitini-Waka programme scheduled for Churchill Park in Lautoka, Ve and Tarika made their respective weights. Tarika went in confident having beaten Nand in a previous fight.

"I'll box and counter his punches right from the first round. I can even go the full distance if he wants to," Tarika said (Sports, 1976).

Like Ve, Basdeo had his eye on Catarogo should he beat Ve, which meant Ve had a lot riding on the fight.

"Basdeo is very confident that he will stop Ve early in the fight and he asked me to negotiate with Catarogo for a crack at his welterweight crown," Sain said on the eve of the fight.

Ve fought Basdeo's fight. Using speed and counterpunching, he managed to avoid Basdeo's knockout hits. Ve to his credit, went the distance against the giant, losing on a split point decision at the end of the ten-round battle, but not without proving himself a worthy opponent. It was his first loss in 11 professional fights.

Basdeo was ready to quit in the sixth, calling on his seconds to throw in the towel at the end of the round. Ve's solid and accurate punching style and solid defence had him in attack mode for most of the early rounds of the fight.

The Fiji Times reported: "On the night Basdeo showed he still had sting in his punches, but his mistakes were in his timing and throwing punches carelessly. This was indicated in the sixth round when Ve's counterpunches caught Basdeo off his guard. Combinations from Ve won the sixth to the tenth round in my card and had the fight gone on for another two minutes, Basdeo would have gone to canvas" (Rabuka, 1976).

"Ve did not box according to our plan for that fight. He went toe-to-toe with the hard-hitting Basdeo when he should have gone for the counter right quick jabs and the two-three-punch combination," Ramos said.

"Ve learnt a lot from that fight not only about his mettle as a boxer but also about what made Basdeo such a tough nut to crack. He was determined that Basdeo wasn't altogether undefeatable, and he worked even harder for the return bout scheduled for a month later in December. This time the clash would be for the newly created, vacant South Seas junior-welterweight title in a 15x3-minute round contest to be held in Churchill Park, Lautoka."

Basdeo, speaking through promoter Brij Sain, said that never in his career as a professional boxer had anyone inflicted such punishment on him as Ve had.

"I've fought Seva Mocesui, Alipate Korovou and Etuate Rabuka, all former champions in their divisions, but never have I been damaged by any boxer as Ve has done to me," Basdeo said (Volavola, 1976).

Ve's loss was softened when Tarika won his title fight against Nand on points over fifteen rounds. The early rounds saw Tarika take the fight to Nand. Tarika maintained his composure, using the advantage of footwork to counter with one-two combinations to Nand's head and strong shots to the body. In the second round, Nand caught Tarika off guard with a combination of punches and it took Tarika to get to the tenth round, to unleash a barrage of combinations that had Nand on the back foot. Tarika's win returned the featherweight title to the Southern division after two decades. In less than two years, Ramos had secured three championship titles for his fighters.

In a post-fight interview, Tarika said that he would hold onto the title until he retired. Tarika also gave credit to Ramos saying, "I am proud to be fighting under the management of such a man who is dedicated to boxing" (Sport, 1976).

On the night, Waka also outpointed Mataitini for the Fiji middleweight title.

"In the lead-up to the Basdeo re-match, negotiations with Sain stalled for a time and by mid-November we managed to talk our way through the contract and agree on a date. Ve was pleased because he was eager to settle the account with Basdeo as to who was the better fighter," Ramos said.

"On that programme, Tarika was to defend his featherweight title against Zamal Azad and Tevita Tui would take on the newly minted Fiji middleweight champion Nemani Waka, in an eight-round contest.

"But before we got to the rematch with Basdeo, I had started negotiations in late October for Ve to fight Catarogo. We knew that Basdeo and his camp would be after the champ as well, but I felt that Ve would provide a more exciting challenge for him because I was confident that Ve would capture the Fiji welterweight title anyway after the Basdeo clash on December 11."

The Fiji Times was quick with review of the proposed match-up: "The Catarogo fight should be a crowd pleaser with two classy champions meeting for the first time in the ring. Both men are crowd pleasers, both have shown their punching power by knocking out Jo Vucago and both are fast, classy boxers. Neither drink no (sic) smokes which means it could be one of the hardest and fastest contest this year" (Sport, 1976).

By early November, all negotiations around a Ve-Catarogo title fight were shelved to concentrate on the re-match with Basdeo to put an end to the media mudslinging that followed the first fight. On offer was a $300 purse for Basdeo.

"In fact, Basdeo has not got this type of purse in his professional career, and it is very attractive too. Ve will be out to prove to the public that he was cheated in the fight. He should have won more clearly," Ramos said (Sport, 1976).

"To prove that Ve was cheated at Lautoka, first referee Mumtaz Ali had to change the timekeeper when the first timekeeper appeared to be cutting out the time to two minutes instead of the normal three minutes in a round. We didn't complain of this at all. In fact, we could have done so because in most of the rounds that were cut short it was Ve who was scoring damaging punches."

Ramos was determined that there would be no confusion as to who the better fighter was. He wanted closure to the Ve-Basdeo discussion.

"We could have gone ahead with our negotiation for the welterweight title fight proposed for December, but we decided that before we take on Catarogo we must shut Basdeo's mouth," he said.

In the meantime, Ramos was preparing light-heavyweight Tevita Tui for a fight against Tonga's Commonwealth-rated middleweight Sam Nagata. The fight was billed as a light-heavyweight contest as both fighters were more likely to make that weight category than as middleweights. The fight was on the undercard of the Luke Sisiwa-Iliavi Bose Fiji light-heavyweight title fight at Lal Square Garden in Sigatoka on November 13.

Ramos knew that Tui was going to have a fight on his hands especially against a Commonwealth-ranked fighter such as Nagata.

"Tui must take the fight to his opponent, and he will be a heavier puncher than Nagata," he said (Sports, 1976).

"We are going to have to slug it out right from the opening round. We have seen Nagata train, and he seems like a scientific boxer in his fighting approach."

A win for the 24-year-old Tui against Nagata would be a career breakthrough after just 11 professional fights.

From the opening bell Tui took command of the fight, scoring with fast left jabs to the head and strong right hooks that shook Nagata time and again. The Tongan came back with bright moments in the second and fourth rounds landing straight rights to Tui's head, but he stood firm (Daunabuna, 1976).

Tui fought a brilliant fight against New South Wales-based Nagata, winning the fight in a unanimous points decision over eight rounds.

Champion Bose did not fare as well, when the fight ended a record 50 seconds into the first round after challenger Sisiwa delivered a solid left to the jaw that put the champ on the canvas for a full count.

Tui's fighting style caught the attention of promoter Raj Kumar Singh who signed him up to meet the newly crowned light-heavyweight champion Sisiwa in a non-title, 10-round contest in Sigatoka on December 16. Singh said that if Tui beat Sisiwa, he would be offered a crack at the Fiji light-heavyweight title next (Sport, 1976).

When promoter Sain returned from Tahiti in the first week of November, he contacted Ramos to go over the Ve-Basdeo return fight. The December 18 date was agreed on and details ironed out (Sport, 1976).

"Ve has expressed his feelings to me and says that he is indebted to Sain for getting this fight together so that he could let everyone see once and for all who the better boxer is," Ramos said after the deal was signed.

Meanwhile, the Fiji junior-welterweight title mooted by Sain was still awaiting approval by the PBWAF. Sain knew there were many boxers who could not get their weight down to lightweight and were not heavy enough for the welterweight division. He wanted to give the boxers something to aim for in their careers.

Tui's win over Nagata had Sain looking to include him on the Ve-Basdeo return programme at the Suva Town Hall. Sain wanted Tui for a supporting bout fight against Fiji middleweight champion Nemani Waka over 10 rounds and Tarika against veteran Sakaraia Qoro over eight rounds (Sport, 1976).

No sooner had Ramos sorted the Ve-Basdeo return programme, he was faced with another challenge after PBWAF announced the contenders for the vacant South Seas featherweight championship contest.

The PBWAF's decision to match unrated fighters Iqbal Azad and Daya Nand for the vacant South Seas featherweight title brought the association into Ramos's crosshairs.

Tarika, the reigning Fiji featherweight champion, was none too happy with that decision as he felt that he would be a logical contender for the vacant title. The title fight was to be included on the Ve-Basdeo return card.

"I'm surprised that the association approved the programme without considering the two boxers who will fight for title. I have beaten Daya Nand for the Fiji title, and I think it's only proper that I should meet him for the vacant crown," Tarika said (Sport, 1976).

Ramos supported Tarika's comment, adding that by overlooking a national champion for the regional title would kill the interest of boxers in the country.

Ramos, who was a PBWAF committee executive at the time, resigned in protest as he felt that Tarika, as the Fiji featherweight champion should have been offered the first opportunity to fight for the vacant South Seas title.

"It surprised me that the association approved the programme without giving Tarika the opportunity as Fiji champion to fight for that title. Tarika had at this point beaten Nand twice, once for the Fiji featherweight title challenge, and Azad was unrated as a featherweight. How was one to justify this?

"I strongly felt that these sorts of decisions would discourage and kill the interest in boxing in Fiji, so in resigning I made a conscious decision to concentrate my time better in looking after the welfare of my boxers and any other boxer who needed my help. At the time I felt also that many boxers in the past had not been cared for well in terms of their welfare and boxers needed an advocate which is what I decided I would now become.

"I had it made known to the PBWAF that they needed to amend their constitution with respect to title fights, to reflect the right of entitlement to contest. I felt also that Fijian champions had the first right of contest or challenge to any South Seas title be it vacant or otherwise. This was the natural progression in my view."

This was not to be the first time that Ramos and the PBWAF disagreed on the administration of professional boxing. In responding to Ramos's comments, PBWAF secretary Mumtaz Ali was quoted as saying that there was no rule in the association's constitution to indicate that champions should have the first chance to fight for the South Seas titles, adding that at the time of Ve and Gul's clash for the vacant South Seas lightweight champion Balwant Singh was the Fiji lightweight champion.

"At the time of the fight neither of them was a Fiji champion ... I'm sure the Fiji champion Balwant Singh was not approached either. If Fiji champions are claiming first chances at South Seas titles, Tonga and Western Samoan champions have equal rights," Ali said.

Ali advised Tarika to find a promoter and issue a challenge to the winner of the title contest.

PBWAF president Raj Gopal Menon also weighed in on the issue, saying that Tarika must honour his contract to fight Qoro on December 18. "Therefore, he cannot fight for the vacant South Seas featherweight title against Iqbal Azad" (Sport, 1978). Although Menon did agree that other than Daya Nand, Tarika was the only other logical contender.

On the night Tarika won the Fiji featherweight title, the unknown Azad climbed into the ring and issued a challenge to the new featherweight champion (Sport, 1976). At the time, Ramos and his seconds spurned the challenge from the relatively unknown fighter.

"No one took him very seriously when he climbed into the ring and challenged Tarika, after all we had never even seen him fight in the ring," Ramos said at the time.

A quick word with other promoters about Azad also yielded the same response. No one had ever heard of him. Tarika invited Azad to watch him take on Qoro later in December. A win by Qoro would have him first in line for a title challenge against Tarika.

With the Basdeo fight back on, Ve had a month to prepare, and he promised fans an entertaining encounter.

"Basdeo is old and slow, and I'll dance him silly," was Ve's way of making light of the tough fight ahead (Sport, 1976).

"I will beat Basdeo well so that there are no other second thoughts about my challenge to Inia Catarogo for the Fiji welterweight title," Ve said.

Catarogo was keen to watch Ve fight. He needed to see up close what he would be up against when he met Ve and the way to do that would be ringside when Ve fought Basdeo (Sport, 1976).

Joining Ramos to train Ve and Tarika for their upcoming fights was former Fiji featherweight, lightweight and welterweight champion, R.D. Shankar (Sport, 1976). Known in his time as the Sugar Ray Robinson of the South Pacific, Shankar was also the first boxer of Indo-Fijian descent to claim a welterweight title when he won it in 1950. Boxing pundits list Shankar as one of the fastest boxers to come out of Fiji (Sport, 1976). Shankar was tipped to be in Ve's corner for this important fight.

"We have been very lucky to have someone of Shankar's calibre as our second," Ramos said at the time, "and according to Shankar, Ve's in top form and I fully agree with him."

Ramos paid respect to Shankar's achievements, describing him as the most scientific boxer of his time and adding he hoped the boxers at the club would take the opportunity to learn from the boxing legend.

With Tarika looking good at training for the Qoro fight, Ramos set in motion plans to have his fighter contest a South Seas junior-lightweight title. There was no such category at the time, but Ramos was keen to create a category to generate greater interest in the light divisions.

"We are not doing this for Fiji boxers only, we are thinking of the South Seas region and by having a junior-lightweight championship, featherweight boxers who find difficulties in keeping the weight limit could fight in that division," Ramos said (Sport, 1976).

Lined up for Tarika in the event the proposal did go through was Rabi Island's Inoke Ratu.

With that in the queue, Ramos was also keen to secure Ve a fight against Catarogo in the new year and was hoping to use the champ's attendance at the Ve-Basdeo fight to lock in that opportunity and he promised the champ that "this fight would be something to see" (Rabuka, 1976).

On the day of the fight, the excitement was palpable with fans packing the Suva Town Hall to capacity. Ve was ready and so was Basdeo.

"This time Ve had to be sharper and quicker," Ramos recalled.

"We put in a plan to work on veteran Basdeo's body starting from the first round to weaken his resolve. In boxing, trainers have a saying 'if you kill the body, the head will die'. This was to be our strategy."

Ve worked the ring, tiring Basdeo. He worked on the body shots, making sure not to get caught on the ropes. This saw the fight go the full ten rounds and this time Ve fought the right fight, winning decisively on points and setting the stage for a grudge match for the vacant South Seas junior-welterweight title the following February.

The fight took a lot out of Ve, but it also cemented his prospects for international opponents.

By the end of 1976, Ve had fought 11 professional bouts winning three on points, seven by knockout and one loss – gaining along the way, the South Seas lightweight title and the Fiji lightweight title.

Nicknamed 'Wili Pony' because of his speed and agility, Tarika, a former Fiji amateur bantamweight, featherweight, and flyweight champion, won the vacant Fiji featherweight title left vacant by Mansoor Ali in 1964. It had been 12 years since Fiji saw another exciting featherweight fighter come along.

"With each fight Tarika stepped up a notch in strength, speed, and counterpunching. I gradually built him to face stronger opponents with each fight," Ramos said.

Tarika notched up nine professional fights in his first year of boxing and was determined to retain his featherweight title until he retired.

"In less than 18 months, I had managed to develop two exciting fighters who between them held three titles," Ramos said.

"For me, building and creating champions was only a part of what I wanted to achieve in boxing. In a time before professional publicists and marketing machines that you see behind many professional athletes these days, my philosophy was quite simple – always give your fans the respect that they deserve and maintain a strong relationship with them and your community by giving back when you can. Such a commitment inspires loyalty and support. Without the support of fans to fill the seats, no professional fighter will be able to earn a living.

"And one of the reasons that Ramos Boxing Club was always remembered with fondness and respect is not only because of the glory and joy that its fighters brought to the fans and to Fiji, but because we always stayed connected with the community by holding exhibition bouts around the country whenever we could to help raise money whether for a school, temples, churches or community halls.

"I knew that in many of these villages and communities, our fans would never have had the opportunity to travel and watch Ve, Tarika, Tui or any of the other exciting boxers from my club in a fight, and by going to see them, meeting them and showing genuine support towards their needs we ensured a loyal following."

During the year, the Ramos Boxing Club participated in the annual Hibiscus Festival by marching in the opening parade and hosting an exhibition match for charity. They also helped raise funds for the Our Lady of Fatima Parish and Kali Temple in Nadera as well as the Methodist Church in Lami.

In a fundraiser for the Suva Crippled Children's Society held in early July, the club members put on exhibition bouts for the children and members of the public who were charged 50 cents for adults and 20 cents for children to watch the programme. All proceeds were given to the Society (Sports, 1976).

"Having established ourselves firmly in the hearts and minds of our fans, it was time to take it a notch higher and to start looking abroad for challengers for Ve and Tarika," Ramos said.

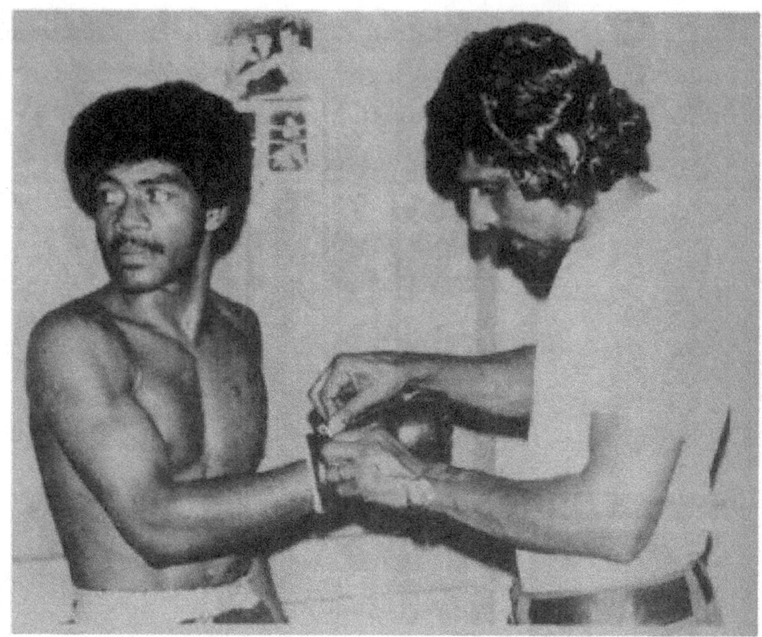

John Ramos (R) tightens Sakaraia Ve's glove at the final workout before Ve's fight against Balwant Singh for the Fiji Lightweight title (Fiji Times, April 26, 1976).

Ramos fighters Tevita Tui (L) and Sakaraia Ve sparring at the Ramos Boxing Club in Belo Street (Fiji Times, January 21, 1976).

ONE of the few times Jo Dawai (right) left himself wide
open to Tevita Tui in their fight.

Fiji Times, July 7, 1976.

Fiji Times, September 20, 1976.

Balwant Singh (R) catches Sakaraia Ve off guard in a rare moment in their return bout (Fiji Times, October 2, 1976).

SAKARAIA VE (left) shows his brilliant counter-punches as he lands a right to Basdeo's jaw in their bout on Saturday night. Basdeo won on points.

Fiji Times, October 25, 1976.

Wili Tarika with his Fiji
Featherweight championship belt
(Fiji Times, October 26, 1976).

WILI Tarika (left) and his trainer, John Marimuttu Ramos, discuss their problems over the vacant featherweight championship of the South Seas. Tarika, the current Fiji champion, was overlooked and Ramos resigned as a member of the PBWA executive committee.

Fiji Times, November 12, 1976.

Chapter 6
1977 – International fights

Nineteen seventy-seven was going to be a bumper time for Ve. In the last 12 months, he had grown in leaps and bounds sealing his place as a champion with two titles securely in his grasp.

In this one year, Ve would have another eight pro fights including three against international fighters - Gilbert Orsaldo, Ali Afakasi and Steve Ayerst. He would also add another two titles to his collection.

JANUARY – TEVITA TUI

The year started out on a great footing as Ve knocked Ramesh Chand out in the fourth round in their meeting at the Suva Town Hall on January 17. This was their third encounter since Ve turned professional.

On that same programme, Tevita Tui, 24, met fellow Fijian and Australian middleweight champion, Semi Bula, 30. Bula opened up a cut over the confident Tui's left eye in the third round and applied his experience and speed to Tui from the sixth culminating with a stoppage in the ninth round after the ring doctor inspected Tui's cut brow as well as a nose and mouth bleed. He advised referee Mumtaz Ali to stop the fight, awarding Bula a TKO (Rabuka, 1977).

After the fight, Ramos said the plan was to get Bula in the early rounds but Tui's preference to box and pace him instead made for a more difficult fight.

"I told him to open him up like he did with Jo Dawai and Luke Sisiwa, but he tried to do the rope-a-dope style and pull Bula into the ropes against him. That was the cause of his downfall," Ramos said (Sport, 1977).

"From the third round I knew Tui could not make it. Tui proved it himself when he started to hit Bula in the fifth round and hurt him. But he did not follow up and lost the edge he had taken in that round. I know Tui has the punch to knock Bula out, but it was just a question of him taking the initiative early. Had he followed our plan the story would have been entirely different."

Ve's win was another step in the direction towards a third fight against veteran Basdeo, who was seen as a warm-up to challenge Inia Catarogo for the Fiji welterweight title.

Ramos and Ve predicted a knockout in the thirteenth round. With a win each in their two encounters, Ve and Basdeo were scheduled for a decider on February 5 at Churchill Park in Lautoka. On the line was the South Seas junior-welterweight title.

"After this fight we are going to wait for Catarogo and then give him the first chance to try for the South Seas welterweight title," Ramos said (Sport, 1977).

Expected at the Ve-Baseo fight was Tahitian lightweight champion Maurice Apeang (Sport, 1977). Sain's contact and relationship with the Tahiti Boxing Association (TBA) was proving beneficial to Fijian fighters as boxers from the French territory were keen to be part of a regional boxing programme. It was anticipated that Apeang would fight Ve in March at the Lambert Hall in Suva for a new title to be donated by the TBA.

Also, on the Ve-Basdeo programme in the undercard draw was Tarika against Zamal Azad in a lightweight contest. In a featherweight bout, Zamal's brother Iqbal would go up against Daya Nand in an elimination fight for the vacant South Seas featherweight title.

FEBRUARY – BASDEO AND THE FIJI JUNIOR WELTERWEIGHT TITLE

With one win apiece, the South Seas junior-welterweight meet between Basdeo and Ve promised to be a cracker with each fighter seeking to settle the score once and for all. Basdeo's trainer and match promoter, Brij Sain said Ve could expect a totally new style from Basdeo when the two met (Daunibuna, 1977). The new strategy from the Basdeo camp was to go for the head.

"This does not mean we will leave his body alone, but a good mixture will be delivered at the right time," Sain said.

Ramos dismissed Basdeo's strategy stating that the last two fights had exposed Basdeo's many weaknesses.

"Basdeo is not strong enough to last the distance when under pressure from the opening round. And if he plans to concentrate his attacks on Ve's head, he will be wasting his strength," Ramos said (Rabuka, 1977).

The build-up to the fight was marred by the appointment of Francis Byrnes as referee, which brought protests from the Ramos camp. Byrnes was also the trainer/manager of Zamal Azad who was meeting Tarika in the main supporting bout. That fight resulted in a draw with Tarika putting on a less than impressive performance. (Sport, 1977).

Ve questioned the impartiality of Byrnes should Azad lose to Tarika, asking for a neutral referee, whether that be former amateur boxer Ilisoni Nate or former Fiji welter and middleweight champ, Kolaia Bauli.

Ramos as well was none too pleased, supporting Ve's call that fighters and their managers should be consulted in the selection of referees for their fights (Rabuka, 1977).

Despite objections from the Ramos camp, Byrnes refereed the much-anticipated decider. There was only one thing left for Ve to do and that was to win. And win convincingly.

"Basdeo hammered – Ve wins in 13," blared *The Fiji Sun* headline the next day.

The fight was a slugfest lasting 13 of the scheduled 15 rounds before referee Byrnes stopped the bout and awarded Ve the South Seas junior-welterweight title on a technical knockout. Both fighters showed great skill and flashes of brilliance in the earlier rounds. Basdeo's solid punches and attacks to the head opened a cut over Ve's left eye at the end of the fourth round. However, Ve's brilliant counterpunches and speed battered Basdeo several times on the head causing the veteran to stagger around the ring in the thirteenth round prompting Byrnes to stop the fight (Sport, 1977).

The cut above Ve's eye put him out for four weeks, delaying his first planned international bout against Maurice Apeang of Tahiti. Ramos said he wasn't risking Ve's career by rushing him into another fight before the cut healed completely.

"Such injury can do harm to good boxers like Ve who is only 21 and already he has won three titles in 14 professional fights over a span of 15 months," Ramos said (Sport, 1977).

Ringside for the Ve-Basdeo fight was the Fiji and South Seas welterweight champion Inia Catarogo. Impressed by the performance of both fighters, he offered to put his Fiji welterweight title on the line against Basdeo and his South Seas welterweight title against Ve if he (Ve) put his South Seas junior-welterweight title on the line as well (Daunabuna, 1977).

Promoter Eric Emberson who flew Catarogo down from Labasa to watch the fight, said that should the PBWAF approve the double title fight, he would begin negotiations with both parties.

Ve's victory was soured by the PBWAF's suspension of Ramos soon after. The suspension came in response to Ramos's public outburst against Byrnes' appointment as referee. Surprised by the suddenness of the suspension, Ramos pledged to continue training his boxers and negotiating fights on their behalf.

"I was rather surprised to hear that the association had taken a tough action against me. I think it is a rather personal one. I would like to make a personal appearance before the committee if they want me to," he said at the time (Sport, 1977). Ramos stood by his comments on referee selection.

The suspension was lifted two weeks later when it was speculated that Ramos intended to stand against Ali, the PBWAF secretary for more than 20 years, at the upcoming February AGM for the association.

Association president Raj Gopal Menon said the committee felt that it would not be fair for Ramos to be under suspension when he had said that he intended to stand for election. The decision was prompted by submissions from Ba promoter Nazir Khan, referee Kolaia Bauli and ex-Fiji heavyweight champion Filimone Naliva at the committee meeting to allow Ramos to stand for election.

"We want to see that those wishing to stand for election should be free, although we are backing Ali to retain his position as secretary," Khan said (Rabuka, 1977).

Ramos, however, was undecided as to whether he would file the nomination papers despite pressure from supporters to do so.

"I was working fulltime band after work I was at the club training the boxers and then I had my young family as well. As it was, I was hardly ever home early during the week. It was a lot to weigh up and I wanted to be certain that if I did stand, I could commit the time but not at the expense of my boxers," Ramos said.

After nominations closed, Ramos made it known he had decided not to stand, stating that there was a huge task ahead of him – to look after his boxers.

"Their careers and their welfare are more important than anything else," Ramos said of his decision (Sport, 1977).

Ali and Menon resumed office unopposed at the AGM as their opponents Lakshman Singh and Joe Lele were disqualified from standing after discovery that their nomination forms were signed by non-financial members.

Five months later, Singh and Lele attempted but failed in trying to set up a rival boxing body despite claims of widespread support (Sport, 1977).

Amid Ramos's suspension and the PBWAF AGM drama, members of the Ramos Boxing Club got together and made a collective gesture of financial support for the family of the late Waisea Tavusa of Labasa who died after his fight against Jo Vucago in 1975. Tavusa collapsed in the ring during the bout and never regained consciousness, passing away in hospital a week later.

Ve pledged to buy a 10-year life insurance policy for the education of Tavusa's daughter, Eleni, who was born three months following his (Tavusa's) death. in addition to a tithe of $20 from each of Ve and Tarika's upcoming purses, other professional boxers from the club also made pledges to contribute into a bank account to be opened by Ve at the Bank of New Zealand where he (Ve) worked.

"As a Fiji boxer and champion, I felt it is my duty to donate something to the family for the child's education. I have promised to open a savings account for the family, and I will be donating $20 from my purse in future fights," Ve said (Sport, 1977). Ramos added that they were also looking to stage a charity fundraiser programme later in aid of the Tavusa family.

Tarika's poor showing against Zamal Azad in the Ve-Basdeo eight-round undercard draw, prompted the Fiji featherweight champion to put his title on the line in a rematch with Azad in April.

"I will prove to the people of the West that I am the champ and there is no one else in the division who can touch me," Tarika said (Sport, 1977).

"I'll prove to his manager, trainer and all his fans over there that Zamal is an overrated boxer."

By the end of February, Ve signed the contract to fight Catarogo at the Lambert Hall in Suva in early April. Ramos was confident of Ve adding a fourth belt to the mantlepiece.

"Ve has been very active in the ring and has taken a lot of heavy punches from Basdeo in close mix-ups which he has managed to weather, while Catarogo has been inactive for a long time," Ramos said (Sport, 1977).

Ramos revealed to *Fiji Times Sport* that the plan was to give Ve night training after gym to get his body accustomed to fighting late at night without tiring easily.

"Ve will box Catarogo from the first to the seventh round and go all out from then on," Ramos said.

MARCH, APRIL – INIA CATAROGO AND THE FIJI WELTERWEIGHT TITLE

The whole of March was for Ve to get his cut healed. Light workouts and no sparring were his preparation for champion Catarogo.

Closer to the fight, Catarogo's camp grew confident that preparations so far would have him at his peak when he met Ve. His manager Ilisoni Nate told *Fiji Times Sport* that Catarogo was doing roadwork morning and afternoon and sparring with partners well over 15 stone (95kg). Nate said that should Catarogo win he would immediately challenge Ve for the South Seas junior welterweight title (Sport, 1977).

Former Fiji middleweight champion Ravuama Roko and former Fiji welterweight champion Seva Mocesui had words of caution for Ve. Having been at the receiving end of Catarogo's hard hits, both men knew all too well what Ve would find himself up against.

Roko, who beat Catarogo once on points for the title, said it would be disastrous for Ve to go right in at the opening bell, advising instead that he keep his distance until after the tenth round.

"Catarogo has a punch, particularly his left hook, and Ve should watch out for him," Roko said (Sport, 1977).

For Ve, having secured the junior South Seas welterweight only a few weeks earlier, making the 10 stone weight limit wasn't going to be a problem. Going into the fight, Ve had the advantage of competing over the last 12 months whereas Catarogo hadn't been active for the previous six months.

Catarogo was ringside for the Ve-Basdeo title fight and was confident that he had sized up his opponent's weakness. He said he was ready to take the fight over the full 15 rounds. Catarogo said, "We are going to capitalise on them (weaknesses) during the fight, but the plan is for the fight to go the distance."

"Ve has tremendous respect for Catarogo's experience and punching strength as a boxer and even though he was only 21 at the time, I knew that his speed, counterpunches and heart would give him victory in the early rounds which was our strategy," Ramos said.

"He may be old but don't write off the left hooks because they could be the deciding factor of the fight. If I was to give Ve any advice, it would be that he should not rush Catarogo in the early rounds," Roko said.

Catarogo, 34 at the time, was a 17-year veteran of the ring. It was not going to be a walk in the park for the 21-year-old Ve.

On the day of the fight, Catarogo knew that he was in for a tough time, but he was optimistic of his chances and refrained from making any predictions of how the fight would proceed. The odds were that the fight could go either way with both boxers given an equal chance of winning.

Ramos, confident that Ve had the edge, noted that with age Catarogo would have lost some of the sting in his punches.

"This is why Ve will be attacking the champion right from the opening round," he said (Volavola, 1977).

And attack from the opening bell is what Ve did, outboxing and outstepping the champion, knocking him out in the fourth round. The win handed Ve, Catarogo's Fiji welterweight title, making him champion of three different weight divisions – lightweight, junior-welterweight and welterweight – in just 15 months as a professional.

The 'Babasiga Terror' was none too pleased with the result, questioning referee Joe Campbell over his decision to stop the fight and award the title to Ve after the fourth-round knockdown. Catarogo felt that the referee should have asked him if he could continue before calling off the fight. So angry was the champ that he threw two punches, one catching Campbell in the chest.

The PBWAF in reviewing Catarogo's conduct in the ring a few weeks later, decided to impose a life ban and thereby stripping him of the South Seas welterweight title. He had 21 days to appeal. Catarogo's team was naturally disappointed by the decision with his manager Ilisoni Nate saying they would appeal the decision (Sport, 1977).

Ramos and Ve came out in support of Catarogo after the announcement, calling on the PBWAF to lift the ban. Ve made known his disappointment with the association's decision. Ramos and Ve knew Catarogo to be a gentleman in the ring his entire career and felt the life ban was excessive.

"I don't blame him (Catarogo) for his action. It must be taken into account that the title was part of Catarogo's life," Ramos said, adding that he and Ve would formally support Catarogo's appeal if requested (Sport, 1977).

After a review at the appeal hearing, the PBWAF lifted the life ban on Catarogo in July, however he would be on 12-month probation (Sport, 1977).

Good to his word, Ve deposited money into Eleni's Tavusa's account after the Catarogo clash (Sport, 1977). He was joined a month later by new professional and stablemate Ami Bavoro, who gave $5 from his $27 purse to help the family (Sport, 1977).

The day after the Ve-Catarogo fight in Suva, Tarika slugged it out with challenger Zamal Azad for Tarika's Fiji featherweight title in Lautoka. The scheduled 15-rounder was a close battle with Tarika winning in a split points decision. A protest followed from Azad's trainer/manager Francis Byrnes when it was revealed that referee Joji Ponipate scored 197-196 to Tarika (Daunabuna, 1977). Understandably, because it was a 15-round fight scored at a maximum of 10 points per round and therefore maximum points awarded could not possibly exceed 150 if contested for the full 15 rounds. Judge Vishnu Deo scored 149-146 to Azad and judge Kolaia Bauli scored 147-143 to Tarika.

The fight controversy did not end there. Azad refused the $30 purse offered by promoter Brij Sain for the fight. Tarika was given a purse of $300, the largest ever negotiated for a featherweight champion. Byrnes admitted that "although they didn't sign any written contract, they had an 'understanding' with Sain to pay a certain amount depending on the turnout of spectators." Sain said that he believed $30 was good enough for Azad adding that he had paid as little as $20 for a boxer who had fought for the title (Sport, 1977).

The Fiji welterweight title win set the stage to find Ve overseas competition. The first contender under consideration was Tahitian lightweight champion Maurice Apeang, who also represented France as a super-featherweight at the 1972 Olympic Games in Munich.

Ramos saw the Apeang fight as a possible stepping stone to challenging Australian Hector Thompson for the Commonwealth light welterweight title (Sport, 1977). However, the fight was called off when it was discovered that Apeang's weight was around 127lbs (57.6kg) as a featherweight while Ve was fighting at 146lbs (66.2kg) as a welterweight. The other fighter also under consideration for Ve was Papua New Guinean super-lightweight and Commonwealth-rated Martin Beni.

Ramos's quest to find quality international fighters for Ve was the next logical step even though local fighters including Mansoor Ali, Log Nadan and Peni Rauga wanted a shot at Ve's welterweight title. Ramos dismissed them as easy knockouts.

Upon reflection of Ve's growth as a professional fighter, Ramos expressed gratitude for Ve's dedication and resilience.

"I don't have any trouble with Ve. He does what he is told, doesn't drink or smoke, no late nights and he is dedicated to the sport. He is very sincere with training, and these are some of the factors that have moulded him into such a perfect boxer. He is like a son to me, and he follows everything I tell him without question," Ramos said.

PBWAF secretary Mumtaz Ali was also supportive of the international search, stating, "Ve will need overseas fights to gain experience against international opponents and this should be done while Ve is still in his prime" (Rabuka, 1977).

Of course, with Ve looking internationally for his next challenge, rumblings within the local ranks spread whispers that Ve was avoiding defence of his four titles, rumours he countered by saying he would like to defend a title each month provided there were decent challengers and a purse to suit (Sport, 1977).

Unperturbed with the continued chatter, Ve signed with Brij Sain in early May to meet Gilbert Orsaldo in Suva on June 3. Ve's contract, as all previous purses negotiated by Ramos, was tax free. At $700, it was the biggest purse of his fight career so far.

"He has the right to hold on to the title at this stage before deciding his next move," Ali said.

JUNE – GILBERT ORSALDO, AZAD BROTHERS

By June, Ve was well into his preparations for his first international fight – against Frenchman Gilbert Orsaldo. Orsaldo, 27, a lightweight, turned professional in 1972 and had 19 professional fights with a 10-5-4 record compared to Ve's 13-1-0 in just 19 months. Orsaldo also won the 1972 silver medal in the European boxing championships for the lightweight division and was the lightweight champion in the French army (Volavola, 1977).

Ve was determined not to let the fight go the distance and it almost did, had Ve not stopped the Frenchman with a TKO in the ninth round.

A week later, Tarika took on Iqbal Azad, Zamal's younger brother, in a 10-round non-title fight at Churchill Park in Lautoka. That fight ended in a points win to Azad. The result raised the ire of Ramos who felt Tarika was robbed.

There were several issues at play here, according to Ramos. One was the appointment of Azad's former trainer, Kolaia Bauli, as the referee and the bias of the other two Western-based referees with one judge, Peni Tora, awarding more than 100 points to Azad when it was only a 10-round contest (Sport, 1977). The tables had indeed turned given a similar result in Tarika's favour when he fought Zamal in April.

"Tarika won clearly. He outclassed his opponent at will and Azad was punching with open gloves. It was one of Tarika's best fights," Ramos said adding, "I don't blame him for what he did to Zamal Azad in the ring."

The older Azad jumped into the ring to declare the decision correct. The declaration turned into flight for Zamal when Tarika charged after him. Both Tarika and Ramos had to be escorted from the ring by police after Ramos also exchanged heated words with Zamal.

Ramos maintained that Tarika scored points consistently throughout the fight with solid counterpunches while Azad missed some good rights. Ramos offered to put Tarika's Fiji featherweight title on the line in a return bout against Iqbal, provided the fight was held in Suva.

The older Azad also challenged Tarika to a non-title contest to settle the score after Tarika challenged both brothers to a contest – on the same night. The older Azad said that he was looking to avenge his narrow points loss in their last meet two months before (Sport, 1977). Ramos dismissed the challenge by the brothers, saying that a fight with either of the brothers would do nothing to enhance Tarika's reputation.

"Zamal and Iqbal Azad's styles are such that if they fought Tarika in Suva, local boxing fans would think we are trying to fight only second-hand boxers," Ramos said (Sport, 1977).

Another Ramos fighter going well in the amateurs was middleweight Setareki Bolatawa. A close cousin of Tarika's from Wailoku Village in Suva, Bolatawa came in the sights of national amateur selectors for the South Pacific Games after a good outing in an amateur fight against Iosefa Kula of Police (Simpson, 1977).

President of the Fiji Amateur Sports Association Les Martin said he was impressed with Bolatawa's "style".

"I would like to see that boy on the Fiji team next year if he does not get battered about too much. He has a good style, and he knows what to do when in a dilemma," Martin said.

Ramos remembers Bolatawa as a very nice, respectable young prospect who went on to become one of Ve's top sparring partners.

JULY – FIJI'S MUHAMMAD ALI

Moving on from the Azad fiasco, Tarika helped Ve with preparations for his first defence of the Fiji welterweight title against Rupeni Vutevute in Suva on July 11.

In planning for the fight, Ramos said that Vutevute would be stopped inside 10 rounds because he wasn't as strong or as rugged at Catarogo or Basdeo (Rabuka, 1977).

"In the case of Vutevute, Ve will have plenty of time to calculate his attacks because his taller opponent throws straight punches only. We know his weaknesses and how to avoid his long overhead lefts and rights," Ramos said, adding that they would be giving thought to a suitable opponent for Ve in the defence of one of his lightweight titles after the Vutevute fight.

Weighing in at 10st 7lbs (66.7kg) to Ve's 10st 8lbs (67.1kg), Vutevute struggled to keep pace with Ve's rapid counterpunches. In keeping close, Ve denied his taller opponent with solid head shots that could have caused serious damage. By the sixth round, Vutevute started to tire and missed some crucial long rights with Ve boxing some brilliant combination of punches to the body and head. Ve's tireless combinations went unanswered. Vutevute's seconds threw in the towel at the bell for the ninth round. A TKO win to Ve and a successful defence of his welterweight title (Rabuka, 1977).

No sooner had that fight ended, the next challenger was queued for Ve. Navosa boxer Ambika Prasad, who had earlier defeated former amateur champion Tomasi Rokoura, was given the nod. Also under consideration was a return bout against Catarogo whose life ban was recently lifted. Ramos reiterated their respect for the former champion's experience and reputation and as such, "We will be quite willing to give him a return bout" (Sport, 1977).

The good performance of boxers in the Ramos stable, prompted Waqabaca Cama, 'Fiji's Muhammad Ali', to request a return to the fold in July after his dismal outing against Vuniivi Namudu in May where he lost on a disqualification in the ninth round. The loss came about in a bizarre incident when one of Cama's seconds, Samu Matainasiga, punched Namudu when he kept hitting Cama after the bell. Referee Mike Ravula claimed not to have heard the bell to end the round.

The lacklustre performance saw Cama step into the ring, a shadow of the former fleet-of-foot and colourful middleweight that he was known to be. Now, fighting as a heavyweight, Cama's added bulk weighed him down to a flat-footed, lumbering slugger. The butterfly was no more, the sting gone (Rabuka, 1977).

After thinking things over, Ramos agreed to let Cama rejoin the club.

"I know that most people in Fiji today would brand Waqabaca as a second-rate boxer, but I know that he has a lot of potential and that he could very well be one of the great boxers for Fiji. At 24, he is possibly the youngest boxer ever to be placed so high on the local boxing scene in the heavyweight division," Ramos said, adding that he already had plans for Cama's training regime and redemption fight (Sport, 1977).

Also, on the road to redemption was Catarogo, who was scheduled to meet Ba southpaw Peni Rauga in Suva on July 22 in his first fight since his life ban was lifted by the PBWAF (Sport, 1977). Catarogo would quietly retire after this fight.

AUGUST – PBWAF SUSPENSION

The South Seas welterweight title vacated from Catarogo by the PBWAF after his suspension, was up for grabs. The rush was on to find the first challengers. The PBWAF ruled that Catarogo had the first right of challenge based on principles of fairness. Plans however, were afoot to bill Ve against Basdeo for the vacant championship with Ramos revealing that Ve had been offered a tax-free purse of $1,100 for the fight (Sport, 1977).

Also bidding for a title fight against Ve was Sigatoka lightweight Ambika Prasad. Ve had not defended his lightweight title since wresting it from Balwant Singh the previous October (Sport, 1977).

Singh, who unfortunately suffered major injuries in a motor vehicle accident in July, challenged Tarika for his featherweight title from his recovery bed. Tarika was up to the challenge, but Ramos had cautionary words of advice for the former champion (Sport, 1977).

"As a friend, I would urge Balwant to hang up his boxing gloves after he recovers from his injuries – especially with the type of injuries he suffered in the car accident," Ramos said.

"If he wants to take on Tarika, it would just be murder on our part for accepting his challenge. His last fight was against Ve in Sigatoka last October and he has been inactive for almost a year now. That coupled with his accident would mean that he is completely out of boxing altogether."

For the Ve-Basdeo fight for the vacant title to go ahead, it required PBWAF sanction, however the association announced in early August that Catarogo would be given the first chance to fight for the title "because he didn't lose it but was stripped of it when he was suspended for punching referee Joe Campbell on April 1" (Sport, 1977).

This angered Ramos who felt that it was a decision that the PBWAF should have made in the first place. He openly criticised the association for not assisting Catarogo find a challenger earlier, instead of blocking the opportunity for Ve and Basdeo to contest the vacant title.

Ramos, in a fit of frustration stated: "The Professional Boxing and Wrestling Association of Fiji would do well to get rid of one of its senior officials if they want to improve their relations with members" (Sports, 1977).

The comment was a clear shot at PBWAF secretary Mumtaz Ali. The statement as predicted, did not go down well with Ali who demanded that Ramos retract his statement or face disciplinary action. Ramos was undeterred.

"I told the truth. I will never retract my statement. I'm fed up with the whole thing. Whenever a person does something against the PBWAF, he is suspended. I was suspended earlier this year while I was away in Lautoka and then mysteriously without my appealing or doing anything about it, it was lifted. Now they are trying to do the same thing again," Ramos said (Sport, 1977).

The public outburst resulted in a summons from the PBWAF for Ramos to appear before the PBWAF committee. The letter to Ramos read:

"You are requested to attend an executive committee meeting on Tuesday, 20th September 1977 at 5pm at the committee room at the New Town Hall, Suva to answer charges made against you arising from your recent press statements as follows:

a. *'You alleged that the association does not want Ve to add a fifth title to his tally*
b. *'You alleged that Professional Boxing and Wrestling Association said Catarogo would get first crack at the title but do not seem to be doing anything about getting Catarogo into the ring*
c. *'You alleged that you are not a member of the association, and you do not care for any disciplinary action*

> d. *'It would be in your own interest to attend this meeting but if you do not then we may decide on this issue in your absence'.*"

Ramos remained defiant, standing by his comments adding that if adverse action was taken against him which would affect his boxers earning a living, he would consider legal action against the association (Sport, 1977).

On September 20, the PBWAF returned a 12-month ban against Ramos for what they described as "mischievous, baseless and disparaging allegations levelled at the association" (Sport, 1977).

According to Ali, "The committee deplored such nauseating remarks and felt these were detrimental to the sport and should not be tolerated." And with that, the association struck Ramos's name off the register with a warning to promoters that if Ramos was found to be negotiating "either in part or in full" with them on behalf of Ramos fighters, they risked not having their programmes approved by the association.

The incredulity of such a decision was that Ramos Club fighters could still appear on PBWAF-sanctioned fight programmes, just not with the man whose club bore his name standing alongside them. According to the PBWAF, Ramos was *persona no grata* as far as they were concerned. But Ramos was not to be silenced by the slap down. The fire in his belly was just warming up.

"By imposing the suspension on me, the association was in fact crippling the future of two of Fiji's top boxers – Ve and Tarika. All because they did not like being criticised because when you fight to get your boxers a better deal, you are not supporting the association," he challenged.

"I resigned from the committee a year ago to concentrate on building my club and helping my fighters' welfare. The association has done nothing to promote boxing in the country. It has failed in every respect to improve the standard of boxing. I'm not concerned for myself regarding the suspension, but I am for my boxers, and I will continue to work in their interest.

"I have spent a lot of my time in the club and a good amount of money in paying rent for the clubhouse. All this I did because I want my boxers to reach a standard to put Fiji's name one the world boxing map and I will continue to fight for my boxers to fight for Commonwealth titles."

In an editorial, *The Fiji Sun* was also searing of the PBWAF's decision opening its editorial with, "This nonsense in professional boxing has got to stop" (1977).

The editorial continued: *"Because of a personality clash between two men; because Professional Boxing and Wrestling Association apparently feel they cannot be criticised; one of the country's finest boxers may not fight here again."*

"Sakaraia Ve yesterday made it clear that he'll head overseas or quit if his manager trainer John Marimuttu is not allowed to continue to look after him. Marimuttu has been barred from any involvement in pro boxing for a year, according to Professional Boxing and Wrestling Association secretary Mumtaz Ali.

"Marimuttu is the man who piloted Ve to four titles and negotiated the champion some of the biggest purses promoters here have been forced to pay. But he has run into a head-on collision with Ali.

"Marimuttu has not hesitated to push the talents of his boxers, and two of them hold championship titles. The former boxer has been quick to criticise anything he thinks is to their detriment. Some people call him a loudmouth. His boxers, however, respect him. Ali is sensitive to any criticism. Unusually so.

"Sports journalists can tell you of his outbursts when he has been angered. So, when Marimuttu spoke out recently trouble was inevitable. Some of Marimuttu's criticisms deserve an answer.

"He has questioned for example, the lack of PBWAF action to look after the families of boxers killed or crippled in the ring. Marimuttu's boxers have been giving their own money to help the family of the late Waisea Tavusa. But as far as many in professional boxing are apparently concerned, Tavusa is dead and forgotten.

"The PBWAF are right to try and maintain some sort of discipline within their organisation. But in suspending someone because he says something you don't like, disciplined? We think not. Maybe Marimuttu is right when he says PBWAF think they are above criticism."

The sentiments of *The Fiji Sun* editorial were also reflected in the letter to the editor column a week later by a fan signing off as "Fed Up, Suva" who had this to say (1977):

"The secretary of the PBWAF, Mumtaz Ali claims that John Marimuttu Ramos should be banned for what he has openly said through the press. Do you

really know what Marimuttu has done to boxing in Fiji? Before Marimuttu came into the eyes of people, boxing was almost fading away in our talented country. He should be credited for reviving the image of boxing. His is the man responsible for making Sakaraia Ve a "world beater," the glamour boy who will carry Fiji's name into the boxing world in the time to come. Not only is Ve under him but there are other big guns in his club. Tevita Tui, Wili Tarika, Cama Waqabaca (sic) and many more up-and-coming young boxers. Why is Marimuttu doing this? The answer automatically is: 'he is doing it for his country.' And yet this man who calls himself the secretary of the PBWAF is trying to destroy a man who has really helped boxing. Now Mr Ali, what have you done for boxing except for self-raising and in an interview with a particular newspaper? You should know by now that it is time you quit and stop ruining chances of other young boxing experts in this country. You seem to like suspending people who seem to be a threat to your post as secretary. Stop being selfish and give John Marimuttu, 'the people's choice,' a chance."

The PBWAF sanction bore no sting as promoters continued to negotiate with Ramos for Ve, undeniably the biggest boxing drawcard in the country, and other Ramos fighters to appear in their programmes. Promoters did not want to risk losing Ve to fighting abroad.

Fiji heavyweight champion, Sunia Cama, who only a month before was handed a $150 fine and a 12-month driving suspension by the Suva magistrate's court for driving his taxi in Suva under the influence of liquor (1977), was critical of Ramos saying that the boxers (Ve and Tarika) should be given credit for their title wins, not Ramos.

"They were at their best when they went to the Ramos club," Cama said.

"No trainer can do much if the boxers themselves aren't that good. I took both titleholders for a while, and I haven't found anything different from what they had been. If ever they go overseas, they will learn more" (Sport, 1977).

The suspension was only the beginning for Ramos. After the public reaction and groundswell of support for Ramos, the association issued a statement calling on Ve to quit his titles if he was indeed serious about moving abroad. Ramos countered with possible legal action if the association saw fit to go that way (Sport, 1977).

The pettiness of the association's response towards Ve only served to reinforce what Ramos had been saying all along about their failure to act for, and in the interest of, boxers.

"If I'm not in the negotiations, my boxers will not fight and (I) will stick to this decision. The fighters only want a fair deal from promoters and any interference from the association officials will jeopardise that," Ramos said at the time.

He proposed the association try to do the same on behalf of Fiji boxers going abroad to fight, who in the past Ramos said, were very poorly paid for their efforts.

"This was due to the failure of the association to negotiate better purses for them. It would have been better if the amount of money spent in sending a manager was added to the poor fighter's purse," he said.

OCTOBER, NOVEMBER – ALI AFAKASI

A week later, Ve started preparations for his second international fight against Samoan Ali Afakasi. A Commonwealth-rated welterweight, Afakasi was seen as Ve's stepping stone to a Commonwealth title fight planned for the following year. Afakasi, the former New Zealand welterweight champion, had fought Catarogo in October 1972 in Tahiti where he knocked out the Fijian in four rounds.

Afakasi was also stripped off his South Seas welterweight title by the PBWAF in June 1975 after he withdrew from a programme at the last minute. Afakasi was scheduled to meet Inia Catarogo in a title defence on the undercard for the Jone Mataitini and Monty Betham Commonwealth title clash in Suva (Sport, 1976).

Afakasi had won the title from Catarogo in 1974 and had not defended the belt since. At the time, he was also the New Zealand lightweight and welterweight champion as well as the Australasian welterweight champion.

To help Ve forge ahead, Ramos decided to not be a second in Ve's corner for the fight. In a letter to the association from Ve, following the association's rejection of the fight card proposed for November 5 in favour of another programme approved for November 7, Ve advised the association that

Ramos would not be in his corner (Volavola, 1977). The letter took association secretary Mumtaz Ali by surprise.

"We did not ask Ve for this statement," he said. "He did it in his own initiative and I'm very glad because he would have jeopardised his own boxing career had he stuck to Ramos."

When asked about Ali's comments, Ve responded that dropping Ramos from his corner did not mean that they were through as a team.

"Actually, we thought the association would have rejected the programme if Ramos was in my corner, so we talked it over. Since this is a very important fight for me, we have decided to take this approach," Ve said.

"Afakasi is in the Commonwealth ratings, and I want to make a good showing against him to prove myself. This is the type of opportunity I have been waiting for and I am not going to let it slip through my fingers."

Ali also expressed surprise at Ramos's decision and respect for the association contrary to his public comments.

"Of course, I respect the association. But I do not respect the people who are running it," Ramos said.

"My solicitor, Ve and I agreed that the best thing we could do was write to the PBWAF saying that I would not be in Ve's corner because we felt that promoter Eric Emberson had put in a lot of money in his preparation for the fight.

"We knew that if Ve did not write that letter Mr Emberson's programme would be rejected regardless of the amount of money he had already put into the programme."

The rejection of the fight card was withdrawn for the November 5 date after Afakasi's manager cabled Ali to advise him that his boxer would not be available for the later date.

Promoter Nur Mohammed, whose fight card clashed with the proposed date for the Ve-Afakasi fight offered to postpone his programme after strong urging from Ali (Sport, 1977).

"I felt that if nothing was done this international fight would not be held here in Suva," Ali said.

"So, I made a strong plea to Nur Mohammed to reconsider his programme, which he agreed to do so."

Promoter Emberson was relieved by the respite saying, "This is Sakaraia Ve's chance to prove himself against a boxer rated in the Commonwealth."

Ramos channelled his energy into preparing Ve for this crucial international fight. Both he and Ve knew what was at stake and Ramos's suspension by the association was not going to stand in the way of that.

A week out from the fight, reporter Eliki Rabuka visited Ve in training and was impressed with the champ's form and wrote this in his report: "I will put my money on Sakaraia Ve to beat Ali Afakasi next Saturday, although I have not seen the Samoan fighter in action. I came out of the Ramos Boxing Club last night confident that Ve will beat Afakasi after seeing his workouts. I have never seen his punching strength so effective. He hammered all his sparring partners in each round including Guam South Pacific Games middleweight representative Salesi Soko" (Rabuka, 1977).

Soko, who also sparred with Fiji middleweight champion Jone Mataitini, said that Ve was a much harder hitter than Mataitini.

Ramos was confident Ve would have Afakasi in the early rounds. A win would get Ve onto the Commonwealth rankings and eventually a shot at the title held at the time by Australian Hector Thompson.

As the fight drew closer, Ramos had a decision to make as Ve wanted him in his corner for the all-important fight. For that to eventuate Ramos had to swallow his pride and make an unreserved apology to the association which he did via his solicitor. In the letter, he also withdrew his earlier negative statements against the association (Sport, 1977).

On receiving the letter, Ali called an urgent committee meeting to discuss possible reinstatement. He also made it clear that there was nothing personal between him and Ramos.

Following their meeting, the association agreed that the 12-month suspension against Ramos be lifted. The decision was met with relief and joy from the Ramos camp (Rabuka, 1977).

Looking back, this fight was to be a watershed moment for Ve who at 17, left his village in Lovoni, Ovalau without his parents' knowledge to move to Suva to pursue his boxing dream. This fight would bring more than 300 of his kinsmen from Lovoni to the Laucala Bay Hangar to watch and cheer on their 'Golden Boy'.

At 30, Afakasi was eight years Ve's senior with a fight record that stood at 27-5-1 to Ve's 17-1-0. Afakasi's amateur record was also impressive with gold medal wins at the 1966 and the 1969 South Pacific Games (now called the Pacific Games).

The fight ended with a sixth round TKO victory for Ve after he opened a cut over Afakasi's eye. His solid hits to Afakasi's head also started an uncontrollable nosebleed in the earlier rounds. The cut and the nosebleed put paid to Afakasi's quest. This was Afakasi's second such TKO loss in similar circumstances. The other being to reigning Commonwealth light-welterweight champion Hector Thompson in the seventh round when they met in July (Rabuka, 1977).

The win also prompted PBWAF's Ali to now actively engage the British Boxing Board of Control to consider Ve for a Commonwealth title shot.

"It is about time the Commonwealth boxing committee looked down here because now we have not only a Commonwealth title contender but also a world contender," Ali said.

After the fight, Ramos said that they were eyeing third-ranked Australian welterweight Kevin Gibbs as Ve's next opponent.

"We don't like rushing Ve to fight Hector Thompson, but I will know by June (1978) whether or not Ve is good enough to take on a world-rated champion," he said.

A week after the Afakasi fight, Ve had two good offers on the table. Lautoka promoter Sain offered Ve a purse of $1,300 for a return bout with Basdeo which could possibly include the vacant South Seas welterweight championship vacated by Catarogo following his suspension.

The other was from Sigatoka promoter Raj Kumar, a purse of $900 to fight Jone Mataitini for his Fiji middleweight title. Neither offer was immediately accepted by Ve as Ramos club members focussed on their charity commitments later that month to host exhibition matches to raise money for Naiyala Junior Secondary School in Wainibuka and Nabua Methodist Youth Fellowship (Sport, 1977).

The plan for a Ve-Gibbs fight fell through after the Australia injured himself. He was replaced by Samoan-Kiwi Steve Ayerst, who had fought and lost against Catarogo in an eighth-round disqualification the previous year.

DECEMBER – STEVE AYERST, PENI RAUGA

In December Ve took on Steve Ayerst then Peni Rauga just before Christmas with Rauga given an opportunity to challenge Ve for his Fiji welterweight title if he fought well (Rabuka, 1977).

Ve was eager to make quick work of Ayerst to maintain his standing and steady progression against international opponents. Neither Ve nor Ayerst have been floored in their career thus far, so the bout would be interesting (Rabuka, 1977).

The programme was set for December 3 at the Lambert Hall in Suva.

"Ve can do it easily," Ramos said, "But we will not rush him because Ayerst is an aggressive fighter who has tackled heavier opponents."

Ayerst was brimming with confidence, seeing the fight as revenge for his friend Afakasi's loss to Ve (Dean, 1977).

"Sakaraia Ve will be no problem for me. The only way we can lose is through unfair judges," Ayerst said.

"He defeated my mate Ali Afakasi, whom I have known for six years, because Ali took the fight too lightly. I will avenge his defeat."

Ramos's good friend Johnny Lewis who was in Ve's corner when he met Balwant Singh for their second fight, was Ayerst's manager.

"This will be the end of Ve's unbeaten run in Fiji," Lewis warned Ramos in good humour (Rabuka, 1977).

For all the bluster from Lewis and Ayerst, the fight turned into a one-sided affair with Ayerst running from Ve. Referee Joe Campbell scored the fight 100-75 to Ve, labelling it "the worst one-sided fight" he had ever controlled (Sport, 1977).

Ramos and Ve were bitterly disappointed with the fight, as they had hoped that it would be a good test in lead-up to meeting Steve Dennis, who Ramos was eyeing for in the new year. Ramos also commented on advice from Afakasi's manager Tom Cassidy and Lewis on what should be done with Ve's professional career (Rabuka, 1977).

"They intend to advise us of what to do with Ve for his future fights, yet their boxers have not proved the reputations they brought to Fiji. It is about time that these people minded their own business as we know what we are doing with Ve's career," Ramos said.

To win back the fight fans after that lopsided showing against Ayerst, Ve knew that a good showing against southpaw Rauga was needed. This was to be the setting stage for Ve against another southpaw, Steve Dennis in January 1978. Dennis was also the reigning Australian welterweight champion.

"We hope to get some southpaw sparring partners soon to get Ve familiar with their boxing tactics," Ramos said (Rabuka, 1977).

"Once he can get used to it, then we will have no problem at all. What we are concerned with is where you should move and how to counter their lefts.

"Ve has got a straight left, but against a southpaw he will be working on his right more often."

In the week leading up to the Rauga fight at the Suva Town Hall, Ve sparred with three southpaws (Sport, 1977).

Rauga also worked hard on his preparations, running seven miles a day and going 10 rounds each time with his sparring partners.

"If I lose the fight, I will have no excuse at all, I had a good preparation and I know I should give him a good battle," Rauga said (Sport, 1977).

Unbeaten in eight professional fights, Rauga was confident that his straight punching would see Ve in trouble when they met on December 19. However, it was not to be, with the fight ending in the second round after Ve knocked him out.

Also walking away with a knockout on the night was Wili Tarika over Jale Fotu in the fifth round. Ramos had nothing but praise for Fotu saying that he had the potential to be a very good fighter (Simpson, 1977).

"His (Fotu's) handlers are rushing him into too many top-rated fights," Ramos said after the fight.

"Given time and a few more fights with unrated boxers, Fotu will be a very promising fighter."

Tarika's win reignited another challenge from Tarika to Zamal Azad for his South Seas featherweight title.

Looking ahead to the New Year, Ramos had Australian welterweight champion Steve Dennis firmly in his sights as a possible international opponent for Ve. Dennis was also amongst Afakasi's list of casualties when they fought for the Australasian welterweight title in September (Sport, 1977).

The year closed out with Ramos club hosting their own interclub awards. The mending of fences between Ramos and the PBWAF seemed to be going well with the association secretary attending as chief guest at the function where he awarded Ve Fighter of the Year and Tarika the Most Promising Fighter of the Year (Rabuka, 1977).

Cover photo: (L-R) Sakaraia Ve with his South Seas Lightweight, Fiji Lightweight, Fiji Junior Middleweight and Fiji Welterweight titles, John Ramos, and Wili Tarika with his Fiji Featherweight Title (Fiji Times, circa 1977).

Sakaraia Ve (R) lands a solid right on defending champion Inia Catarogo in their Fiji Welterweight Title fight (Fiji Times, April 1, 1977).

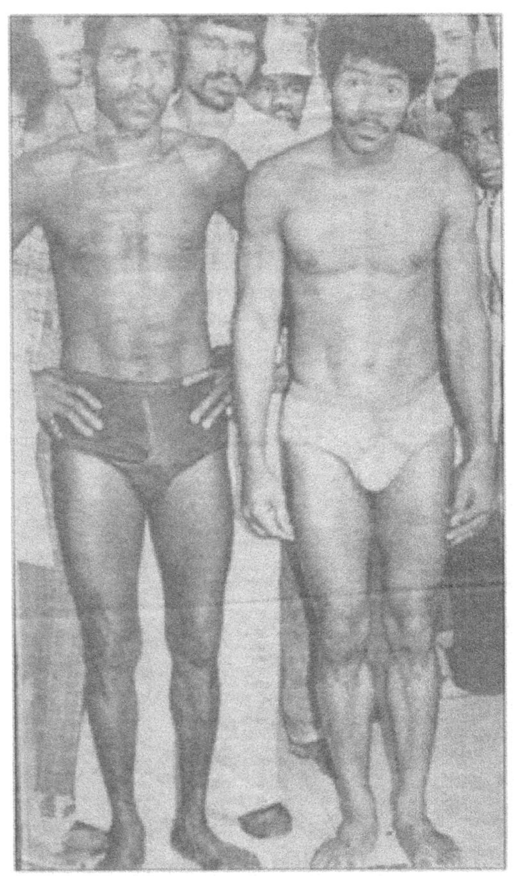

Basdeo (L) and Sakaraia
Ve at the weigh-in
before their clash in
Lautoka (Fiji Sun,
February 16, 1977).

Sakaraia Ve (L) defends his Fiji Welterweight title against Rupeni Vutevute (Fiji Times, July 13, 1977).

Sakaraia Ve (L) takes on Steve Ayerst in Suva (Fiji Times, December 4, 1977).

Chapter 7

1978 – The Commonwealth title fights

The Christmas and New Year break wasn't much of a respite as Ramos ploughed ahead with his plans for Ve and a coveted Commonwealth title fight. His approach to a few promoters did not get the reception he expected mainly because of the costs involved in staging such a major international title event (Rabuka, 1978).

"It reached a point where I was willing to put up my own money to make the title fight happen because the promoters all cited financial difficulties when I put the proposal to them," Ramos said.

Ramos's ambitions for Ve were driven by seeing how hard Ve worked at being good at his craft. From his humble beginnings in Lovoni, Ovalau, Ve had fought his way to national representation in the amateur ranks and as a professional, shown that he had the discipline and the skills as a boxer to make it to the world stage. As he worked to perfect his fight skills, Ve also managed to hold down a full-time job as a bank officer with the Bank of New Zealand.

"Ve had a great work ethic. He was always in the gym training hard to the schedule that I had set for him. This work ethic resulted in the successful run he'd had in his professional fight record so far. His dedication to this training saw him develop a quick right counterpunch, which is one of the best that I ever seen or trained since," Ramos recalled.

"We also shared a mutual understanding of where we wanted to go in terms of his fight career, and this made everything so much easier."

JANUARY – STEVE DENNIS

Ramos knew that if Ve beat Steve Dennis, who was third in the Commonwealth welterweight rankings and reigning Australian welterweight champion, on January 14, the Commonwealth title taken by Lawrence "Baby Cassius" Austin from Hector Thompson the previous September, was the next logical step. Ramos was keen to strike while the iron was hot.

A bigger venue, the Ports Authority shed along the Suva waterfront was eyed as the venue to host the Ve-Dennis fight in hopes that the larger venue could accommodate Ve's die-hard fans who had to be turned away from his three previous international fights because capacity had been reached.

Ramos was also in contact with Johnny Lewis to arrange an Australian featherweight to fight Tarika.

Ve's preparations included researching the kind of boxer Dennis was. With a record of 17-2-0, 15 by knockout, compared to Ve's 19-1-0 with 16 knockouts, Dennis was known as a scientific boxer with a fast right, a deadly left and great footwork. Both trainers predicted a win for their fighters between the sixth and eighth rounds. This was primed to be a meeting of equals.

Ve knew that he had to prove that he deserved a Commonwealth title shot and overcoming the Australian welterweight champion would be a great stepping stone towards that goal.

Ve's reputation as a hard hitter had made its way across the Pacific to Australia. His wins over Orsaldo, Afakasi and Ayerst made him a fighter to watch. Sydney-based Fijian boxer Sakaraia Bale, who had never seen Ve fight professionally, was impressed with Ve's fifth round KO of Afakasi back in September and had this to say: "He must be good to stop the veteran Afakasi whom I have always admired as a good fighter" (Rabuka, 1978).

Afakasi had beaten Dennis for the vacant Australian National Boxing Federation Australasian welterweight title just four days before meeting Ve. For Dennis, a win against Ve would get him a shot at a return fight against Afakasi for the Australasian title.

Dennis, 24, was confident that he would take out Ve. His manager John McColl expressed surprise that Ve beat Afakasi (Daunabuna, 1978).

"Ve must be pretty good to win against his three overseas opponents. We are not treating this fight lightly, especially against a man who has beaten Ali Afakasi," McColl said.

The day of the fight saw the PAF shed filled to capacity. Men, women and children came to see Fiji's favourite son take on the Australian.

In the first two rounds, both fighters gauged each other with a few combinations thrown. True to form, Dennis worked on Ve's body while Ve worked on Dennis's head. In the third round, Ve took the fight to Dennis, standing toe-to-toe much to the delight of the fans. In the fourth round, Ve amped up the pace rocking Dennis with a few strong rights to the head followed by a right hook and a flurry of combinations to Dennis's chin and jaw.

Dennis made a comeback in the fifth and sixth rounds, sinking everything he had only to be met by Ve's brilliant counterpunches. Ve took command of the seventh round as Dennis landed a series of solid combinations to Ve's body and a few attempts at the head.

In the eighth, it looked like the Ve-bomb was going to fizzle as Dennis connected a powerful left to Ve's jaw followed by two right jabs and a left as Ve missed with his counterpunches. Ve knew at this point that he needed to re-establish his dominance and Dennis probably thought the same as well as both fighters came at each other with everything they had with Dennis catching Ve on the ropes a few times.

In the final round, Ve went in at the bell as Dennis waited for him in the middle of the ring. Through a tight guard, Ve rocked Dennis with short left and right jabs, switching midway to working Dennis's midsection stopping when he thought the bell had gone, only to be signalled by referee Mike Ravula to continue. Ve finished off the Australian with a smashing right and a flurry of body shots that gradually sank the champion to his knees to be counted out (Rabuka, 1978).

"Ve fought calmly and on his own initiative. Because he was never in trouble we did not try and put a lot of tactics into his mind," Ramos said.

"After all, Ve was in command of the fight throughout and there was no need for further coaching. After each round, he would come and say he was not worried. I knew we had the fight after the sixth. I could see that Dennis had slowed down. His punching speed was not the same as in the fourth and fifth."

Dennis admitted after his defeat that Ve was a fighter of great potential.

After the win, the conversation returned to negotiations with Lewis to arrange for Ve to meet Lawrence 'Baby Cassius' Austin in April. In a parallel arrangement, Ramos was also in talks with his brother Adi Narayan, for the No.2-ranked Canadian lightweight at the time to meet Ve if the Baby Cassius deal fell through (Simpson, 1978). Narayan and his family had family migrated to Toronto, Canada a few years earlier.

While the deals percolated, Ve turned his focus to his next title fight, against Jone Mataitini in February. Mataitini, the South Seas middleweight champion, didn't pull any punches when he brushed aside comments that he stood a slim chance of holding onto his title when he goes up against Ve (Daunabuna, 1978). Ve would fight Mataitini for his South Seas middleweight title.

"I doubt Ve can beat me through his speed and his fighting approach," Mataitini said, adding "The only way I can lose is if I am not in top fighting condition."

The week after Ve fought Dennis, Tarika defended his title against Tomasi Rokoura, the former South Seas featherweight champion in Subrail Park, Labasa. This was to be Tarika's second title defence since winning it from Daya Nada two years before. Tarika had lost previously to Rokoura on points in a non-title clash a year ago.

Only a few months earlier Rokoura had lost his South Seas featherweight title to Zamal Azad on a technical knockout (Simpson, 1978). Ramos had plans for Tarika to meet an Australian featherweight if the fight against Rokoura went well.

The South Seas featherweight title win gave Azad renewed confidence. He issued a non-title challenge to Tarika and a title challenge to Ve for the Fiji lightweight title claiming Ve could not possibly make the weight limit (Daunabuna, 1978).

FEBRUARY – JONE MATAITINI AND THE FIJI MIDDLEWEIGHT TITLE

Getting right back into training, Ve was focused on adding to his trophy cabinet. The Fiji middleweight title would look spectacular next to the South Seas lightweight, the Fiji lightweight, the South Seas junior-welterweight and the Fiji welterweight belts he had collected over the past 26 months.

Ramos, as always, would work five steps ahead in organising opponents for Ve as well as other fighters in his camp. While the Canadian and Austin deals were in progress, he added Australian 'Big' Jim West, the former Australian bantamweight and former Commonwealth flyweight champion, to the list of potential opponents for Ve. West vacated the Commonwealth championship after he could not make the weight division.

"Records in the past have shown that most boxers increase their weight divisions as they continue to train hard. What happened to West can be said of Ve, who started as a featherweight and was now in the junior-welterweight or welterweight division," Ramos said (Rabuka, 1978).

A Ve-West match would be either at junior-welter or welterweight. The choice of West was to ensure Ve had the proper pre-fight build-up with more seasoned and experienced boxers. West had at that point, a 39-16-7 record, with seven by knockout. Ve on the other hand had 21 professional fights under his four belts, a 20-1-0 record, with 17 by knockout.

The fights planned for West and Baby Cassius did not eventuate in the end as Narayan managed to get a look-in that would give Ve a very real shot at Commonwealth welterweight champion, Canadian Clyde Gray. This was a turning point. The brass ring was within grasp.

Narayan recommended that Ve's build-up to the Gray championship fight be at super-lightweight against African American Saoul Mamby instead in April. Ranked 27 by the World Boxing Council and No.3 in the USA, Mamby had narrowly missed out on winning the WBC world super-lightweight title from Saensak Muangsurin of Thailand the previous year when he lost on a split points decision (Sport, 1978).

The push to host a Ve-Gray fight in Fiji was now foremost in Ramos's mind. The thought of taking Ve to Canada to fight Gray was not a consideration. Ramos's preference was to bring Gray to Fiji, where Ve would have the home advantage and support from fans to power him on inside the ring.

Ramos also knew that he would be doing Ve's fans a great disservice if they were not able to attend the fight and show their support. In a time when there was no television in Fiji or the rights to view a live televised broadcast other than a live radio crossover, the decision was the right one. Ramos also knew that fighting in Fiji put Ve in a better bargaining position for his purse than if he were to fight abroad in Canada or the United States. As with all other decisions, it rested on Ve to make the final call and upon hearing Ramos's advice, Ve decided to remain in Fiji to host those fights.

Ve's local fight record did not go unnoticed by the British Commonwealth Boxing Board (BCBB - later changed to the Commonwealth Boxing Council). To be considered as a serious contender for a Commonwealth title, a fighter had to be ranked in that weight division. At the end of January 1978, the BCBB ranked Ve the No.4 welterweight, replacing Ali Afakasi whom Ve stopped in the fifth round the previous September.

Ali, the PBWAF secretary, wrote to the BCBB following the Afakasi and Dennis fights to have Ve considered for a Commonwealth ranking. Ali viewed the BCBB's ranking as "tremendous" (Rabuka, 1978).

"It will make me put more dedication into my boxing career to achieve my goal – that is to win the Commonwealth title, and possibly even a world championship," Ve said at the time of the recognition.

Ramos said he was pleased with the outcome and acknowledged Ali's support and effort in getting the BCBB to recognise Ve.

Tarika was also looking forward to defending his Fiji featherweight title against Tomasi Rokoura in Labasa on February 11, but the fight was cancelled as promoter Rennie Mohammed's licence was suspended by the PBWAF following the promotion of the Ve-Dennis fight in January. The suspension by PBWAF of Mohammed's promotor licence stemmed from the over-sale of tickets for the Ve-Dennis fight at the PAF shed in January.

The cancellation turned Tarika's sights to Zamal Azad and his recently acquired South Seas featherweight title. It was a fight that Tarika was keen to get.

Planned to feature in the Tarika-Azad programme was Peni Tabua, a former Ramos Boxing Club stablemate of Tarika's who was now living and boxing in Australia. Tabua was to meet Tongan middleweight Papani Makihele in a supporting bout. Another Tongan also lined up in the programme was former amateur heavyweight Tevita Tau'fa'ou against Waqabaca Cama in an eight-round clash. Engineered by suspended promoter Rennie Mohammed on behalf of promoter Jubar Khan of Lautoka, the inclusion of Tongans in the Fiji professional boxing programme was seen as a fostering of the Fiji-Tonga relationship (Dean, 1978).

In the meantime, Ve got ready for the mother of all battles against the reigning Fiji middleweight champion Jone Mataitini for his title. A confident Mataitini said Ve would have to do more to succeed in that weight division.

"I must admit, Ve is a good boxer, which he has proved in his recent fights, but he will have to perform a miracle to beat me in the middleweight division," he said (Sport, 1978).

At 21, Ve put in the hours at training with sparring partners Waqabaca Cama and Tevita Tui in preparation for the fight against Mataitini, 29, scheduled for February 25 at the Laucala Bay Hangar.

"I'm ready now. I'm satisfied with all the training I have done for this fight," Ve said (Rabuka, 1978). "I have done all that is required and that includes tactics to counter the champion's speed punches."

"We know Mataitini is fast with both hands, but Ve has the art to keep him within his reach," Ramos said of their strategy going in.

Training in Dratabu, Nadi, Mataitini said he has prepared well, predicting that Ve would not last past 10 of the 15 rounds scheduled.

The Ve-Mataitini fight had its sceptics notable among which, was former Fiji welterweight champion (1959-63) Wate Nacigalevu who felt that Ve was out of his league by fighting in a heavier weight division (Sport, 1978).

"He shouldn't go so quick in his bid to win titles and money. My piece of advice to him is that his own life is more important than anything else," Nacigalevu said at the time.

Ve was not put out. He mentioned that many supporters felt the same way and he took their views on board, however, the decider would come on the day of the fight if he should fight in the middleweight division in the future.

"If I know I can't fight as a middleweight I will concentrate in the welterweight division," was all Ve had to say on that matter.

On the day, fight fans packed out the Laucala Bay Hangar to watch Ve take out the Fiji middleweight champion in the fourteenth round making Mataitini, Ve's eleventh victim in the ring.

Reporter Eliki Rabuka described the fight as "cruel and hard fought". Ve (10st 10lb, 68kg) had wanted to quit after the eleventh round because Mataitini (11st 5lb, 72.2kg) was too heavy in the clinches.

"I had to follow instructions from my trainer in those final rounds or I would have lost the fight," Ve said (Rabuka, 1978).

"I told him to switch tactics. To keep away from him (Mataitini) and to tire him. This, Ve did well because he noticed that Mataitini was running out of stamina," Ramos said.

After the thirteenth round, Ve recovered enough to want to end the fight in the fourteenth.

"When the bell came for the fourteenth, Ve indicated that he wanted to finish the fight," Ramos said. "He did it because he knew he was in a better physical condition than the champion."

Rabuka reported that Ve came out strongly in the fourteenth to withstand Mataitini's attacks. "Mataitini connected with a long left and a right, but Ve caught him (with) a good strong counter to the head. They clinched as they exchanged short punches to the body. Then Mataitini came out with a left and to his surprise, Ve caught him with a well-timed combination to the head, another left and right to the jaw, followed up with a left to the body. Then Ve let fly a series of combinations to the head which put Mataitini down for the full count."

At the end of the day, Ramos and Ve did not regret the decision to take on the champion.

"It was wise because it would have tested Ve's punching strength. Ve will be meeting some welterweights in future who punch like middleweights or even heavier," Ramos said.

Ve was now the proud title holder of the South Seas lightweight, Fiji lightweight, the South Seas junior-welterweight, the Fiji welterweight and now, the South Seas middleweight titles. The only other Fijian to hold five titles simultaneously was Isimeli Radrodro between 1954 and 1961. Radrodro was the heavyweight champion of the Orient, light-heavyweight champion of the Orient, heavyweight champion of Fiji, light heavyweight of Fiji and heavyweight champion of Vanua Levu (Radrodro, 1978).

The Oriental and Pacific Boxing Federation (OPBF) previously known as the Orient Boxing Federation was formed in Japan in 1952 and had membership from the Asia and Oceania region including Fiji. The OPBF helped form the World Boxing Council in 1963 and to date, remains affiliated to the WBC.

Ve's win did not come without a price. To make weight, Ve increased his fluid intake. After the fight, he asked for a month off before getting ready for his next welterweight fight in April.

Reflecting on this fight, Ramos said that "Mataitini was the best local fight opponent that Ve had met."

"Ve was the underdog and Mataitini was the best middleweight in Fiji at the time. He had the height, weight and reach advantage in his favour. When Ve agreed to this fight with promoter Raj Kumar, we both knew that it was going to be a tough fight, but Ve had the edge to beat Mataitini because he knew not to allow Mataitini to use his hold and clinch but to instead, use his (Ve's) speed and peek-a-boo style of boxing.

"I had advised Ve to follow up with his counterpunches which he did and as a result stopped Mataitini in the fourthteenthround to become the South Seas middleweight champion. That was one of the best fights in my book, as manager and trainer."

MARCH – LINING UP THE CHALLENGERS

No sooner had the referee counted out Mataitini, the challenge for a rematch echoed across the Suva Harbour. A challenge from middleweight, Nemani Waka was in the mix. Ramos knew that the fight against Mataitini took a lot out of Ve, and he wasn't too keen in getting him another fight in the middleweight division anytime soon so he issued a statement to the media which he hoped would give Ve some breathing room.

"Ve is entitled to keep the title for the next six months before he is forced to defend it. Ve is still undecided at present whether he will fight as a middleweight," Ramos said (Sport, 1978).

While Ve took the well-deserved time to recover, Ramos was busy at work to secure the next fight.

Other than American Saoul Mamby as an opponent for an April bout, Ramos through Narayan, contacted boxing manager, promoter and Canadian Boxing Hall of Fame alumni Irving Ungerman about the possibility of Ve meeting with Chris Clarke, the ninth-ranked Commonwealth welterweight. Clarke would go on to beat Clyde Gray for the Commonwealth welterweight title in August 1979.

Among Ungerman's stable of fighters were two notable Canadian champions, George Chuvalo and Gray. Ungerman's love for amateur and professional sports was boundless and his savvy in identifying and exploiting financial opportunities in boxing was legendary.

While Ungerman suggested two fights for Ve in Canada in May with televised rights, Ramos was reluctant to consider the option as Ve had a fulltime job and this would take him away for longer than usual and possibly at the cost of his employment. Instead, Ramos decided to give serious consideration to a fight against Australian Jeff Malcolm for April.

Known as "Flash", Malcolm was a southpaw with a 37-14-9 record, eight by knockout and Ve was 22-1-0 with 18 by knockout. Malcolm normally fought in the lightweight division, but he went on to fight and win several Australian, Pan-Asian and world titles in the lightweight, super-lightweight, welterweight and light-middleweight divisions.

Finding a promoter willing to shell out a $3,000 purse to Ve was not easy. Ramos agreed for Ve to fight Malcolm for $2,000 tax-free after negotiations. Raj Kumar Singh agreed to promote the fight.

Malcolm, the No.2 Australian light-welterweight contender, had just lost a fight to the former Commonwealth super lightweight champion, Hector Thompson in February. Ramos felt Malcolm was a great stepping stone in Ve's Commonwealth ambition given that Malcolm went the distance against Thompson. The date set was April 15.

Also, on the programme in a supporting bout was Tarika's defence of his Fiji featherweight title against Kaminieli Vunimasi of Lautoka.

Ve's record and fights against reputable opponents did not go unnoticed abroad. In the wake of Samoan-Kiwi Monty Betham's shock loss of his Commonwealth middleweight title against Fijian Alipate Korovou in Suva in March and Ve's defeat of another Samoan-Kiwi Ali Afakasi the previous September, the search for two fighters to headline a revived Auckland Boxing Association (ABA) programme was on.

Afakasi approached Ramos for a return bout with Ve in Auckland in May. Ramos turned down the offer as Ve already had three fights lined up for the next few months. The reputation and quality of boxers produced in Fiji at this time had the ABA thinking of the quality and entertainment value these fighters would bring to their programmes.

APRIL – JEFF MALCOLM

Jeff Malcolm was a highly regarded opponent given his scientific style. The southpaw's split points loss in a 12- round battle against Hector Thompson made him a worthy opponent for Ve's next fight.

Ve had only one thing in mind: to prove that he was a better fighter than Thompson by stopping Malcolm.

Malcolm's trainer/manager John McColl was confident that Malcolm would win by piling on the points despite Malcolm not being a big puncher (Rabuka, 1978).

"He is good mover, which should make Ve miss his big punches just as he did to Thompson last month. He concentrates on speedwork, with combinations and footwork. That makes him a difficult target in the ring. And he makes use of the ring too," McColl said adding that watching the way Ve demolished Dennis in January, Ve's approach and style were very similar to Thompson's which should make for a good fight.

Ve and Tarika had several sparring sessions as they prepared for their big fights. Also joining in was Ramos light-heavyweight Waqabaca Cama, who was also eager to prove his form against the South Seas light-heavyweight champion Josaia Dawai in the same programme.

Regarded as the best defensive fighter in Fiji at the time, Dawai wasn't going to be an easy opponent, but Cama was determined to get that rematch against Samoan-Australian Fossie Schmidt.

Vunimasi predicted he'd knock out Tarika in the third round of their 15-round clash. Vunimasi's trainer John Buadromo said the 19-year-old was running six miles and sparring 20 rounds each day (Rabuka, 1978).

"Vunimasi will be a big surprise for Tarika this time," Buadromo said. "He is faster and hits harder than any featherweight around."

A year younger than Ve, Malcolm arrived with cyclonic bluster into Nadi three days before the highly anticipated fight. Ve said that his plan was to work on Malcolm's body in the first few rounds. Known for going the distance, Ve knew only too well what was at stake when he got in the ring with the Australian southpaw.

The Tarika-Vunimasi fight ended controversially after going the distance. Vunimasi was crowned the new Fiji featherweight champion, effectively ending Tarika's two-year reign on a points decision. As expected, Tarika wanted a rematch, but Buadromo wasn't having any of that, telling Tarika to first beat Jale Fotu before taking another stab at the title (Sport, 1978).

Cama didn't fare any better either as he was outpointed by Dawai over their eight-round affair.

Ve went the distance with Malcolm winning a tough 10-round bout on points. Ve suffered a bicep strain during the fight.

After the fight, Ramos considered taking Ve to Toronto to fight Canadian Chris Clarke in preparation for a bout with Clyde Gray. The trip didn't eventuate due to financial reasons. Other fights against Australian Neil Patel (also styled as Neil Pattel) and Papua New Guinean Martin Beni that were in negotiation also fell through.

Another fighter who was keen to meet Ve was the former New South Wales state welterweight champion, Mark Barnett.

The proposal to match Ve against Barnett came from former Ramos stablemate Peni Tabua who was boxing in Australia alongside Barnett. Sharing the same trainer/manager in Ben Hall, who also trained Semi Bula and Tony Mundine, Tabua said the idea came about in a discussion with Hall about his (Tabua's) possible meeting with Samoan William White (Simpson, 1978).

On the home front, Ramos and Margaret prepared for the birth of their third child, a daughter, Donna Evelyn Regina who arrived just after midnight on April 30.

MAY – JO DAWAI

May started quietly for the club. Ramos worked furiously behind the scenes to get Ve a crack at the Gray's Commonwealth title and possibly a few more fights before then.

Tevita Tui surfaced with a challenge to Fiji light-heavyweight Jo Dawai despite cautions from doctors to give up the square circle after it was discovered that his eyesight was failing. His response when asked was: "I know what I'm doing" (Sport, 1978). Dawai decided, instead, to take on Tongan Tevita Taufoou, the younger brother of former South Seas light-heavyweight champion Malupe Taufoou.

In early May, Gray's management indicated to Ramos that Gray would accept Ve as a challenger if he (Gray) successfully defended his title against Englishman Dave Green in June. Gray had been under pressure from the BCBB to defend his title or risk being stripped off it (Sport, 1978). Since winning the vacant Commonwealth welterweight title in February 1973, Gray had defended it only five times.

As negotiations continued with Gray's camp, Jone Mataitini challenged Ve to a return bout. Mataitini said that he didn't sign a return bout match in the initial contract because he never expected to lose (Daunabuna, 1978). In response, Ramos said that Ve had several international fights planned through until December and "by then Ve's weight may have gone up to junior-middleweight grade and he may keep the title for good till somebody wins it from him".

On May 22, eight years after he started his professional boxing career, 32-year-old Basdeo won his first title, the vacant South Seas welterweight championship over Nadroga slugger Ambika Prasad. By outpointing a determined Prasad over 15 hard-fought rounds, Basdeo became the second champion at the Rail City Centre Junior Boxing Club in Lautoka (Rabuka, 1978).

JUNE – ROSS EADIE

The anticipated fight between Gray and British Dave Green was called off after Green injured his hands in training. This was the third postponement between the two. This delay opened the door to serious consideration for Ve as a worthy opponent.

The confirmation for Ve as an acceptable challenger for the Commonwealth welterweight title came from the Gray camp on June 8. Ramos's persistence and an inordinate number of phone calls to Adi Narayan finally paid off. Ramos remembers the sense of elation when he got that call.

"It was the biggest moment in my boxing life and the boxing life of promoter Raj Kumar Singh who agreed to stage the fight at the Laucala Bay Hangar," Ramos said.

August 18 was the date agreed and Ramos wasted no time in getting Ve ready for what was to be the biggest fight of his career. They finally had a chance to get their hands on a Commonwealth title.

Western Promotions headed by Singh, came on board and the search for a venue with a 12,000-13,000 capacity was on. The fight confirmation also came with good news from the world rankings in the latest issue of *Ring* magazine had Ve listed at number eight in the welterweight division and Gray at number seven (Rabuka, 1978).

But first, the fight against Australian Ross 'Bronco' Eadie in Suva on June 17 was to take place. Five years older than Ve at 28, Eadie came with a 33-25-6 record with six by knockout. Eadie had more experience and faced quality opponents in the past including Hector Thompson for the Australian super-lightweight title and the Commonwealth super-lightweight title in December 1976, which he lost by knockout in the seventh round.

In May, Eadie had beaten Mark Barnett to win the New South Wales state welterweight title by a third-round knockout.

'Golden Boy' Ve, was not fazed. Ramos predicted a sixth-round knockout. Ray Bucknell, Eadie's manager and trainer, said that they were looking forward to the fight because Eadie preferred to score with punches at close quarters where his left hook worked out to a greater advantage (Rabuka, 1978).

The fight drew mixed reviews. As always Ve was in devastating form, but Eadie failed to deliver as expected. Although the fight went 10 rounds and Ve won on points, Ve said after the fight he felt like he was in a "wrestling match" (Simpson, 1978).

"Eadie is not an in-fighter as he said he was. He is good but is more of a slugger than an in-fighter," Ve said afterwards.

After six overseas opponents and six clear wins, Ve acknowledged that Steve Dennis was to date his toughest overseas opponent.

With the Eadie fight now over, Ve and Ramos focused on getting ready for Gray. The negotiations, preparations and money that goes into staging an international fight of this calibre is quite substantial. Bringing someone of Gray's standard to fight in Fiji would mean paying a larger than usual purse. Following crafty negotiations, Gray's purse demand was reduced from US$15,000 to US$12,000. Then there was the advance payment for preparation which in this instance, was US$2,000 non-refundable. Gray also asked to be in Fiji at least a week before the fight so he could adapt to the weather and finish his preparations.

The determination to see the fight happen went as far as Narayan offering to pay Gray's purse in advance if that's what it took to have the fight happen (Rabuka, 1978).

With everything in place, the question then became what to do with the two months left before Ve's Commonwealth title shot.

AUGUST – CLYDE GRAY AND THE FIRST COMMONWEALTH TITLE FIGHT

Ve's intense preparation since the Eadie fight included over 10 rounds of daily sparring, five days a week. He worked on his speed, power and the timing of his counterpunch. He sparred with Tarika, ni-Vanuatu fighter Phil Kating, and Salesi Soko to name a few.

In early August a mild case of the 'flu caused a slow-down but did not altogether stop the preparations. On the days that he was unwell, Ve did light training instead.

Given the enormity of the fight and its significance for Fiji, the sport, and fans, Ramos and Ve were given three weeks off work by their respective employers to concentrate on the fight.

Nasinu Teacher's College, two kilometres from Ramos's Nadera home, was kind enough to provide the training venue for the five-week preparation.

Five days before the main fight, the Lord Mayor of Suva at the time, Noor Dean, offered Ramos the Old Town Hall as a training venue so that the public could come and see the 'Golden Boy' and 'Ve-Bomb' prepare for the fight of his life.

The Old Town Hall proved a drawcard as fans gathered daily to watch Ve do his light workout from midday to 3pm. Gray also used the venue for his workout from 4pm to 6pm with an autograph session afterwards. This arrangement not only generated greater interest with fight fans but also made the fighters accessible to them for it's not often that a British Commonwealth boxing champion came to Fiji for a fight.

"Ve is fighting for Fiji and not for himself. He is in great shape. He is 100 per cent better than when he fought Steve Dennis in January," Ramos said, adding that Ve's speed, youth and punching power were his greatest assets against the 32-year-old Gray (Rabuka, 1978).

Joining Ramos and Soko in Ve's corner for this fight was school principal and Catholic priest Father Brian Wilson. A New Zealand national amateur welterweight champion, Father Wilson's presence was a boost to the champ's preparations, Ramos said.

On fight day, August 19, 7,000 hard-core boxing fans packed the Laucala Bay Hangar in Suva. Befitting an international fight of this calibre, the pomp and pageantry set the tone with the Royal Fiji Police Force band entertaining the crowd before the main fight.

Ve entered the ring carrying a Fiji flag, cheered on by supporters. Ramos, alongside, was expressionless. Like Ve, he too reflected on the past three years and the path taken to arrive at this moment. History is going to be made today, Ramos thought to himself.

Gray followed with his small team including manager Ungerman to the ring. The maple leaf flag caught a gentle breeze as he entered the battleground. Referee Mumtaz Ali stood with the fighters and their seconds as the Police band struck up *O Canada* followed by *God Bless Fiji*. The Fiji Times report of this moment summed up every international event since, where we've watched our athletes attempt to sing the Fiji national anthem.

"The Canadians joined in lustily singing their anthem. When the band played the Fiji national anthem, the home crowd remained silent. Probably because not one person there knew the words of our anthem" (Rabuka, 1978).

In the audience were Fiji's deputy prime minister Ratu Sir Penaia Ganilau and other public service and political dignitaries as well as former and current heavyweight champions Mike Ravula and Sunia Cama respectively.

The fight lasted eight rounds. The result was a disappointing technical knockout in Gray's favour. Up until that point, The Fiji Times scored the fight evenly in the first, second and sixth rounds. The newspaper felt Gray won the third and fifth rounds with solid punches to Ve's body and head.

Ve won the fourth and seventh rounds with an attacking style that allowed him to deploy his left hook and send through a volley of counterpunches as Gray was forced to defend.

The eighth round started with Gray on the attack, landing two straight lefts in a row to Ve's jaw. Ve returned that with a well-timed left to Gray's head. Another left opened a cut under Gray's right eye and above his nose. Recovering on automatic from the barrage, Gray unleashed a flurry of blows to Ve's face and head. Ve turned and walked back to his corner. The crowd gasped then fell silent. What happened next will forever be one of those 'coulda, woulda, shoulda' stories. The unthinkable happened. After Ali checked on Ve, he walked back to Gray and raised his arm, declaring Gray winner by technical knockout. The fans were confused.

It turned out the cause of Ve's retreat were his new dentures for his missing upper central incisors. In the flurry of shots Gray despatched to Ve's face and head in the eight, a well-placed punch cracked the denture plate and sent a piece towards the back of Ve's throat where it lodged in his upper palate.

Ramos was livid. Livid at having missed a seemingly innocuous appendage such as Ve's dentures as a potential hazard. Livid at Ali for declaring the fight without first consulting with the ring doctor as technically Ve wasn't decked to the canvas or sluggish due to concussion or had broken any bone. Whichever way one was to view this, the fight result would probably have been the same.

"Ve was hurting Gray with his speed and counterpunches. I honestly believe to this day, that Ve would have stopped Gray had they fought the full 15 rounds. I was very disappointed. Ve was disappointed. The whole of Fiji was disappointed and in shock," Ramos said later.

"If only Ve had told me of his new dentures before the fight, things might have turned out differently. This was a fight where Ve met one of the top 10 welterweights in the world. The same top 10 fighter who in 1973 fought and lost on points for a title challenge against the WBC world welterweight champion Jose Naples and again, in 1975 against Angel Espada for the vacant WBA world welterweight championship."

They had come so close, and a momentary oversight had cost Ve and Ramos the Commonwealth welterweight championship. Referee Ali and ringside judge, Mike Ravula had the fight scored evenly at 67-67 and 66-66 respectively. The third judge, Australian Boxing Federation president, Ray Mitchell had the fight scored at 68-66 to Gray (Rabuka, 1978).

When Ali raised Gray's hand, Ve graciously accepted the decision and walked over to congratulate the champion. After the fight, Ungerman said that he would be happy to consider a return bout with Ve.

"We will be happy to give him another shot at the title. The people of Fiji have been good to us and that is another reason why we want to come back," Ungerman said (Rabuka, 1978).

Gray described Ve as a brilliant fighter, a good mover and a hard puncher.

Criticising how local judges scored the fight, Australian journalist Frank O'Callaghan decided to stick the fork into Ali and Ravula in a scathing article written in The Courier Mail after the fight, labelling them "over-zealous", based on factually incorrect information that the two had Ve ahead on points while the Australian judge, Mitchell had Gray leading (Rabuka, 1978).

It appeared that O'Callaghan got his news from Australian fighter Neil Patel's trainer Reg Layton. Patel was one of several overseas opponents lined up for Ve. The Courier Mail reported Layton as saying: "You don't go to countries like Fiji expecting to win unless by a knockout. But that is where the money is and that is what the game is about." Ali, as secretary of the PBWAF, wasn't having any of it.

"There is no such decision in Fiji as a 'hometown' decision. If Layton and Patel don't want to fight in Fiji under our own judges, they are not welcome here," Ali said.

"We, judges in Fiji, do our best to judge a fight to give a fair verdict, whether or not one of our boxers is fighting."

Judge Mitchell, Ali said, had seen for himself what the situation was with boxing in Fiji and knew what Ve was capable of.

"He told me that when he goes back to Sydney, he will fix those people who complained of decisions in Fiji and say that Ve can't fight. I want to make it clear that if people like Layton and Patel think they will not get a fair verdict here they should forget about coming to Fiji. And that goes for anyone else for that matter."

In a sports editorial after the fight, veteran journalist Stan Ritova acknowledged that Ve put up a strong fight believing that had the false teeth incident not happened, "Gray would have got the hiding of his life" (1978).

"Ve's accomplishments so far shows that Fiji boxing is on the threshold of some big things in the sport. Ve has carried the sport out of proportions in Fiji and those boxers of ours who in the past considered it as a way of earning a few bucks to buy booze should re-think," Ritova wrote.

As Gray and his team prepared to return home, negotiations re-started for a return bout in December. Ungerman, the shrewd businessman that he was, upped the stakes when it came to Gray's purse.

"We will not treat Ve lightly should the deal come off for another title fight. He is a puncher and a very clever boxer too," Ungerman said (Rabuka, 1978).

Judge Mitchell agreed that Ve deserved another crack at Gray's title.

"Ve can throw any punch from any position. This impressed me very much," he said adding, "All these reports from boxers and managers who have fought here I find them baseless. He is the best prospect for a Commonwealth title from this region."

A veteran referee of more than 5000 fights including three Commonwealth title deciders, Mitchell felt that Ve needed more experience with fighters of Gray's calibre, noting that he believed Ve could beat Gray in a rematch.

In meeting Gray's demand for a larger purse for the return bout, Ve was equally determined in his stance that he would not lower his purse if asked by the promoter. Ve also felt that his purse of $5,500 was less than what he deserved as challenger for the Commonwealth title (Rabuka, 1978).

"The championship fight was well organised, and the people of Fiji gave Gray the best fight reception he had had in his boxing career, despite the fact that they were cheering for their local hero Ve," Ungerman said.

He said a copy of the film of the fight was sent to the BCBB in the event a dispute over the decision was lodged with the board.

In three years, Ramos had taken Ve to five national and South Seas championships and a Commonwealth title fight, an achievement for boxing in Fiji. In that time, he had also moulded Ve into a drawcard, sought after by every promoter on the local boxing scene.

"The promoters who promoted Ramos boxers were Raghunath Singh, Eric Emberson and Rennie Mohammed from Suva; Noor Mohammed from Nausori; Raj Kumar Singh of Sigatoka; Dr Raj Bali of Ba; and from Lautoka, Brij Sain, Bala Subramani and Dass," Ramos said.

"This fight was just another chapter written in the history of Fiji where you also had nine of the top boxing promoters vying to promote Ve and boxers from Ramos Boxing Club."

By the end of August, promoter Brij Sain threw his hat in the ring to host the Ve-Gray return bout. On Ali's advice, Sain began negotiations with Gray's camp. Ve agreed to a purse of $7,000 and Gray was in for US$15,000 plus first-class travel for five, hotel and a neutral official as judge for the December 2 clash.

Ve's loss to Gray caused a seismic shift on the local boxing scene. The 'Golden Boy' had feet of clay. He could be beaten.

First cab off the rank to challenge the 'Ve-Bomb' was welterweight Paula Namosi fresh from his points win over South Seas welterweight champion Basdeo in August. Namosi told *The Fiji Times* that it was time that Ve took on a local fighter for a change (Rabuka, 1978).

"Perhaps next Saturday if Namosi wants it quickly – I'm ready and I would like to give him a chance to prove himself," Ve said. "But first, he must get a promoter who can pay my purse of $2,000 – no more, no less plus travel expenses if the fight is outside Suva."

Namosi felt that he earned the right to challenge Ve for either his South Seas junior-welterweight or South Seas middleweight title after winning against Basdeo. The two did eventually meet in April 1979.

Meanwhile the race by promoters to get the Ve-Gray return fight was on with Lautoka's Sain leading the negotiations with Ungerman and his team after Ve declined to support the proposal by Sigatoka promoter Raj Kumar Singh.

In a *Fiji Times* report, Ve said that he told Singh he would not fight under his promotion after the treatment given to him by the promoter (Rabuka, 1978).

"I have made it clear to Kumar that I will not fight under his promotion. And I will not accept any purse less than $7,000," Ve said.

The strain in the relationship with Singh and the delay by Sain in locking in the return bout, prompted PBWAF secretary Ali to send an urgent telegram to Ungerman as the deadline approached.

"Monday (September 18) was the deadline given by Ungerman for Ve and any promoter to come up with an agreement. I have asked Ungerman to wait for two more days. I don't care which promoter – Kumar (Singh) or Sain – as long as they come to an agreement within the next two days or else Ve's chances to have another crack at the Commonwealth title will slip away," Ali said.

Another challenger looking at Ve was unbeaten light-middleweight Silio Tiko, who had had 12 fights. Promoter Nazir Khan was quick to step in with an offer to promote such a fight were it to go ahead for either Ve's welterweight or middleweight title. Ve did eventually meet Tiko in May 1984 when he defended his South Seas middleweight title. Ve walked over Tiko with a second-round knockout.

Ve's preparations for his next fight, against Mark Barnett, met with a minor hiccup when his tracksuit was stolen off the clothesline outside the Ramos clubhouse on Des Voeux Rd in Suva where Ve rented a room.

A 26-year-old unemployed man from Lami was later convicted of the September 22 theft, all thanks to a vigilant Tarika who found the man wearing the tracksuit jacket at the Suva bus stand a few weeks later. A search by police of the man's home uncovered the bottom half of the suit, which he claimed he found lying on adjacent McGregor Road. Seems the magistrate didn't believe the story and handed the man a $30 fine in default of one-month imprisonment.

OCTOBER – MARK BARNETT

While negotiations progressed for the Ve-Gray return bout, Ramos lined up Australian welterweight Mark Barnett. Barnett, with his fight record of 21-6-1, with eight by knockout against Ve's record of 24-2-0, with 17 by knockout, stacked the odds in Ve's favour.

Ramos saw the fight as a recovery effort after Ve's loss to Gray as well as a pre-Gray return bout warm-up. A quick win would help restore Ve's confidence and of course give Ve's fans reason to keep faith in him.

With promoter Noor Mohammed on board, the fight was scheduled for October 14. Also featuring on the programme was Tarika against Kini Nabiri of Navosa. Tarika hoped for a win before challenging Vunimasi for his previously held Fiji featherweight title (Rabuka, 1978).

As Ve was now fighting in the welterweight division, recently retired South Pacific Games silver medallist Esala Vula criticised Ve for not vacating the Fiji and South Seas lightweight titles to give other boxers a chance (Rabuka, 1978).

Ramos rubbished the claims saying that Ve was fighting in the heavier, welterweight division because he had run out of competition in the lighter weight category. He also said Ve would have no problem making the 9st 9lb (63.2kg) weight limit should a promoter willing to pay Ve's purse came forward.

As September ended, so did Adi Narayan's long negotiations with Ungerman to secure Gray for the return fight. A delighted Ramos broke the news to the Fiji public, "Narayan has done it again!" (Rabuka, 1978).

The resolution came about after Ungerman's push for Singh as promoter was resolved to accept Sain. As a condition of agreeing to Sain as the promoter, Ungerman demanded that Sain pay a deposit of US$5,000 once the contract was signed.

Sain had also agreed to meet all the conditions including first-class air tickets, accommodation and expenses. Ve too was delighted at getting a second crack at the title.

"I will do my best this time. I believe I deserve another crack at the title and Gray knows it," he said.

Sain, excited by the prospect of Ve becoming the next Commonwealth welterweight champion, offered to pay Ve $15,000 for the opportunity to promote Ve's defence of the title if the time came.

With the return bout locked in, the focus could now be turned on Ve's next fight against 22-year-old former New South Wales welterweight champion Barnett scheduled for October 14 at the Laucala Bay Hangar.

Rated by former WBC world featherweight champion John Famechon as the best welterweight in Australia, Barnett had fought the likes of Ross Eadie to whom he lost his championship title the previous May. Barnett's manager Bernie Hall was quick to dismiss Ve as a credible opponent for his fighter.

"Mark is a hard puncher with either hand. Watch him work on Ve on Saturday. He will be a hard man to beat," Hall said (Rabuka, 1978).

"We don't know whether Ve is a puncher. If he should rely on his skills, then he is making a mistake."

Ramos laughed off Hall's comment by saying: "It remains to be seen who the hitter is of the two" (Sport, 1978).

Ve as always was ready to make his mark known. "I'm feeling good and very sharp for Saturday's battle. I hope Barnett doesn't run away like Jeff Malcolm and Steve Ayerst. I like to fight busy fighters."

A win for Barnett over Ve would give him an opportunity to get Commonwealth ranking recognition from the BCBB and a possible chance to challenge Gray for his welterweight title.

On the day of the fight, Hall was not about to be outdone in the challenge exchange, telling the media, "He will make sure that this afternoon that Sakaraia Ve does not enter the ring wearing his false tooth" (Rabuka, 1978).

"We don't want that as an excuse this afternoon," Hall said. "Barnett gives and takes. That makes him a very tough opponent. I'm very confident of a good win today."

A fan's perspective of the Ve-Barnett fight is worthy of a revisit of Stan Ritova's op-ed column "From the Sidelines" at the time in which Ritova wrote about how, "Sakaraia got me to the church on time".

"From my ringside seat I watched Mark Barnett as he sat in his corner waiting for the start of the fight. With his fine features – in fact he is pretty – I thought while studying him, that he should have been a film actor and not a boxer. And he's got height and beautiful physique.

It's a pity that Ve had to pound those fine facial features to win by a KO in the fourth round after Barnett could not take any more. I knew that the 10-rounder would not last too long. And it wasn't a hometown decision.

As Barnett sat in his corner before the fight, he didn't look too happy. There was a look of despair in his face. He had that faraway look. I made up my mind that the fight wouldn't last more than three rounds. I wasn't too far wrong.

In fact, I was due at a wedding ceremony at the Centenary Church at 5.30pm to shoot some wedding photographs. Soon after the fight was underway, I asked the man next to me for the time. It was about 5.05pm. I told him the fight would end before 5.30pm so I could be 'at the church on time'. My neighbour doubted me.

Barnett was just no match for Ve, and after the news of his pitiful defeat gets back to Australia, anyone from there in Ve's class will think twice about coming to Fiji to take him on.

Towards the end of the third round, Barnett could hardly defend himself. Then came the big slaughter in the fourth and it was a big mistake on referee George Ponipate's part to allow the fight to continue when it was so obviously a one-sided affair.

I looked hopefully at Barnett's corner and saw manager Bernie Hall's hand suspended in mid-air with the towel obviously hoping for a last-minute change in the gruesome situation. He finally threw it in, but a few seconds too late as a battered Barnett lay on the floor.

Now, where are you Clyde Gray?

I hope the news of Ve's victory has been relayed to him. It should give him some food for thought.

As I said after Ve's surprise defeat on a TKO by Gray earlier this year, Ve will beat him when they meet again, and I will shadow spar all the way along Victoria Parade if he doesn't" (Ritova, 1978).

The fourth round TKO of Barnett impressed Hall so much that he let it be known that Ve could easily demolish any Australian fighter in the welterweight category including former Commonwealth super-lightweight champion Hector Thompson and current Australian welterweight champion Neil Patel.

"He will beat any Australian welterweight fighter. Take my word for it. None of those in Australia could stand up to Barnett's aggressive tactics," Hall said.

The comment prompted Ramos to secure Thompson for Ve's next fight after Gray. Now that the Barnett warm-up was done with, the focus would now be on Gray in December.

The Ve-Gray return fight was fixed for December 2 at Churchill Park in Lautoka where a 12,000-capacity crowd was expected to attend.

Meanwhile, Tarika's fight against Kini Nabiri of Navosa fell through and Tarika went up against Esala Vula, whom he despatched quickly in a third round TKO. Hall was also 'impressed by Tarika's style and offered him a crack at Johnny Aba of Papua New Guinea, the Commonwealth junior-lightweight champion at the time.

Before meeting Vula, Tarika's peaking form and the stubbornness of South Seas featherweight champion Zamal Azad in not putting his title up for challenge had Ramos on a mission.

"If a champion has not fought for the past 18 months he should be stripped of his title," Ramos said (Sport, 1978).

Tarika also wanted Azad to defend the title or have PBWAF strip him of it. Tarika's challenge to the current Fiji Featherweight champion Kaminieli Vunimasi also hit a brick wall with Vunimasi's manager John Buadromo demanding a $600 purse for a return fight with Tarika.

According to Ramos, Lautoka promoter Brij Sain had approached Buadromo twice to set up the fight. Ramos said Tarika gave Vunimasi a crack at his title on the understanding that he got a return bout within three months.

"No promoter will be prepared to pay $600 to Kaminieli to defend his title. It's too much. He is not a drawcard like Sakaraia Ve," Ramos said.

When Tarika fought Daya Nand for the title he received $300, Ramos said. And when he defended it against Vunimasi he earned $400. In frustration, Ramos said that if Azad and Vunimasi did not come to the party, he would ask the PBWAF to create a junior-lightweight division so Tarika could take on fighters in that weight category.

NOVEMBER – JAY EDSON

The back and forth between Ramos and the Vunimasi camp ended with Ramos declaring that Tarika would not be fighting Vunimasi any time soon. Given the contractual agreement for a return bout in three months if Tarika lost, Ramos accused Vunimasi of dodging Tarika.

"It is now more than six months since he won it from Tarika. It is time that they put the title at stake," Ramos said (Sport, 1978).

With Sain all-in for the Ve-Gray return bout, the idea of an Australian lightweight contender for Tarika's next bout went on the backburner. Instead, Tarika was scheduled to fight Prem Chand of Nadi in a supporting bout.

The Ve-Gray pre-fight promo gained momentum when Sain revealed former world middleweight champion, the great Sugar Ray Robinson, could be coming to Fiji as a judge for the fight (Sport, 1978).

"I spoke to him last week on the telephone," Sain said. "He is really interested to come to Fiji to watch the title fight."

Sain added that if Ve did well against Gray, he would lead negotiations for Ve to meet the current World Boxing Council welterweight champion Carlos Polomino of Mexico.

In the contract signed by Ve with Sain, Sain would get to promote Ve's next Commonwealth title defence against Gray, if Ve won this second encounter. The contract also recognised Ramos as Ve's manager, a role that the PBWAF did not acknowledge. This was a hangover from Ramos's last suspension in February 1977 after he challenged the PBWAF decision to appoint Francis Byrnes as the referee for the Ve-Basdeo title fight.

The return bout provision in the contract, however, hit a bit of a hurdle when the British Boxing Board of Control ruled it would not recognise such provisos in contracts (Sport, 1978).

The board ruling was made after a contract between Commonwealth lightweight champion Jeff Malcolm – whom Ve had beaten back in April – and Lawrence "Baby Cassius" Austin for their fight scheduled for December 12 in Australia.

The ruling threw Sain for a loop as he had deferred to Gray's manager Irving Ungerman's knowledge and experience of such negotiations to know better. According to Sain at the time, Ungerman signed the contract so "he must think it's all right".

The announcement spun the PBWAF into action with Ali seeking legal advice as well as support from Commonwealth delegates to the Oriental Boxing Federation who would be meeting in Manila the following January (Rabuka, 1978).

Coming just a few weeks before the December 2 fight, the PBWAF secretary sought clarification from the board as to whether the contract with Ungerman voided the return title fight with Ve.

Ramos cleared up the confusion saying that Ungerman already had approval from the Commonwealth Titles Committee in London when he reported that Gray had successfully defended his title against Ve (Rabuka, 1978).

"At the same time Ungerman requested the permission, which was approved, for them to give Ve a second shot at the title," Ramos said, adding that it was Ungerman's suggestion that Ve fight Barnett before the return title fight.

"This was to be in accordance with the ruling made by the Commonwealth Titles Committee that Ve must prove himself again in a fight. This Ve did in pounding Barnett in four rounds," Ramos said.

"There should not be any problems. The fight is on, and the Commonwealth welterweight title is at stake."

The fight's go-ahead was also confirmed by Ali who added that any return bout fight between Ve and Gray should Ve win, is a matter to be sorted when the time came.

Ve's fight record and crowd appeal had him in an enviable position when it came to bargaining power with promoters. A fighter of Ve's ilk had other boxers with titles also seeking the same considerations which raised an interesting discussion in Stan Ritova's "From the sidelines" column in which he asked, "How much is a boxer worth?"

The Fiji Professional Boxing and Wrestling Association has always looked after the interests of boxers in the past and its high time they had a relook at the purses of small fighters who have no bargaining status with promoters.

The more important boxers are taking their cue from our Golden Boy Sakaraia Ve who is in a position to name his price for a fight. But he is a boxer of different stamp.

He works hard for what he wants and boxing enthusiasts, no matter where they live in Fiji, pay high prices and fares to see him fight. Some of our better-known boxers don't bother training very hard and go into the fight just to earn money for a booze-up. As a result, they become very unpopular with people who follow boxing closely. When they are billed on a programme people just don't go.

Result: A promoter with a hole in his pocket.

I wonder if (Luke) Sisiwa is genuine in his demand for $4,000 to defend his two titles, or is it just a lurk (sic) to frighten promoters away because Cama is such a formidable opponent" (1978).

The commentary followed Sisiwa's defeat of South Seas light-heavyweight champion Josaia Dawai on November 11 for the Fiji and South Seas light-heavyweight titles.

Sain's unwavering confidence in Ve securing the Commonwealth welterweight title had him working two steps ahead. Sain had started talks with former boxer and now United States promoter Don Elbaum, who promoted some of Sugar Ray Robinson's last fights. The negotiations were for Ve to meet the WBC welterweight champion Carlos Palomino should Ve beat Gray this time round. The fight would be held in Fiji (Sport, 1978).

Ve's preparations for the return fight with Gray continued at the Nasinu Teachers College where a capacity crowd of 200 people turned up to watch him go through his paces every day. Gray arrived in Nadi two weeks before the fight, this time without his wife Evelyn and with a new trainer, Lee Black (Rabuka, 1978). A purpose-built $1,200 ring was made just for the Commonwealth champion to train in at the Sugar City Hotel.

Also lined up to watch the fight was Ramos's former trainer John Payne with whom Ramos formed the Duavata Amateur Boxing Club with back in 1965 (Sport, 1978).

One of Gray's sparring partners was South Seas welterweight champion Basdeo, who admitted that Gray had the punches: "I got one good hook on the head. It came through the headguard. If I had a weak jaw, it would have been broken" (Sport, 1978).

Ve, too, was working hard on his punching speed and strength, having scheduled two workouts a day.

"Watch it this time. The champion will be caught with more accurate and pistol-like punches," Ramos said.

Basdeo's session with Gray boosted his confidence, prompting him to challenge five-title holder Ve, to a fight for both their welterweight titles (Sport, 1978).

After his eighth round TKO loss to Ambika Prasad on November 18, Basdeo claimed that the loss came because of a swollen eye that started with him sparring with Gray. The referee's decision to stop the clash against Prasad came at the urging of Basdeo's manager Brij Sain after Prasad worked on the injury from the sixth round.

Basdeo had the upper hand earlier in the fight when he floored Prasad with a solid left hook in the second round but failed to follow up. In the fourth round, Basdeo opened a cut over Prasad's left eye with a well-timed right hook, but Prasad saw the swelling in Basdeo's left eye and decided to make that his mission, which he did brilliantly to his advantage by closing it totally by the eighth round.

Not to be distracted, Ve did not respond to the challenge, instead focusing on getting it right during sparring sessions with Tarika and Setareki Bolatawa, the Fiji amateur middleweight champion at the time.

Ritova, brilliant as always in accessing the inner thoughts of his subjects, captured the relationship between Ve and Ramos in conversation perfectly with his op-ed "From the sidelines", titled: "A quiet chat boosts my hopes".

"Right out of the blue – it's a normal question that a Fiji-ite would think of anyway – I asked about his diet (because I'm worried about mine and have been for a long time) and the reply was: "Always grilled steak and a bit of chips."

And before the fight? "Four hours before I get into the ring it's just over two kilos of grilled steak."

I had a long talk afterwards with Ve's long-time friend, manager and trainer, John Marimuttu.

"I've got to be strict with him. It's a personal relationship and I think brother Ve appreciates this," he said.

"We've been friends for a long time and I think it's a contributing factor to his success."

I agreed because I felt that communication is the greatest thing in life, as well as dedication" (1978).

What Ritova did not capture at the time was that the steaks were prepared at Ramos's home by his wife, Margaret who along with their three children, were Catholics while Ramos was a practising Hindu at the time.

Two decades later, Ramos converted to Catholicism.

Ve's legendary status extended beyond Fiji into the neighbouring Pacific islands where in Tonga, his upcoming fight with Gray was followed with much anticipation. Backing the 'Ve-Bomb' going in, the Tongan Amateur Boxing Association (TABA) formally asked for Ve's help in getting their national team to the upcoming South Pacific Games to be held in Suva the following year, if Ve won the Commonwealth welterweight title (Rabuka, 1978).

Ramos and Ve accepted the invitation for an exhibition match in Tonga to help their games fundraising effort.

"We are willing to help any amateur boxing association," Ramos said.

TABA president Bill White said: "The people of Tonga will love to watch Ve if he wins the title."

As fight day neared, the search for a third, neutral official was becoming more urgent. After the media fiasco of the last Ve-Gray fight, it was important to the PBWAF to make the selection process more transparent.

Several names were put forward including TABA's White, but he was unavailable. American Jay Edson was nominated by Gray's camp to referee the fight. Ve strongly objected to the idea of an American controlling the fight (Sport, 1978). Ali was not going to be the referee this time round.

Ve's objection to Edson's appointment stemmed from that fact that he wasn't from a Commonwealth country (Sport, 1978). Ali promised to investigate Ve's concerns.

Ramos was more concerned about the close friendship between Ungerman and Edson saying, "anything can happen, and I am not prepared to take any chances with my fighter" (Naidu, 1978).

"We don't want to upset Ve's mind at all. We don't want Ve to worry about fight officials when he enters the ring," Ali said.

Edson arrived in Fiji a few days before the fight with Gray's manager Ungerman. It was Ungerman's request that Edson, a veteran referee of 43 championship fights, be the neutral official on December 2.

Edson, who went on to referee 49 championship fights including the December 2, Ve-Gray fight, was posthumously inducted into the Florida Boxing Hall of Fame in 2010 alongside Muhammad Ali following his death from pancreatic and liver cancer in early December 2001 at age 77 at his home in Naples, Florida.

Edson retired from refereeing in 1979, going to work instead as site coordinator for Bob Arum's Top Rank Promotions. He was also a recipient of the James J. Walker Award for meritorious service to boxing (BoxRec, 2017).

The return bout against Gray was Ve's road to redemption after the false teeth mishap that cost him the fight in August. Fight pundits and Ramos were confident that it was going to go Ve's way with a knockout predicted.

"Since we know Gray's fighting tactics now, we are pretty confident in our plan to counter his attacks," Ramos said (Rabuka, 1978). Gray said the fight wouldn't go the distance.

Ungerman was confident that the choice of Edson as referee was the right one.

"Sain asked me to bring a referee of world reputation and Edson is one. In fact, Fiji is lucky to have a referee of Edson's calibre," Ungerman said (Rabuka, 1978).

Ungerman's trust in Edson to officiate neutrally came from his experience when Edson refereed Gray's fight against World Boxing Association welterweight champion Jose Napoles in 1973, a fight that Gray lost on a unanimous points decision.

Ungerman added that the fight in Fiji was not about the money, but to fulfil a commitment they made earlier. He said Gray's win over Ve had moved the Canadian up the world raking to No.2 contender for the WBA and WBC welterweight titles.

Edson said he was happy to be a judge instead if that was what the PBWAF wanted (Daunabuna, 1978).

"The promoter sent me the ticket and not the association or anyone else, but I would abide by the decision of the association. I am also willing to be the neutral judge, but then again, it would not be proper because I was brought here to referee," he said.

Edson's impressive record included refereeing several world title fights including Muhammad Ali and Jimmy Ellis in 1971. Edson had also refereed the Tony Mundine (Australia) and Bunny Sterling (England) fight for the Commonwealth middleweight title in Brisbane in 1976.

"The Australian Boxing Association invited me specially to referee the fight which shows that had confidence in my reputation. My record speaks for itself. They even went without a ringside judge in this fight but only the referee's decision," he said.

DECEMBER – CLYDE GRAY AND THE SECOND COMMONWEALTH TITLE FIGHT

The day before the fight, Gray went on record saying that he had between three to five different plans as to how he was going to tackle Ve (Sport, 1978).

"I've fought a lot of fighters who are heavier punchers than Ve and they could not knock me out. But if Ve thinks he can do it tomorrow, I wish him luck," Gray said.

The PBWAF sent the decision as to who was to referee the fight to a special committee. Ve's camp picked Ali as referee with Edson as Gray's nomination (Rabuka, 1978).

Ali was confident that whatever the decision, it would be fair and in the interest of the sport.

At the eleventh hour a decision was made. Edson would be the referee. The PBWAF-appointed committee met members from the two camps and after discussions, Ve's team withdrew their objections paving the way for Edson to be named referee (Daunabuna, 1978). The meeting also appointed Ali and Byrnes as ringside judges with a fourth person to be decided just before the fight.

The rules agreed for the fight included a waiver of the three-knockdown rule, the referee had the power to stop the fight if he felt the fighter could not continue, the mandatory fight count must be had for any knockdown and in the event of a double knockout, however rare, that the fight be called a draw.

Both camps also agreed that in the last five seconds, except the final round, a fighter could not be saved by the bell meaning that if a countdown was in progress, that the referee would continue even if the bell had rung to signal the end of the round. It was also incumbent upon the referee to consult with the ring doctor for an opinion in the event of injury with the referee stopping the fight if the doctor recommended. Ve weighed in at 10st 4.5lbs (65.6kg) and Gray at 10st 6lbs (66.2kg).

Ritova in his "From the sidelines" column that weekend reminded everyone of his promise to shadow-spar along Vitogo Parade if Ve lost. A tongue-in-cheek footnote from the editorial team noted: "We only hope that we don't have to change the name of his column to 'From the roadside'" (Ritova, 1978).

The day arrived with torrential rain, but fans were undeterred, packing the stands and ground at Churchill Park in Lautoka to witness what they hoped would be Ve bringing home the Commonwealth welterweight championship at age 22.

The fight was not without controversy to say the least. Where the first fight ended with the dislodgement of Ve's false teeth, the second ended with what Ve and Ramos claimed came about because of a low blow.

The fight went nine of the scheduled 15 rounds with Ve going down two minutes and 47 seconds in the ninth round after he claimed Gray dealt him a low blow that referee Edson did not caution Gray (Rabuka, 1978).

"He is a damn good fighter," Gray said afterwards.

"He has got some pretty good hooks. One really hurt me in the fourth round. If I have to describe this fight, I will say it is one of the toughest, shortest battles I have had in my career.

"I'm fine. But Ve has developed his boxing ability since we met in August."

"We had expected him (Edson) to warn Gray but he did not," Ramos said of certain perceived foul tactics by Gray.

"Ve was doing exactly what we had planned but he did not continue when Gray landed the punch below the belt, which gave him a lot of pain.

"He was even limping while trying to get into the car after the fight."

To his credit Ve said that Edson did not see the punch.

"The refereeing was good, but he did not see the punch. I had expected him to warn Gray. But when he didn't, I was rather angry and fought back hard. But I could not continue because the pain was too much," Ve said.

"Gray brought his world-class experience into the fight. He moved side to side and worked on Ve's body from the first round with hard body shots, but Ve fought back in each round, hurting Gray with his left jabs and right counterpunches. Some of Gray's punches hit Ve below the belt and Ve did complain," Ramos said.

By all description, the fight did go point for point in each round with *The Fiji Times* describing the ninth round as: "Gray and Ve stood toe to toe with short, sharp lefts and rights. Ve landed three lefts in a row and right to the jaw. But Gray came in with three strong lefts to the body in a neutral corner, one of which Ve claimed to be well below the belt. Ve went down for an eight count. Then Ve and Gray stood it out with Ve connecting some solid punches to Gray's head and body. However, Gray pounded three more hard lefts to the body and Ve decided to go down to the canvas for the full count" (Rabuka, 1978).

The loss by knockout was the first ever for Ve in an otherwise sterling fight record of 26-2-0 which included 17 knockouts.

"The second attempt at the Commonwealth title slipped away, but I will always be proud of my young fighter, Ve. He put up a good fight and he belongs up there as a world-class fighter. Ve fought a high-calibre fighter in Gray, who was in the top 10 world ranking," Ramos said.

Not so impressed with the fight was Ramos's former trainer Maurice Payne who flew from Auckland to watch ringside.

"Ve's performance left something to be desired," he said. "But he's 22 years of age. Ve still has a long way to go. There's no denying that Ve had got class. He will be among the world's best should he be put in the right direction" (Rabuka, 1978).

The hunger for the Commonwealth title did not abate with that loss. Ramos pursued a third attempt with Ungerman.

"I don't think Ve will fight Gray for another year or so. Gray is tough and is too experienced," he said (Rabuka, 1978). Ramos added that if Ve was ever to beat Gray it would have to be by knockout.

"But Gray in 77 professional fights has only been knocked out twice. That shows how tough he is."

Ungerman, like all other trainers and managers of Ve's opponents, also encouraged Ve to gain international exposure by fighting in the United States or Canada.

"He is a world-class material ... but he must fight in Canada or the United States and against different fighters and be prepared to face different systems of training," he said.

Ungerman said that they now had their sights on WBC welterweight champion Carlos Palomino of Mexico for a title fight.

Gray went on to have seven more fights before retiring in August 1980 after winning the Canadian welterweight title against Allen Clarke by knockout in the tenth round. Gray's next three fights after Ve were against Tommy Hearns in January 1979, which he lost by TKO in the 10th round, and American Pete Ranzany in June for the North American Boxing Federation welterweight title which he lost by TKO in the fifth round. In August 1979, Gray lost his Commonwealth welterweight title against Chris Clarke, in an 11th round TKO.

Gray challenged Clarke to a return bout three months later in November and won back his Commonwealth crown by TKO in the 10th round. Gray never did get that fight against Palomino as Palomino lost his WBC crown to Wilfred Benitez in January 1979.

Ve's loss also meant that Ritova lost his bet. Ritova shadow-sparred down Namoli Avenue in Lautoka the day after, "but with a very heavy heart". In his column that Monday, Ritova laid bare some of the theories behind Ve's loss.

"Irving Ungerman, Clyde's manager, I think is partly to blame. He pressured Ve into signing that contract for a return fight if Ve won the title. If not, the fight was off. The Gray camp held the upper hand, and whether Ve and manager John Ramos liked it or not, they had no choice.

But what a way to treat an up-and-coming world-class boxer. Well to be in a game like this, one has got to learn the very hard way.

There's another story of Ve being starved. One man that was very pointed about this was Fiji Professional Boxing and Wrestling Association secretary Mumtaz Ali. I mentioned two weeks ago how Ve was being fed steak and chips. I mentioned although it wasn't published how I was very surprised that he wasn't into his natural food – hunks of tapioca, dalo and fish. Mr Ali agreed with me. During that after-the-fight talk, he said that he was concerned about Ve's performance. He just wasn't the Ve we know of the past.

World famous ref Jay Edson has a lot of faith in Ve. He told me that he would put in a report to the World Boxing Council about Ve.

'Although he was beaten, he wasn't disgraced. The boy should go a long way,' Edson said.

I always thought that. But he considers that Ve shouldn't be based in Fiji. I'm right behind that. I consider that a year's stint in America, Canada or even

England would do the boy a lot of good. Edson thinks so, Ungerman thinks so, and I think a lot of other people think so" (Ritova, 1978).

Understanding the pros and cons of carbohydrates and proteins in the modern athlete's diet puts rest to the starvation theory as maintaining weight and building lean muscle is central to a boxer's conditioning before a fight.

Edson was so impressed with Ve that he made Ve and Ramos an offer to talk to Angelo Dundee, Muhammed Ali's long-time trainer, to get Ve a place in his gym (Daunabuna, 1978).

"If Ve wants to go up the ladder to a world rating, he has got to get away from the island to fight and train overseas. A man of Ve's calibre should get more experience to be considered in the WBC and WBA ratings," he said at the time.

Edson also offered to negotiate fights for Ve with promoters, Hawaiian-based Sam Ichinose and Florida-based Chris Dundee, Angelo's older brother. Ramos was appreciative of the offer preferring that any training abroad be kept to a short period. The decision he said, was ultimately Ve's.

Ramos explained that a shorter training stint was preferable to a longer stay to fight in places like the United States because the nature of the contract negotiations in the US was such that fighters became tied to a promoter for a certain number of fights.

"There are always a lot of points to be considered before we can agree to get training overseas," Ramos said.

"I want Ve to be a 'free' fighter rather than be bound to a long-term contract. If Ve signs to fight under a particular promoter for a single fight, he is likely to fight another six fights under the same promoter because he is bound by their way of contracts."

He said such contracts would be like selling Ve's freedom. As Ve and Ramos had no binding contract with each other than that forged on each other's word as gentlemen, Ramos said that any decision on Ve's part to seek further experience overseas, would be his alone to make.

"I have no binding contract with him to fight under me for life," Ramos said (Berwick, 1978).

Ramos did point out that if Ve went overseas, he would be starting again at the bottom of the ladder, fighting for $500 purses and trying to win fight fans so he can demand a higher purse. Historically, Ve at the time was, and still is, the only Fijian boxer to be trained, managed and based in Fiji to fight for a Commonwealth title. Fiji's former Commonwealth middleweight champion Alipate Korovou was based out of Australia.

In a separate interview with The Fiji Times, Ve said that he was not interested in going overseas for further exposure, turning down Edson's offer to have him train with Angelo Dundee (Berwick, 1978).

"I doubt if I will learn anything new by going overseas," Ve said. "The only problem I have is the lack of proper training facilities."

Ve continued that he had developed his own fighting style which he had used to demolish several Australian boxers, and he doubted that he would be able to adapt himself to changes which he would have to face if he went overseas.

"For this reason, I have no intention of going overseas," he said.

Ve also reaffirmed to The Fiji Times that he would maintain his current relationship with trainer/manager Ramos as he was happy with the arrangement in that Ramos did not get a share of his purse, "which normally managers got".

The bad weather that marked the Ve-Gray fight in Lautoka, led to an investigation by the PBWAF after $15 ringside ticket holders complained of not getting seats when they turned up (Rabuka, 1978) .

PBWAF secretary, Ali said he would await the report of the association's ring official before commenting further. Promoter Sain said he was prepared to give affected ticket holders a 20 per cent discount to tickets for a Ve and Dave "Boy" Green fight if it went ahead. Green was the British and European super-lightweight champion at the time.

Ve's second loss also brought forward local challengers for his titles. First up was Paula Namosi who wanted a go at Ve for his Fiji welterweight title. Namosi's manager Francis Byrnes, who was a ringside judge in the Ve-Gray return fight, said that Namosi was unimpressed by Ve's form (Rabuka, 1978).

"We are confident that after Saturday's performance, Ve can be beaten," Byrnes said.

Ve said that after a short break, he'd be ready to take on either Namosi, Ambika Prasad or Silio Tiko for a purse of $4,000.

And, where other promoters had failed, it appeared that promoter Sitiveni Niumataiwalu had made some headway in getting Vunimasi to agree to a title defence against Tarika for $400 (Sport, 1978). The fight would be billed along with a Sisiwa-Cama battle royale for the Fiji heavyweight championship on December 23.

The year ended with news of the retirement of former Fiji welterweight champion Seva Mocesui at the age of 34. Mocesui had fought as a welterweight and middleweight during this career (Sport, 1978).

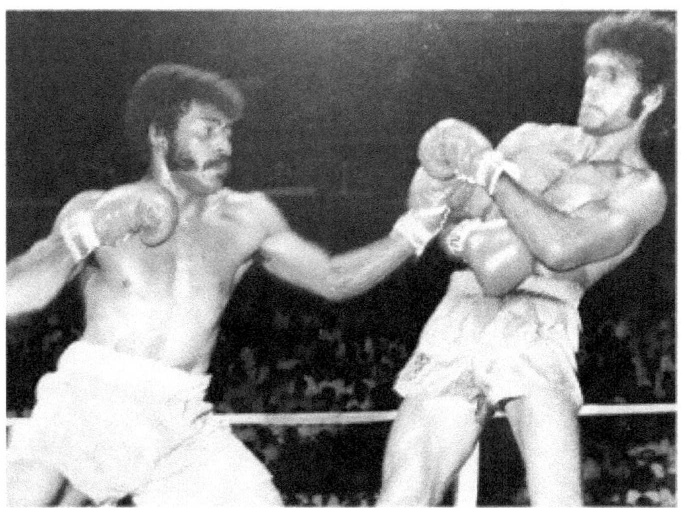

Sakaraia Ve (L) in the ring against Steve Dennis in Suva (Fiji Times, January 14, 1978).

Referee Maika Ravula counts out defending South Seas Middleweight champion, Jone Mataitini in the fourteenth round of the scheduled fifteen rounds fight against Sakaraia Ve (Fiji Times, February 27, 1978).

Clyde Gray (facing camera) and manager Irving Ungerman make their way to the ring to defend his Commonwealth welterweight title against Sakaraia Ve in Suva (Fiji Times, August 19, 1978).

Sakaraia Ve (second from right) taking a moment for the national anthem before his Commonwealth welterweight title fight against Clyde Gray at the Laucala Bay Hangar in Suva. Ve is flanked by his second, Father Brian Wilson (R), trainer/manager John Ramos and Wili Tarika (Fiji Times, August 19, 1978).

MUMTAZ ALI ...backed by Sakaraia Ve and his camp.

JAY EDSON ...backed by Gray and his camp.

PBWA Secretary and referee Mumtaz Ali and veteran American referee, Jay Edson were opposing options to referee the second ve/Gray fight, which Edson was eventually selected to do (Fiji Times, circa November 1978)

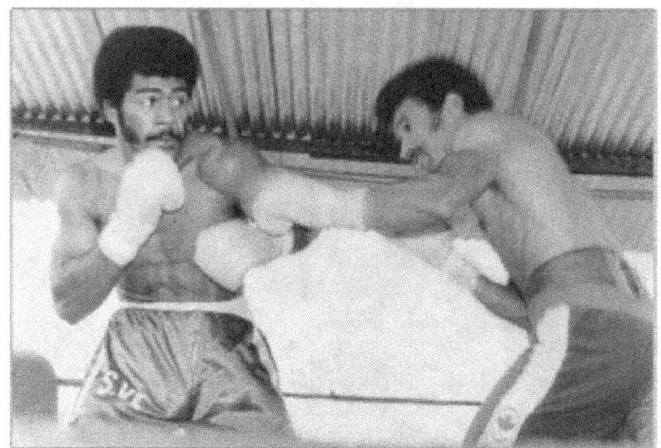

Sakaraia Ve (L) and Clyde Gray go toe to toe in their second Commonwealth welterweight title fight in Churchill Park Lautoka (Fiji Times, December 3, 1978).

Sakaraia Ve on the canvas in round nine of his second Commonwealth welterweight challenge against Clyde Gray, Churchill Park Lautoka (Fiji Times, December 2, 1978).

Commonwealth welterweight champion Clyde Gray (L) with his manager Irving Ungerman after his fight against Sakaraia Ve, Churchill Park Lautoka (Fiji Times, December 2, 1978).

John Ramos (L) and Sakaraia Ve sign the contract for the Hector Thompson return fight. Looking on is promoter Dr. Raj Bali (circa November 1978).

Chapter 8
1979 – Winds of change

Ve took two months off after his second failed Commonwealth title attempt. It was time enough for him to regroup, refocus and determine where to next. Ramos also took the time to look at a few fight prospects for Ve when he was ready to return to the ring. Among the possibilities were Dave Green, the British super-lightweight champion; Neil Patel, the holder of the Australian super-welterweight and welterweight titles; and Hector Thompson, the former Australian and Commonwealth super-lightweight champion.

The year would also see Ve slowdown in the fight stakes, entering the ring only five times in the year following his marriage to Una. This also allowed Ramos to spend a bit more time with his other boxers.

JANUARY – WHO'S NEXT?

After the New Year, it looked as if the Ve-Green fight was going to happen but Green's commitment to English promoter Mickey Duff created problems in securing a date. A win against Green, rated No.6 to WBC welterweight champion Carlos Palomino, would have added pressure on Gray to give Ve another shot at his Commonwealth championship title (Rabuka, 1978).

Neil Patel on the other hand, who had lost to Hector Thompson on points the previous October in Brisbane, Australia was demanding an A$4,000 purse while Thompson asked for A$2,000 – initially. Depending on which fighter Ve decided on, Ramos would approach their camp for a suitable lightweight to go up against Tarika in preparation for a possible challenge for the Commonwealth super-featherweight title held by Papua New Guinean Johnny Aba for later in the year.

"I wanted in on a team basis to give Tarika enough experience because we are also negotiating with Johnny Aba to defend his title that same year," Ramos said.

As Thompson's purse demand grew to A$5,000, Ramos spoke to Bernie Hall, Mark Barnett's manager and vice-president of the Australian Boxing Federation, to speak to Thompson and his manager Brendon Tapp to accept a purse of A$3,000 instead. This followed Ramos's initial problems in getting direct contact with Tapp (Rabuka, 1978).

"Thompson is still known as the best welterweight in the South Pacific. It is important for Ve to beat him to win world recognition," Ramos said.

Hall warned Ramos of the danger Ve would face going up against Thompson.

"Hall told me that Thompson is a work-in fighter and a very powerful body puncher, even stronger than Clyde Gray," Ramos said.

"Now we know what to expect from Thompson. We know that he is a world-class fighter and very experienced, being once rated top in the lightweight division."

Thompson lost his first attempt at the world title against Panamanian Roberto Duran for the WBA lightweight championship in 1973 and again in 1975 against Colombian Antonio Cervantes for the same title.

Thompson was not to be underestimated by any measure. His punching power had ended the lives of two of his opponents. The first was fellow Australian Roko Spanja in October 1970 in what was Roko's thirteenth professional fight. Thompson won that fight by a 10th-round knockout. It was reported that repeated blows to the head sustained by Roko, led to his untimely death not long after the fight.

Then in April 1976, Thompson beat American Chuck Wilburn in a seventh round TKO after Wilburn collapsed mid-fight. Wilburn suffered a brain haemorrhage and died a few days later. It was Thompson's sixty-third professional fight and Wilburn's seventeenth (AAP, 1976).

On the undercard for the Ve-Thompson fight, Tarika would go up against Sydney lightweight Gary Rosen. The fight would be the first international fight for Tarika.

Former Fiji heavyweight champion Leweni Waqa was not convinced that Ve had made the right decision to not train in the United States (Sport, 1979).

"Ve is a good young fighter but has to still develop his fighting style and this is exactly where he would gain more style, skill and a modern approach to the game," Waqa said.

"They have the best trainers and consultants in building a boxer which will help Ve in his future."

As an alternative, Ramos considered inviting Dundee to Fiji to train Ve should the Dave Green fight go ahead. The Dundee invitation was conveyed by Edson in an official letter (Rabuka, 1979).

The practicalities of this arrangement rested on Ve and Ramos getting time off from their respective jobs to take on boxing as a full-time occupation.

"We are both very much interested in our work. It is too early for anyone in Fiji to make boxing a full-time profession," Ramos said.

"A full-time professional means earning your living from boxing and that is what Dundee is doing in the United States as a trainer and manager with millions of dollars."

Ramos said the club would try to raise $2,000 before making the Dundee invitation official.

"We are also asking Edson to ask Dundee for his charges for the period he will spend in Fiji," Ramos said adding that his wish list to Edson also included enlisting his help approaching the British Boxing Board of Control to lock in the Ve-Green fight.

In the meantime, Ramos drew up a wish list of equipment and facilities needed to be brought in from the United States including a medicine ball for stomach exercises and a swivel for the speed ball mounting.

The Noor Mohammed card for the Ve-Thompson fight hit a snag after the February 10 date selected clashed with the Andrew Millar programme for Sunia Cama-Mani Vaka heavyweight fight set for the same date (Sport, 1979).

After a discussion with Thompson's camp, the fight date was changed to February 17 (Sport, 1979).

The Thompson fight was critical for Ve after his second loss to Gray. Thompson, a nine-year veteran in the professional ranks, had a record of 71-9-2 against Ve's barely three years in the paid ranks with a record of

25-3-0. The fight was either going to be a one-sided affair or an entertaining road to redemption for the 'Ve-Bomb'.

Ve was now seventh in the WBC rankings. Ramos said that if Ve lost against Thompson, efforts would be made with Edson and Dundee to get Ve fights with Americans rated in the thirties (Thomson, 1979).

To pique public interest in the Ve-Thompson fight, Ramos spoke with ABF vice-president Bernie Hall about the possible creation of a South Pacific welterweight title which Ve and Thompson could fight for. The non-affiliation of the PBWAF and the ABF made fights for titles by boxers from the other association impossible. This new title would rank higher than Ve's three national titles and two South Seas belts, all governed by the PBWAF; and be open for contention for boxers from Fiji, Australia, New Zealand and Papua New Guinea.

The proposal met with ABF approval and all Ramos needed was the PBWAF's OK (Sport, 1979).

"I'm happy that it has gone through the Australian federation. This is the start to a move to get more Australia and New Zealand boxers to fight our local boys," Ramos said, adding that Fiji boxers did not qualify to fight for Australasian titles while PNG, Australia and New Zealand did not qualify to fight for the South Seas championship.

It was agreed that the winner of the new title would have to defend it against Australian Eddie Buttons as the top challenger.

While the PBWAF mulled over the proposal, Ramos met quietly in a non-publicised event in early January with Joe Tokabai, Tahitian businessman and boxing promoter Louis Aitemai, and Tongan businessman Joe Mateale. Australian trainer John McColl could not make it for the meeting. Ramos said the meeting was to get endorsements from boxing members from around the South Pacific region to recognise the proposed South Pacific title.

In an interesting international boxing development at the time, the BCBB, abolished separate titles for blacks and whites in South African boxing (AAP, 1979). This was an effort to lessen discrimination in boxing in South Africa where apartheid was practised at the time. The former champions would be given the first opportunity to reclaim a unified titled for their weight divisions.

FEBRUARY – TAKING ON THE 'BRISBANE BOMBER'

Thompson came to Fiji with one mission – end Ve's unbeaten record against Australian fighters, according to his manager Brandon Tapp (Thomson, 1979). Tapp, the former New South Wales State and Tasmania state welterweight champion, had retired only 10 years earlier.

Having watched Thompson fight in Australia in 1974, Ramos was confident that Ve could counter the strong body punches that were Thompson's hallmark, by building stamina and using his elbows better to protect his trunk.

"Thompson has a reputation as a rib-smasher and we will be watching him closely in the first round," Ramos said.

Having the inside track on Thompson's weak spot, the area above his brow which opens easily, Ramos was confident that Ve could weaken Thompson by working on his body which would cause his head to drop then following that through with well-placed head shots to open him up. Until then, Thompson had lost only three fights by TKO because of a cut above his eyes.

At age 29 with 71 professional fights behind him, Thompson was still a considerable force in the ring. By comparison at age 22 and only 25 professional fights, Ve looked like a 'babe in the woods'.

The Tarika-Rosen fight was also building up interest. At age 26, Rosen (born Alipate Natoba in Fiji and based in Sydney), had 29 professional fights with five losses. Tarika at 22, had 26 professional fights with five losses.

After defeating Ve in December the previous year, Gray met 20-year-old American Thomas Hearns in a 10 round non-title fight in Detroit on January 11. Before departing Fiji, Ungerman indicated a third title shot might be a possibility for Ve, but that would be later down the line. However, Gray's tenth round TKO loss to the much younger Hearns, led Ungerman to express an interest in returning earlier for that third fight against Ve sometime in June or July instead of a later date (Thomson, 1979).

Hearns went on to win the WBA world welterweight title in August 1980 after beating Mexican champion Pipino Cuevas (born José Isidro Cuevas González).

Ve, however, had his sights set on Dave Green. To take that next step, he would need to first overcome Thompson, known to his fans as the 'Brisbane Bomber'.

Thompson arrived in Suva with Rosen a week before the fight. Brimming with confidence, the former Commonwealth super lightweight champion said he was looking for a knockout against Ve when they meet at the Laucala Bay Hangar (Rabuka, 1979).

Only a week earlier Rosen had drawn with the top New South Wales state title contender, Joey Collins. Rosen left Fiji in 1975 after completing his education at Provincial School Northern in Taveuni and Ratu Sukuna Memorial School in Suva.

Looking forward to his first international fight, Tarika had put in seven solid weeks of training for the eight-round clash. Tarika wanted nothing more than a clear outcome against Rosen when they met in the Ve-Thompson undercard draw at the Laucala Bay Hangar.

"I have never been so fit in my career. I have worked hard for seven weeks to get into top form. It should be a good fight. I will be giving away weight and height on Saturday but that will not worry me at all," Tarika said (Rabuka, 1978).

Ramos said Tarika had developed a tremendous punching combination which could decide the fight. With Rosen's record, Ramos deemed the challenger a worthy opponent.

"Tarika must win this fight if he is to take on the overseas line-up that has been set up for him," Ramos said.

Ve returned to his normal routine of going to his day job as a bank teller at the BNZ Bank branch in Cumming Street during the day and training for 2-3 hours after work every evening. Keeping a quieter approach to the upcoming fight after his successive defeats by Gray, Ve wasn't making any predictions other than to say: "I'm no Muhammad Ali. I don't like to talk or make predictions before any of my fights. But this much I can say, it will certainly be a good hard fight" (Rabuka, 1978).

Having recently married Unaisi Naqio, the niece of the Tui Wailevu, Ratu Isikia Rogoyawa, Ve was more focussed on regaining his fight form after the Christmas break. Thompson's manager Brendon Tapp was not so gun shy about making predictions, saying confidently that Thompson would end the fight between the sixth and tenth of the scheduled 15-rounds bout (Rabuka, 1979).

Tapp said Thompson had been cut only once in his professional fight career.

"This was when current junior-welterweight champion of the world Antonio Cervantes cut him in the last 10 seconds of the eighth round with an uppercut to the eyelid," Tapp said.

Tapp continued that Thompson's fight against former world lightweight champion Roberto Duran in 1973 placed Duran in hospital for a week but not before Duran sent Thompson packing with a TKO in the eighth round.

"He trains hard, works hard as a supervisor in a construction company and is very friendly," Tapp said of Thompson.

The new South Pacific welterweight championship was a shield and not the traditional belt. For Ve, given that everything was on the line including a fight against Dave Green, losing was not an option.

Knowing that, Ve went into the fight against Thompson on February 17 with classic shades of his attacking style and brilliant counterpunches, rocking the Australian several times early on.

However, the follow through was just not there on the day. Ve, to the disappointment of fight fans and Ramos, lost by TKO in the eighth to the more experienced Thompson, handing his opponent the inaugural South Pacific welterweight championship.

"Hector Thompson should consider himself lucky that Sakaraia Ve was not wearing his killer instinct on Saturday ... otherwise he would have ended up on his back on the canvas in the third round," said Stan Ritova in his "From the sidelines" column the following Monday (Ritova, 1979).

"Ve, after counterpunching beautifully, had the veteran Hec in trouble and I think the Australian knew it. But our boy eased off. Why? I don't know."

PBWAF secretary and fight referee, Mumtaz Ali said, "Just a couple of good body punches would have finished Thompson."

The scorecards had Ve leading the fight up until then. Ali had Ve winning at 69-66. Judges Joe Campbell and George Ponipate scored it 68-66 for Ve (Rabuka, 1979).

The fight ended when Ve did not emerge in the eighth round because of vision problems.

Ramos said that Ve complained he couldn't see properly out if his right eye at the end of the sixth round after Thompson connected with a solid left (Rabuka, 1979). Ramos poured water in Ve's eyes but by the end of the seventh, Ve told him that he preferred not to continue because his vision did not improve.

Given the vision problems that fellow stablemate Tevita Tui now had, perhaps Ve thought the same was or would happen to him and decided to quit the eighth round as a precaution.

The fight fans were bitter about the loss and the way the fight ended.

"It has been reported that Ve was missing training before the fight. If it is true and he wasn't fit and he didn't want to lose face by being knocked out in the final rounds of the scheduled fifteen, then former fans would be justified in saying that they had just watched a $4,000 write off," reporter Richard Thomson wrote in *The Fiji Times* (1979).

Thomson the writer, didn't end his attack on the champ there. He continued that now Ve was married and had a job in banking, perhaps he should stay and make his career there.

Thompson the fighter, was more encouraging in his remarks after the fight.

"If Ve is to progress through the ranks, then he must go overseas for further training," adding that remaining in Fiji would limit his capabilities (Rabuka, 1979).

Thompson also believed that turning down the offer to train with Angelo Dundee in the United States was the biggest mistake of his career.

"I suppose because he is now married and wanted to continue in his banking career. But if he is to become world champion, the answer is to go train under a world reputed trainer."

He on the other hand, heaped praise on Ve after the fight saying that Ve landed some good punches.

"He has the potential, but I think he should become a junior welterweight. He is too short to be a welterweight."

The loss, the second in a row, set Ramos and Ve back on their world and Commonwealth title plans, with Ramos recognising that Fiji promoters may now not be as forthcoming to promote Ve's fights. Ramos had a plan to do so himself, if it came to that.

"If I can get a licence, I can get overseas fighters to fight Ve. This is to build him up again. It is not the end of the road for us. We will continue from here with our aim at fighting for Gray's Commonwealth welterweight title," he said. The anticipated fight against Green was put on hold.

Looking back, Ramos felt that Ve gave Thompson too much open room during their encounter and the experienced champ took advantage of the exposed rib area round after round.

In a post-fight interview with *The Fiji Times*, Ve was quoted as saying that boxing took second place in his life. First and foremost was his career as a bank officer and his family (Berwick, 1979). That did not sit well with a boxing fan who sent this letter to the editor:

"Sir, - I refer to the Fiji Times (February 20) and wish to ask Ve, the Golden Boy of Fiji a few questions.

1. If he thinks that boxing is only a hobby, why doesn't he fight three and six rounders only, not title fights?

2. Why can't he give the titles he has won to the association if boxing is just a hobby?

3. Why is he demanding a lot of money if he thinks boxing is just a hobby?

I wish to know why Ve has put boxing and his family first. If I remember, he had said earlier that boxing came first. – Asivorosi Waqa, Suva."

The off-handed comment undoubtedly lost Ve a few more fans, but the reality was that boxing was not his 'job' in the traditional sense, as earning a living through professional sport was unheard of in Fiji at the time. His daily job was as a bank officer, the boxing worked around that. Correlating that to doing something that he loved when he was not at work, could only perhaps best be described as a "hobby" in Ve's manner of thinking.

When Thompson returned to Australia, he announced his retirement from professional boxing on March 31. A few weeks later, he had a change of heart and called his manager, Tapp to say he wanted a few more fights (Sport, 1979).

Tarika fared better in his fight, taking out Rosen by TKO in the seventh round.

The fight was entertaining with Tarika clearly superior in skills and experience. He battered Rosen for six rounds of their eight-round encounter ending with Rosen not coming out for the seventh. Tapp, who was in Rosen's corner for the fight, suggested to Ramos afterwards that Tarika fight Brian Robert, a former Commonwealth junior-lightweight champion, as his next opponent (Sport, 1979).

In a post-script to this sub-chapter, Hector Thompson passed away on Brisbane on 20 May 2020 at the age of 70 years. Ramos was saddened by the news of his death, reflecting on his memory as "a great boxer, great champion and a great person".

MARCH – KAMINIELI VUNIMASI, ANGELO DUNDEE

Tarika's victory over Rosen in his first international fight opened new opportunities for the 22-year-old. No sooner had Tarika recovered from the six-round encounter, than an offer from New Zealand came his way. The proposed opponent, Jeff Smith was a super-featherweight offered by the Auckland Boxing Association to Ramos as a suitable next opponent for the former Fiji featherweight champion (Sport, 1979). Offered $300 for the 10-round fight, Ramos was cautious about accepting the offer at face value.

"The money is right but there are some terms in the contract that need to be clarified," he said.

Tarika's focus, Ramos said, was the upcoming return fight against Vunimasi for the Fiji featherweight championship on March 17. "Tarika was robbed of the title when he fought Vunimasi in 1978. Vunimasi will return to Lautoka without the title on March 17."

Paula Namosi's wish to challenge Ve for the Fiji welterweight title also came true. Ve agreed to give Namosi the opportunity to fight for the title. This was to be Ve's second title defence after winning the vacant belt against Inia Catarogo in April 1977. He had only defended it once since, against Rupeni Vutevute in August 1978. Ve would get a purse of $2,500 for the fight.

Also, interested in Tarika was Australian-based Papua New Guinean Commonwealth junior-lightweight champion Johnny Aba (Rabuka, 1979). Aba was trained and managed by Bernie Hall, the same man who brought Mark Barnett to fight Ve the previous October.

But Tarika wasn't the only aspirant to the Commonwealth title, Vunimasi also wanted a fight with Aba if he beat Tarika in their return bout.

The offer to Tarika came via a letter from Hall to Ramos. In the letter Hall said that Aba had a fight scheduled on March 24 against Australian bantam and featherweight champion Paul Ferreri. On a date yet to be decided, Aba was to also meet the then world junior-lightweight champion Eusebio Pedroza in PNG.

"He (Aba) will then be free, and the chance is ours. Hall has told me to write to him as soon as Tarika is ready to fight. The fight will be in Suva, and they have agreed to this," Ramos said.

Also planned for the year, according to Ramos, was a fight between light-heavyweight Joe Dawai and the New South Wales light-heavyweight champion Al Gattling in Pacific Harbour. Ramos also had former Australian featherweight champion Guinea Hillier in his sights for Tarika.

Ramos also heard back from Angelo Dundee on his (Ramos') proposal for the world-renowned boxing trainer to visit Fiji to train Ve. In his letter, Dundee said that he would not be available until October as he had several world title fights coming up for his fighters.

Angelo and his older brother Chris, who was also a boxing promoter, ran the Fifth Street Gym in Miami, Florida.

Tarika's preparations leading up to the return fight against Vunimasi was intense. The 'Wili Pony' was determined to regain the Fiji featherweight championship at the Laucala Bay Hangar. Ramos was confident that Tarika would win by a knockout. Vunimasi's team believed it would be Tarika on the canvas.

"We have worked on how to counter Vunimasi's fast two-fisted attack from a long range," Ramos said (Rabuka, 1979).

The day arrived, greeted by typical Suva heat and humidity. The corrugated frame of the old Hangar trapping the heat generated throughout the day, set the stage for a heated and often entertaining exchange of the featherweights.

Tarika was coiled as a tightly wound spring. That much was evident when at the opening bell of the first round Tarika charged in with a flurry of well-timed shots to Vunimasi's body.

The first round must have been Tarika's as his vicious left and rights hammered into Vunimasi's body (Dean, 1979). The second round was the same with Vunimasi coming off worse in the clinches. By the third round, Tarika's head shots were worked off by Vunimasi's dancing feet and upper cuts that didn't seem to worry Tarika. Vunimasi came into the fifth round with some fast combinations before Tarika got the better of him with three well-timed lefts to the head. The fifth and sixth were Tarika's as he forced Vunimasi on to the ropes and continued to deliver solid punches to the head. By the end of the sixth, Vunimasi's right eye had started to close from Tarika's relentless pounding.

The fight lasted the entire 15 scheduled rounds. Respect and credit were due to Vunimasi, who despite having one eye completely closed and the other partially closed because of Tarika's assault, stood his ground like the champion he was and saw the fight through to the end.

The fight ended with a split points decision with judge Pundit scoring an equal 150-150, judge Veramu Dikidikilati, 147-136 to Tarika and judge George Ponipate, 144-143 to Tarika.

Fans of the losing camp claimed they were robbed.

"That comment is utter nonsense. If Vunimasi is ready to fight Wili tomorrow, we are willing to put the title at stake. But the young boxer from the west will not be fighting for some time after the beating he received from Wili," Ramos said.

However, Vunimasi's trainer/manager John Buadromo was magnanimous in saying, "It was a close fight, and the decision was fair."

Reclaiming the title was bittersweet for Tarika.

By all accounts, Tarika and Vunimasi put on a good fight. The fact that Vunimasi lasted the 15 rounds despite his obvious facial injuries was a testament to his mettle. Even Ramos conceded that the young man had class and was "a good fighter. A good prospect who just needs experience".

With one fighter recognised at Commonwealth prospect level and another embarking on the same path, the Ramos Boxing Club had put itself firmly on Fiji's boxing map in three short years. Ramos's exchange of letters with Angelo Dundee and continuing telephone contact with Jay Edson also helped cement the recognition of Fiji boxing on the international scene.

At the time, Dundee, born Angelo Mirena in Philadelphia, Pennsylvania on August 30, 1921, was training Muhammad Ali, the reigning WBA world heavyweight champion. Dundee's impressive resume over the years saw him train several world champions including Jimmy Ellis, Trevor Berbick, Sugar Ray Leonard, George Foreman, Jose Napoles and Sugar Ramos, Ramos's own boxing idol. In all, Dundee trained 15 world champions. His legacy in boxing earned him the mantle of being one of the greatest boxing trainers of all time.

By late March, a visit by Dundee to Fiji looked to happen sooner rather than later as Edson relayed to Ramos that Dundee had made arrangements for the training of his fighters and wanted to be in Fiji in late May (Rabuka, 1979).

The plan devised by Ramos and Edson to utilise Dundee's visit was to schedule a fight between Ve and Dundee's 12th-ranked US welterweight, Jimmy Heair who had a fight record of 72-17-1, 27 by way of knockout. An eight-year veteran, the 26-year-old had an impressive record and looked to be a great opponent for Ve. Accompanying Dundee and Heair would be another fighter, a featherweight to fight Tarika on a June 2 card.

Upon hearing of Dundee's availability from Edson, Ramos was elated. He described the impending visit as a "tremendous boost" to Fiji boxing. Edson had arranged for Dundee to spend a week in Fiji after the fight to train Ve and Tarika.

The planned visit and fight card were starting to gain a heavy outlay. Heair wanted a US$4,000 purse with another US$1,000 for the featherweight by the Dundee camp. With airfares and accommodation for Dundee and the two fighters, it was going to be quite an expense, which thanks to Shore Promotions' interest, looked likely to happen. Shore Promotions patron was Shore Buses Limited owner Raghunath Singh, a former employer of Ramos back in the '60s and a respected local businessman.

During the visit, Dundee was to run boxing clinics for other interested fighters and Edson was to coach fight referees and judges.

"I'm hoping to give other professional boxers in various clubs a chance to have Dundee train them while he is here," Ramos said.

With Edson's experience in refereeing and judging world title fights, Ramos suggested the formation of a separate association under the PBWAF for referees and judges as a means of helping develop the talent pool so that it would also improve the standard of boxing in Fiji.

Ramos felt that it was time that referees and judges sat examinations before qualifying to judge fights so that they could make the right decisions.

"If the standard of refereeing and judges improved, the standard of boxing would improve too," he said, adding that he had been disappointed many times when good up-and-coming boxers were robbed of their victories which discouraged them from continuing with a boxing career.

Vunimasi's manager John Buadromo agreed with Ramos's suggestion saying: "If boxing is to improve, refereeing and judging should be improved."

Buadromo was also receptive to the idea of coaching clinics for trainers, encouraging others like him to take advantage of Dundee and Edson's planned visit.

PBWAF secretary Ali agreed with Ramos's suggestion for the referees and judge's clinic, however it would not be practical as there were only a handful of judges and referees, and the association did not have the personnel to run it.

Ali said that the system used by the association was the worldwide system and a good one. He pointed out an incident during the Tarika-Vunimasi programme when the PBWAF ran short of referees and judges.

"I nearly ran into the ring with my own cloth, but fortunately someone came up to do the job," he said, adding that he would look into the suggestion, nevertheless.

APRIL – PAULA NAMOSI, PAUL BAKER

As the PBWAF annual general meeting on April 4 grew nearer, a disaffected band of PBWAF members, led by suspended promoter Rennie Mohammed, met in Suva on March 20 to devise a plan to unseat Ali from the association during the AGM (Rabuka, 1979).

Mohammed questioned the validity of the association's financial members, a query that Ali brushed off as "wasting his time" given that Mohammed was still suspended by the association. At this point Mohammed's suspension had been year-long after charges of overselling tickets for the Ve-Dennis fight.

Ali, with 20 years as secretary for the PBWAF, was not fazed by the influence of the dissenting group who had invited Ramos to their meeting.

"I have been with the association for 20 years and I will be here for the next 20 years as secretary," Ali said as he challenged Mohammed and his group to put up a nominee for secretary at the AGM.

"I hope they do that to prove who is popular with the financial members."

Ramos distanced himself from the group saying that he was only invited to listen to their grievances. His only focus at this time was to obtain his promoter's licence and to train Ve and Tarika for future Commonwealth title fights.

As quickly as the planned Ve-Heair fight was put into motion, so came its cancellation a week after its announcement. Instead of meeting Ve, Heair was keen instead to fight the WBC and WBA lightweight champion Roberto Duran in a non-title fight anticipated for April 8, a fight Heair lost by unanimous points decision when they met at Caesar's Palace in Las Vegas.

The message was relayed to Ramos by Edson who said that Dundee would look for another welterweight for Ve (Rabuka, 1979).

Edson told Ramos: "He will be one of the products of Dundee's famous camp from Miami Beach, Florida." Tarika's opponent was also still unnamed.

As Ramos sorted through the logistics for Dundee and his camp, Ve continued his preparation for his Fiji welterweight title defence against Paula Namosi scheduled for April 7 at Churchill Park in Lautoka.

In the throes of negotiating fights for his professional boxers, Ramos had not lost sight of the amateur fighters in the club. He always saw them as the foundation, the future of professional boxing and worked with a select group from within the club to organise their internal amateur championship tournament. With the support and sponsorship of Rewa Dairy, several trophies were donated for the tournament.

"It was important that I had this amateur event on the club calendar because you have to set a clear pathway for these boxers to build on their skills and experience before going into the national tournament," Ramos said.

Meanwhile, Tarika's planned fight against Hellier scheduled for April, was also cancelled and Hellier replaced by Australian super-lightweight Paul Baker for a fight on April 28 in Suva (Dean, 1979).

Ramos said he was informed by Aba's manager Bennie Hall that Hellier had been inactive for some time and therefore was not available. Hall did inform him that Baker was the tenth-ranked Commonwealth lightweight and had lost by knockout to Aba in the tenth round the previous November.

Ramos said that if Tarika beat Baker, Hall promised Tarika a crack at Aba's title. Tarika would earn $500 for his fight with Baker. Shore Promotions would promote Tarika's second international fight.

Ramos predicted Ve would knock out Paula Namosi in the fourth round of their 15-round clash in Lautoka on April 8 (Sport, 1979).

"Anybody who says that Ve has had it must come to Lautoka on Saturday, where he will prove that he is still the best fighter in Fiji today," Ramos said.

At just 23 years of age, and seemingly a lifetime of boxing behind him, the three losses suffered in his past four fights within six months would have worn down a lesser man. But for Ve this was just another chapter he needed to write to prove that he was still the 'Golden Boy'.

Unbeaten in three years, Namosi was confident that Ve's form was at its nadir and the time was right to wrest the Fiji welterweight title from Ve's steel grasp.

"I feel great, and I know that I can win. If I do not win by TKO or knockout I will win the fight on points – but I will win," Namosi said, confident that his preparations for the fight had gone well and he was ready for whatever Ve had.

"If Ve wants to stand toe to toe, I will be for it but I want to win the fight because this is a chance of a lifetime and I have been waiting a very long time for this opportunity," Namosi said, stopping short of giving his fight plan away.

Ramos knew that Ve's form was good, and he had done the work required to retain his title. Ve had fought top-shelf boxers the calibre of Gray and Thompson, while Namosi who had been inactive for a period, missing the exposure to tough fights.

Ve completed his preparation with a light workout the day before the bout. A lot was riding on this fight given recent losses.

Ramos's previous claims that Ve was the best fighter in the country was met with criticism by Fiji heavyweight champion Sunia Cama, who said that such claims gave the public the wrong impression of Ve (Sport, 1979).

Cama said that "because of this Ve has to suffer a lot from people who blamed him for his three defeats in his recent fights". Ramos did not respond to Cama's comments.

Ve's stock was still of value despite the recent losses, as Patel's people offered him a $3,000 purse to meet Patel in Brisbane in June. However, with the planned June fight as part of the Dundee programme still on track, Ramos turned down the offer.

On the day of the Ve-Namosi fight, former Fiji and South Seas middleweight champion Jone Mataitini challenged Ve for a return bout (Rabuka, 1979).

"I have seen Ve fight Clyde Gray twice for the Commonwealth welterweight title, and also against Hector Thompson. I now know his weaknesses. And should we meet again, I will beat him," Mataitini said adding that he was the only logical middleweight contender apart from Nemani Waka.

As predicted by Ramos, Ve stopped Namosi in the fourth round by TKO when ring doctor Welby Korwa declared Namosi unfit to continue (Daunabuna, 1979).

Ve was not taking any prisoners on the day. He entered the ring focused on what he needed to do to quiet the criticism of why he wouldn't fight local boxers. Namosi ended the fourth round with a bloody nose that Ve started in the first in addition to a cut above his right eye and a puffy left eye. His face was a bloody mess by the end of round three.

"Paula was no match for Ve and no local fighter in the welterweight division can beat him now – at least for another two years," Ramos said. "And to prove what I have said, Ve is willing to defend any of his five titles against any local challenger."

Namosi's manager Francis Byrnes admitted that the fight wasn't Namosi's best – "in fact it was his worst fight in his professional career".

"I was just getting started when the fight ended. Paula is a good fighter, but he did not hurt me much with his punches and I knew it would be a short fight after the first round," Ve said.

Ve returned to his hotel room after the fight to a 30-minute workout and a bit of shadow-sparring to wind down.

The win raised the possibility of an October meet with Gray for a third attempt, but Ungerman wanted Ve to prove himself first with a few more overseas opponents before they would consider coming back, Ramos said.

No sooner had the perspiration on the canvas dried from the Namosi fight, the rumour mill, fanned by Brisbane journalist Frank O'Callaghan, was in gear. O'Callaghan had written a report in *The Courier Mail* that Ve would soon be migrating to Australia (Sport, 1979).

It was reported by *The Fiji Times* that O'Callaghan had said: "Brisbane could get a readymade drawcard from Fiji. 'Sakaraia Ve, who twice last year fought Clyde Gray for the Commonwealth welterweight title, is interested in moving here'," the report said.

"I have no intention of leaving Fiji," Ve said, describing the report as "baseless and unfounded".

Ve did say he intended to spend his annual leave in Australia at some point.

"But I have not made up my mind when I will go. This depends on my future fights," Ve said. "I must make it clear that I have no intention of settling outside Fiji."

The as-yet-unnamed US opponent from Dundee's camp finally came through. Sammy Masias, 26, from Florida, who had a 19-9-1 record with eight by knockout, would be Ve's opponent for the June 2 fight (Sport, 1979).

With 19 fights under his belt since turning professional in 1975, Masias would be meeting Ve, who at this point had a fight record of 26-4-0, of which 18 were by knockout. Edson informed Ramos that talks were also in progress for a featherweight to meet Tarika in the main supporting bout.

Trained at the same gym as Muhammad Ali in Florida, Masias would be the first US opponent for Ve. Until this point Ve's only international opponents were Canadian Clyde Gray and a host of boxers out of Australia.

Preparations for Tarika's fight against Australian Baker were in gear. The main supporting bouts were John Krishna Chotka, a former Fiji soccer captain, and Peni Tabua, a former Ramos Club member, who were both based in Australia.

Chotka would meet Jone Mataitini and Tabua would fight Tomu Baca over 8x3-minute rounds at the Laucala Bay Hangar.

The Chotka-Mataitini grudge rematch was a long time coming for Chotka, who suffered a sixth-round knockout in their 1976 title fight (Rabuka, 1979).

Chotka was Australia's No.2-ranked middleweight after another Australian-based Fijian Apimeliki Rainima. Both had fought and lost against Wally Carr, the Australian middleweight champion. Carr beat Chotka for the Australian middleweight title in February 1978 with a third-round knockout.

Tarika was confident of beating Baker and getting that chance at Aba later in the year.

"We are confident that he will be on top of Baker. We know that Baker comes from a good training camp, but Tarika is very fit," Ramos said.

To ensure that Tarika was mentally prepared, Ramos had him check into the Grand Pacific Hotel in Suva the day before the fight (Sport, 1979).

"This is the most important fight. We are taking into consideration the fact that Baker went to the tenth round with Commonwealth junior-lightweight champion Johnny Aba before being knocked out in Port Moresby in January this year," Ramos said.

Ramos said that Tarika had been working on hitting harder and they were confident that they would prevail against Baker.

"This should give Tarika a good chance of being considered a top contender for Aba's title," Ramos said.

Tabua had advice for Tarika against Baker, describing the latter as a "walk-in" fighter who could be dangerous at close quarters (Rabuka, 1979).

"Tarika should take advantage of his speed if he is to beat Baker," he said.

On the eve of the Tarika-Baker fight, Edson came back with a name for Tarika's US opponent – Jose Chavez, an American Mexican also from the Dundee camp. Tarika would meet Chavas in a scheduled 10-rounds.

Glad that he had his next opponent lined up, Tarika was focused on his fight with Baker, predicting an early knockout (Rabuka, 1979). Keeping his fight plan close to his chest, Tarika said: "I'm going in there to win. If I knock him out so much the better."

The fight, however, took a different turn and went the distance. Trading blow for blow, Baker's style of fighting was everything Tarika was warned about, but the Fijian kept his head especially after a powerful right cross from

Baker in the third round took out Tarika's mouthguard with such force that it shot outside the ring (Rabuka, 1979).

Tarika kept his distance, making sure to stay out of reach of Baker's right cross, using his stamina to outpace and outpunch the Australian who by round eight, was struggling to maintain vision out his right eye as a cut opened by Tarika in the earlier rounds continued to trickle blood down his face. The last two rounds had Baker throwing everything he had to earn himself a knockout, but Tarika steered away from him, outpacing his opponent to a unanimous points decision win. The two judges and the referee scored the fight 97-94, 97-94 and 98-93 to Tarika.

Ramos was elated. The plan it appeared, was on track for Aba's title. Two more international fights and Tarika would be ready.

Baker was complimentary of Tarika after the fight. "He has all the guts in the world. In the third round I had him down, but he came back to fight a good fight."

Meanwhile, Chotka did not fare as well as he hoped to against Mataitini, who was out to prove that he was still a worthy challenger for Ve's South Seas middleweight title. Mataitini's hard jabs and crosses to the face had Chotka down on the canvas twice in the third round and with a cut opened under his left eye by the fifth, Chotka's quest for a win against the veteran wasn't looking too good. Chotka took one more knockdown in the sixth from which he tried to recover, groggy and dazed as he took the count. The referee decided enough was enough and stopped the fight.

On fight day, Tomu Baca was a no-show, so Petero Yavala stepped in as challenger for Tabua. The fight ended in a knockout win for Tabua.

JUNE – SAMMY MASIAS, JOSE CHAVEZ

In early June, Ramos boxer Aisake Buka participated in a pre-SPG amateur boxing event in Suva. The programme also hosted amateur boxer Peni Vai from Tonga (Rabuka, 1979). Vai met and lost to the Fiji amateur welterweight champion Joe Nitiva.

The sole Tongan delegate to the event was Tongan Boxing Association Secretary Tuileila Tapueluelu better known as Ila (Rabuka, 1979). At a dinner hosted by Ramos at his home for Ila and Vai, Ila was surprised to discover that there were South Seas titles in existence and that Ve held two of them.

The discovery prompted Ila to call for the formation of a boxing body separate from the PBWAF to look after the titles. At the time, the PBWAF were the administrators for all the South Seas titles. Ila was surprised that other member countries – Tonga, Western Samoa (now called Samoa), New Caledonia and Tahiti – knew nothing of its existence.

"My association has not been aware of these titles being fought in Fiji. By rights, we should have been informed by the Fiji body that these titles have been fought here," he said.

The only South Seas title Ila was aware of was the one held by heavyweight Fossie Schmidt, which he won by beating Tonga's Luke Veikoso.

"If we should organise ourselves and have a good body to look after the affairs of South Seas titles, I'm sure the standard of boxing in the region will improve," he said. Ila said he would put forward a proposal that if the light-heavyweight title were to become vacant, that all countries with eligible fighters have a championship elimination contest before identifying the two top contenders.

The comment followed South Seas light heavyweight champion Luke Sisiwa's legal troubles, a conviction that he was in the process of appealing. At the time, the South Seas title holders were Fossie Schmidt of Western Samoa (heavyweight and junior-heavyweight), Luke Sisiwa of Fiji (light-heavyweight), Sakaraia Ve of Fiji (junior-welterweight and lightweight), William White of Western Samoa (junior-middleweight), Basdeo of Fiji (welterweight) and Zamal Azad of Fiji (featherweight).

The fights with the American boxers moved from June 2 to June 30. As Tarika and Ve prepared to meet them, Ramos was already negotiating Ve's next fight, this time against Lawrence 'Baby Cassius' Austin of Australia (Rabuka, 1979).

Cassius had beaten Thompson in September 1977 to win the Commonwealth and Australian super-lightweight titles. The Perth-born slugger went on to lose the Commonwealth title to Jeff Malcolm a year later on points. Ve had also outpointed Malcolm when they met in April 1978.

"I think the fight with Cassius will be a good test for Ve, especially against a boxer who has beaten Thompson," Ramos said.

As the fight day against Masias drew nearer, Ve was keen to have that over with a quick knockout (Rabuka, 1979).

"We are going for an early knockout, and we are confident we can do it this time," Ramos said, adding that Ve's experience against Gray and Thompson had him at an advantage.

As Ve shadow-boxed, built stamina and skipped his way to peak fitness, Adi Narayan contacted Ramos from Toronto to tell him that Gray had been forced to defend his title against fellow Canadian Chris Clarke in two months.

The decision of the BCBB was either Gray fought Clarke or give other top contenders a fight sooner rather than later. Narayan's advice to Ramos was for Ve to knock out Masias early so that Ungerman would agree to give Ve that third shot. Ungerman was more likely to agree to this as Gray would get a better deal in Fiji than in Canada.

The pressure on Gray to defend his title followed his fifth round TKO by American Pete Ranzany on June 13. Ranzany was ranked third in the world at the time. This was Gray's second successive loss after beating Ve the previous December.

Gray eventually fought Clarke on August 28, losing his Commonwealth title after a TKO in the 11th round.

Tarika, fresh from his win against Baker, worked hard to maintain his fitness for the Chavez fight (Sport, 1979). With a 26-4-0 record, the Fiji featherweight champion was ready for the Mexican American with the 12-0-0 record. His wins all by knockout.

"He is a knockout fighter all right, but he will not put me down," Tarika said.

"I'm punching with more speed and power than in my last bout with Paul Baker. I will fight to the last minute, and I'm prepared to take him the distance."

Masias and Chavez arrived a week before their fights but without their manager Chris Dundee who was expected to arrive a few days later due to a fight promotion he had that weekend (Dean, 1979). Accompanying them was referee Jay Edson.

Masias, when asked about Ve said: "I don't know anything about the guy. I have never heard of him, but I will try for an early knockout."

The 26-year-old had fought Pete Ranzany in February and lost by knockout in the third round. Yes, the same Pete Ranzany who beat Gray earlier in the month.

At 23, Chavez was also confident of beating Tarika, citing his right hand as his weapon of choice.

As promised, Edson didn't waste time and got on to running clinics for referees and judges during the week of the fight. In his 37-year career, Edson had at the time, controlled 45 world title fights for the World Boxing Council.

However, despite the opportunity to learn from one of the most experienced and internationally recognised referees in boxing, only a handful of people turned up to take advantage. Among the few was Fiji Amateur Boxing Association secretary, Abraham Thomas (Rabuka, 1979).

Edson told the small gathering that to be a good referee, one had to be honest, calm and impartial, plus having the ability to do simple arithmetic as fight points were allotted for each round.

"A first-class referee will do his work unobtrusively," he said. "He must never try to make himself part of the ring picture by taking the pay away from the contestants by being overly energetic and rushing about within the ring. The only ones the fans want to watch are the boxers doing the fighting."

Edson told the participants that a referee also looked beyond just measuring blows landed during a round.

"They must consider ring cleverness, agility, dodging and ducking, countering, blocking – and the amount of damage inflicted," Edson said.

"The average fight fan looks for heavy hitting as the most pleasing part of a boxing match. But there is more to boxing than hitting power.

"To such fans it seems that the man who is fighting all the time by forcing matters in every round and trying desperately to knock his opponent out should be declared the winner.

"This, despite the fact that his opponent, on the defensive all the time, has landed the cleaner jabs and counters, has often made his man miss and has been effective."

Edson said that if a fighter was knocked out of the ring, he should not be assisted back into the ring.

"If the fighter has not re-entered the ring when the count reaches 10, the decision should be a knockout," he said.

Chris Dundee didn't make it down for the fight this time, sending Kevin Conlan in his place. It was probably just as well that he didn't because the 'Ve-Bomb' and the 'Wili Pony' express disposed of his two fighters in rounds two and one respectively (Dean, 1979).

Both the bouts were scheduled 10-rounders. Tarika, in the supporting bout, entered the ring dancing and throwing quick jabs to Chavez's face. A low blow from Chavez bought Tarika 30 seconds from referee Edson. With the rest over, Tarika stepped on the gas and unleased a flurry of lightning left-right combinations to Chavez's chin which saw him fall like a tree on to the canvas, a minute and 58 seconds into the first round. Edson gave Chavez the full count.

Ve also wasted no time getting on to Masias from the opening bell. A hard left and a right cross to the chin saw Masias down on the canvas in the first round. No sooner had the eight-count ended, Ve found a sweet spot on Masias's head with a right uppercut and the American was down on the canvas again. By the end of round one, Masias had a cut above his nose and another on his right cheek.

Round two didn't go any better for the American. Ve's hammering blows to the head started a nosebleed and two minutes in a well-timed and executed series of rights, lefts and finished with an uppercut soon floored Masias for the full count.

The quick end to both fights left the fight fans disgruntled and called the fights 'a proper mismatch' as they left early. After the fight, Masias had nothing but praise for Ve.

"I am a strong puncher myself, but he was too fast and punched even harder," Masias said, adding that he did not expect Ve to be so fast. Masias said that Ve should fight abroad for better recognition.

Conlan agreed that Ve was a world-class fighter, and that Ramos should get him more fights with overseas boxers. Edson was also impressed with the Ramos boys.

"Let me make one thing clear – Ve has got the talent to beat Clyde Gray or a top-ranking world welterweight," he said (Rabuka, 1979).

"He has everything, but he needs to improve on a few basic skills of the game."

Of Tarika, Edson said: "I was very impressed with his punching speed, and I am sure given good coaching he should be punching harder and 100 times more than he did to Chavez."

While he was disappointed with the Americans' performances, Edson said there was nothing that they could have done against two good Fiji boxers.

"Take it from me, for Ve to knock out Masias is something that world-rated fighters like Pete Ranzany, the number five in the world, will talk about," he said.

With more overseas opponents, Ve should be able to beat Gray, Edson said.

With Tarika's convincing win over Chavez, Ramos would look at Australian Brian Roberts as his next opponent.

Having proven their dominance over the Americans, there was one other matter that required a better ending. Negotiations for a re-match against Hector Thompson was started with Shore Promotions on board to promote the fight in September. Ramos also wanted the Tarika-Roberts fight on the same card.

JULY – THE FIJI BOXING COUNCIL

Also jousting for a shot at Ve was lightweight Zamal Azad who had asked the PBWAF to strip Ve of his Fiji and South Seas lightweight titles as he hadn't defended them since winning them both in 1976 (Sport, 1979).

In response to Azad's letter, the PBWAF secretary wrote to Ve asking him to defend either of his lightweight titles soon.

Ramos said Ve was happy to defend the titles provided a promoter, willing to pay Ve a purse of $3,000, came on board.

"If he wants to have a crack at Ve and gets a promoter with the purse Ve is demanding, we will take him on anytime," Ramos said, although he had doubts that any promoter would be willing to stage such a title fight as they would be gambling on making any money at the end of it.

"Let me make it clear to Azad that should the fight come off, it could be the end of his boxing career."

Ramos proposed instead that Azad defend the South Seas featherweight title he won in 1977 against Tarika, the Fiji featherweight champion.

"We have offered him $700 to defend it against Tarika, but he keeps running away. Before taking Ve, Azad should fight Tarika first to prove himself," Ramos said.

The inroads made by Ramos and Ve with the two Commonwealth challenges must have had something to do with the invitation to PBWAF secretary Mumtaz Ali to attend the BCBB annual convention in London in August (Rabuka, 1979). Ali was delighted and honoured by the invitation, a first for Fiji.

"I certainly would like to attend the convention because it would be beneficial to Fiji boxing," he said.

At the end of the day the association was run by volunteers and as such did not have the funds to make the 16,248km journey on such short notice.

"In the event of me not going, I will prepare a paper on Fiji and the South Seas region boxing and have it read at the convention," Ali said.

"In the paper I will also mention the fact that we have some potential Commonwealth title contenders such as Wili Tarika in the featherweight class and heavyweight Sunia Cama. Of course, we also have Sakaraia Ve, who is already rated in the welterweight division."

Given the importance of the forum, Ali was happy to endorse anyone else who could attend at their own expense as a Fiji representative.

After that, the PBWAF and the Tongan Boxing Association (TBA) declared the South Seas heavyweight title vacant following Samoan boxer Fossie Schmidt's refusal to defend his title. The two associations announced Luke Veikoso and Sunia Cama as the challengers. The two associations had ordered Schmidt to defend the title within 30 days.

"Unfortunately, Schmidt was not prepared to accept these terms," PBWAF president Raj Gopal Menon said.

Also, Luke Sisiwa was on the verge of losing his South Seas light heavyweight title after his jail sentence for rape (Dean, 1979). The PBWAF and the TBA announced Tongan Leveni Tufui and Fijian Ananai Curubera as the likely contenders if the title was to be vacated.

This did not sit well with Ramos, whose fighter Jo Dawai lost the title to Sisiwa six months prior. Ramos described the decision as 'unfair' as Sisiwa was yet to give Dawai a re-match after the loss.

"I don't know why Ali hates my boxers, but his attitude certainly indicates that he holds some grudge against them," Ramos said of the decision.

"Dawai should be given the first crack at the title if it is declared vacant since Sisiwa failed to give him a return match. If this fight (Curubera-Tufui) is held with the title at stake, we will take the matter to court."

Dawai also felt the same way after confirmation that the PBWAF and the TBA had officially stripped Sisiwa of the South Seas light-heavyweight title (Sport, 1979).

"By right, I should be given the first chance to fight for the title as a former title holder. I am still the first contender for the title if it is vacant," Dawai said.

"Everything is against me just because I'm a member of John Marimuttu Ramos's club. If Ali is against Ramos, then let it be between them. It should not affect the boxers. What is happening now is that we boxers have to suffer for it."

Dawai said he should fight Tongan light-heavyweight champion Naelesoni Taufa for the vacant South Seas light-heavyweight title.

The PBWAF had already put together a programme for the two vacant South Seas titles featuring Cama and Veikoso for the heavyweight bout, and Curubera and Tufui at light-heavyweight. The programme was to also raise funds for Fiji soldiers in Lebanon.

Ali did approach Ve to be on the card, but negotiations broke down when a suitable purse could not be negotiated.

The breakdown in purse negotiations was considered a snub by the PBWAF and added to the discord between the association and Ramos Boxing Club with a letter writer to *The Fiji Sun* calling on Ve to fight for free.

This drew a biting response from Ve fan, Peter Edwards (1979).

"Sir – I refer to P. Ledua's letter of 20.7.79 and I would like Mr. Ledua to know that he should get his facts right before putting pen to paper. If Ledua was in Ve's shoes he would have reacted the same way. I think Mr. Ramos made a

very clear statement of how Mr. Ali's approach was made to Ve to fight for the Lebanon Fund.

Ve and Ramos Boxing club boys have done a lot for charity and just recently Mr. Ali tried to stop them from raising funds for a Catholic church in Taveuni. Is Ledua acting like one of Ali's puppets jumping to conclusion? Does Ledua know what the word "professional" means?

I would suggest to Ledua that he go to Laucala Bay Hangar and have a sparring session with Ve and any money raised should go to the Lebanon fund. How about it Ledua? Would you like to be punched around free of charge? If so go and see Mr. Ramos and I'm sure he would be too pleased to promote a fight for you (free of charge of course).

Mr. Ramos and Ve do not be offended with such comments, you both have done a lot for Fiji boxing, especially Ramos if it were not for your good and faithful guidance Fiji boxing would be nowhere. Maybe an 'MBE' honour would be next."

Ali said that the PBWAF, the TBA and the Western Samoa Boxing Association were in talks to form a South Seas Federation that would oversee the South Seas championship titles. Ali said that the TBA were taking a strong stand on the South Seas titles not being defended.

It would only be a matter of time before the PBWAF would turn the spotlight on Ve regarding the two South Seas titles that he held for the lightweight and junior-welterweight categories. Since winning those titles and the three Fiji titles for the lightweight, welterweight and middleweight divisions, Ve had at this point defended the Fiji welterweight title only twice – in April 1977 against Rupeni Vutevute and in April 1979 against Paula Namosi.

The best contender for the South Seas middleweight title at the time was ni-Vanuatu boxer Phil Kating, a 1975 South Pacific Games gold medallist. Kating was in good form after beating Mataitini in a fifth round TKO at Churchill Park Lautoka on July 14. (Daunabuna, 1979). Ve beat Mataitini for the South Seas middleweight title back in March 1978.

Kating's manager Luke Nasaroa wasn't as keen, wisely saying that he hoped to give his boxer two more fights before sending him up against Ve.

"I don't want to rush Kating to fight right now, but probably towards the end of the year after having two more bouts," he said, adding that he would look for worthy middleweights for Kating to fight before Ve.

Ve was happy to entertain Kating's wish to challenge him – but for the right price, according to Ramos (Sport, 1979).

"Ve had to fight for these titles, and he will only defend them if it is worthwhile," Ramos said.

As Kating joined the queue seeking a go at one of Ve's five titles, Ramos negotiated a deal for Ve to meet Thompson again in September (Rabuka, 1979). Ramos also was looking to bring Neil Patel if Thompson couldn't make it.

In the meantime, Ramos put in efforts to organise a Jo Dawai-Al Gattling programme in Pacific Harbour in a Las Vegas-like setting where tables were sold with food and drinks to fans as they watched boxing.

Ramos's outspokenness regarding decisions made by the PBWAF administrators saw him suspended for it twice before. With a third suspension likely, following his outburst regarding their decision not to award Dawai first dibs for the vacant South Seas heavyweight title, the relationship between Ramos and the administrators of the association deteriorated once again. As a result, Ve was stripped of all but the Fiji welterweight title. The reason given was that he hadn't defended them since winning them. According to Ramos, it was all political and designed to hurt him further for standing up for the rights of his boxers.

"I called Jay (Edson) in New York to seek his counsel on how I might be able to form a Fiji Boxing Council to be affiliated with the World Boxing Council of which Jay was a representative. Jay said, 'Give me two days and I will call you back,'" Ramos recalled.

"He made some enquiries, called me back and said, 'Go ahead. I'm sending you the rule book. All you need now is people who are knowledgeable to run the council.' I received the rule book a few weeks later and cobbled a constitution together to provide the governing framework and got the council established with Joe Tokaibai as the president, Timoci Naco as the secretary, Michael Low as treasurer and four other committee members."

The Fiji Boxing Council was formed in Suva on July 21, 1979.

"The first order of business was to restore the titles to Ve and other boxers who had suffered a similar fate. We also started to look for promoters to register with the FBC and in no time, promoters with PBWAF crossed the floor and asked to join the FBC which was not only affiliated to the WBC but also recognised by the Commonwealth Boxing Council secretary, Ray Clark OBE," Ramos continued.

The Commonwealth Boxing Council (CBC) was formerly the British Commonwealth Boxing Board (BCBB).

"The FBC wasted no time in getting fights going around the country. We had a full calendar of programmes and were excited by the breath of fresh air that was now running boxing. The PBWAF on the other hand had started to slow down," Ramos said.

The formation of the FBC sounded a death knell for the PBWAF leadership, stagnated perhaps by a select few who had ensconced themselves in key positions for far too long. The FBC aimed to be better than the PBWAF when it came to boxers' welfare. That was the foremost pillar in its establishment. The council would also endeavour to promote amateur boxing as a pathway to the professional ranks.

Interim council president Jo Tokaibai announced that joining the FBC were two national champions, Sakaraia Ve and Wili Tarika, and Jo Dawai, the former South Seas light heavyweight champion – all from Ramos Boxing Club (Rabuka, 1979). Tarika and Ve handed back their Fiji titles to the PBWAF, but Ve held on to his two South Seas belts.

The exodus from the PBWAF gained momentum when 11 members of the Liakat Boxing Club led by Silio Tiko, Peni Rauga and Iqbal Azad said that they would join the council. Following closely were promoters Raghunath Singh, Eric Emberson and Bala Subramani in addition to the Fiji Amateur Boxing Association (FABA).

"We will not register any promoter who will give us a bad name in future by failing to pay purses for boxers, whether overseas or at home," Tokaibai said.

Built into the FBC cards would be five amateur bouts for which FABA would get $100 from the council to help with its finances.

"We have decided that if the amateur body wants to raise funds for an overseas trip for its boxers, the council will ask one of its promoters to promote a fight," Tokaibai said.

Established at its first meeting was the fight purse which Tokaibai said would be higher than that offered on the PBWAF cards. The increase would be at a minimum increase of $7.50 with purses now set at: six rounds winner $40 ($30 PBWAF purse), loser $30 ($15) and draw $30 each ($22.50); eight rounds winner $60 ($40), loser $30 ($20) and draw $45 each ($30).

The referees also were on the list for increased compensation with 10 rounds getting $30 ($20 PBWAF), six rounds $15 ($5); title fights $40 plus expenses of $30.

"It's been long overdue to increase boxers and referees' fees," Tokaibai said adding that a drive was on to also boost financial membership of the council.

"We have 300 people all waiting to register as members and it's a healthy sign for the council," he said.

The council announced that its first fight programme would be at the Tropic Sands Resort in Deuba, Pacific Harbour in August between Jo Dawai and Australian southpaw Al Gattling, who was the New South Wales State light-heavyweight champion. With Ramos as the architect of the Vegas-style programme, the fight was to be promoted by Praneel Dass of Lautoka. The 10-round contest would be the first of its kind to be hosted at a resort venue and promised to be an experience for fight fans.

All boxers who were title holders and leaving the PBWAF to join the council were promised to be reinstated with an equivalent title by the council, according to Tokaibai (Rabuka, 1979).

"Once they return the titles to the PBWAF and join us, they will automatically become our national champion," he said, confirming that Ve and Tarika would be the council's first national champions at welterweight and lightweight for Ve, and featherweight for Tarika.

Where there were no champions in a particular weight category, Tokaibai said the top contenders would be invited to challenge for the title. The categories included the addition of the junior-lightweight, junior-welterweight and junior-middleweight divisions alongside the traditional weight categories for featherweight, lightweight, welterweight, middleweight, light-heavyweight and heavyweight.

The formation of the council was applauded by fight fans, with one letter writer to the *Fiji Sun*, penning this (1979):

"Sir – Allow me to hail the initiative of my friend Jo Tokaibai, and others with him, in forming the new Fiji Boxing Council. I see in it the salvation of Fiji Boxing. Such an institution has been long overdue. I am a great boxing fan. But I have been saddened and disillusioned by the sometimes overly ridiculous paternalistic attitude of the parent powers-that-be in Fiji boxing who sometimes give the impression that boxing is their personal property. Almost invariably one reads in the papers statements of the type which indicates this.

It must be clearly understood that institutions are created by the people for the people. It is the people who give an institution – any institution its dynamism, its credibility, its durability and its other '…ities'. Without the people, institutions are virtually worthless.

All too often, however. We tend to very quickly lose sight of this simple, yet important and undeniable fact. I therefore wish to thank my friend Jo Tokaibai and others in that group like my old boss Ratu Inoke Lesuma, my friends Jim Naco and Eric Emberson and the 'Great' John Marimuttu Ramos, for their courage and initiative in taking this step.

This is the revolt mobilisation that will revolutionise boxing in Fiji and rescue it from the abyss it is fast sinking into because of the egotistic manipulations of 'empire builders'. Keep it up, gentlemen, you are not short of supporters."

AUGUST – PHIL 'SPIDER' DAVIS, AL GATTLING

Ve's first fight under the FBC banner was to be against the new NSW light-middleweight champion, Phil 'Spider' Davies on August 25 in Suva (Sport, 1979).

Davis had just beaten the No.1 Australian middleweight contender Torkano Marcos (aka Apimeleki Rainima) in a fifth-round knockout in Sydney on July 31. Davies had also fought and denied former Ramos club member Peni Tabua the vacant NSW light-middleweight title when they met in March where Davies beat Tabua on points.

At six feet tall, Davies had a height and reach advantage over Ve.

A week out from the planned Dawai-Gatling meet, the FBC's application to the Fiji Police Force for a permit to host the event met with a minor obstacle as the police took some time to consider its permit request due to "certain legalities" but FBC president Tokaibai wasn't too concerned (Sport, 1979).

"It's just a normal thing to do. You have to apply to the police force to stage a fight because it becomes a public gathering," he said.

In the meantime, Ramos expressed confidence that Dawai would do well in the fight as he was fit and had prepared well. A win over Gattling was also an opportunity for Dawai to earn himself a Commonwealth ranking in the light-heavyweight category (Rabuka, 1979).

At the time, Gattling was top contender for Tony Mundine's Australian heavyweight title. Tony (snr.) is the father of Anthony Mundine jnr., the former WBA super-middleweight (2003-2008), IBO middleweight (2009-2010) and WBA interim super-welterweight (2011-2012) champion.

Mundine snr. was also the former Commonwealth light-heavyweight champion who at the time, was ranked tenth in the Commonwealth.

Dawai had fought international opponents previously in New Zealand, but Gattling was to be his most experienced opponent thus far. Their 10-round contest would see a portion of the gate takings go towards helping the Nailewa Catholic Church on Taveuni.

"If he can get through Gattling and beat him, the Fiji Boxing Council will write to the Commonwealth ratings committee in London to consider Dawai," Ramos said.

Police reviewed the paperwork and issued the permit a day before the fight after meeting Tokaibai and treasurer Michael Low (Sport, 1979).

Tokaibai had to clarify with police that the FBC was not a breakaway body, "but formed after boxers and their supporters wanted to form a separate body to give them a better deal".

The event took place at Tropic Sands Resort in Deuba, Pacific Harbour, a 45-minute drive outside the capital Suva on the way to Nadi. Pac Harbour as it is commonly referred to, was a newly developed estate with villa style homes and resort hotels that was set up to draw tourists into the region. The rare fine weather added to the atmosphere as hundreds gathered to share in this new boxing experience.

Dawai prevailed over Gattling, winning the 10-round contest unanimously on points (Rabuka, 1979). There were no knockdowns in the fight, but Dawai's fast lefts opened a small cut over Gattling's left eye at the end of the second round.

Realising that he needed a knockout to beat Dawai, Gattling came out in the tenth with everything he had. It worked for a short time as this forced Dawai to back-pedal midway through the round but not before Dawai landed some well-timed hits to the head. The win was Dawai's second under the Ramos banner.

"He is a very confident fighter now. He picks his punches, and he's dedicated to his training," Ramos said of Dawai.

The win prompted Ramos to cast his eye on Commonwealth light-heavyweight champion, Gary Summerhays as a future opponent for Dawai after a few more international fights.

The Deuba programme also saw Ramos club members Tevita Ravuravu and Isikeli Veitala win their first professional fights, against Jo Vucago and Panapasa Bune respectively. Both opponents were knocked out in the third round. Ramos middleweight Setareki Bolatawa also knocked out J. Tau in the second round.

After his loss to Dawai, Gattling warned Ve of Davies' non-stop attacking style and big hits, saying that the Australian also had a height advantage that could cause an upset when the two meet in Suva the following week (Rabuka, 1979).

Ramos was not perturbed by the warning, saying that they had a plan.

"This will be the big test for Ve. Ve like all boxers who walk in and if Davies is that sort of fighter then it should be a tough battle," Ramos said.

The Ve-Davies fight on August 24 at the Laucala Bay Hangar in Suva was a split point decision, with BoxRec recording it as a draw (BoxRec, n.d.).

A knockdown in the dying stages of the fight almost gave Ve the decision. A well-timed right cross at the end of the tenth round sent Davies to the canvas. Referee Kevin Conlan reached a count of nine when the bell rang to end the fight. Davies was literally saved by the bell and after the scores were counted, Conlan awarded the fight to Ve on the narrowest split points decision.

Throughout the fight, Davies used his reach and height advantage to keep away from Ve. The crowd were not impressed with this strategy, booing the Australian. Between the seventh and the ninth rounds, Ve managed to penetrate the lanky guard, in the process connecting some well-placed hits to the head and body until that wonderful right cross crashed Davies to the canvas.

The fight was scored 96-96 by referee Conlan and judges Paula Cokanasiga scored the fight 98-97 for Ve and Ilisoni Nate scored the fight 97-97 (Rabuka, 1979).

The decision was met with derision from PBWAF secretary Mumtaz Ali who said that according to international rules, it should have been declared a draw (Rabuka, 1979).

"The decision to award the fight to Ve on points was deplorable, shocking and beyond this world," Ali said. "Never have I seen such atrocity, which only indicates the lack of knowledge of the Fiji Boxing Council."

The bite back was inevitable, and Ali was correct. The fight was technically a majority draw decision as two judges had scored the fight a draw and one in favour of Ve (BoxRec, n.d.).

Ramos did not respond to Ali's criticism but offered instead a review of Ve's performance saying Ve took it too easy until the last round, adding that an opponent of Davies' calibre was also a good experience for his fighter.

Davies' manager Wal Bentley, who was also training Thompson for his comeback, told Ramos that he would return to Australia and ask Thompson if he was interested in a return bout in October.

Ramos boxers Setareki Bolatawa and Mataiasi also did well in the supporting bouts. Bolatawa took out the former Fiji middleweight champion Jone Mataitini with a second round TKO. Mataitini did not emerge for the third round. Mataiasi also drew with Simi Liston.

After the fight, Ve decided to take a three-week break before preparing for his next fight.

Meanwhile, Kating and his manager Nasaroa who took on Ve's challenge to find a promoter for the middleweight challenge, were not rewarded for their efforts (Rabuka, 1979).

Kating reported that promoters rated Ve's demand for $7,000 as 'unreasonable'.

"They told me they cannot risk putting up so much money because Ve is no longer a drawcard," Kating said after he and Nasaroa approached three promoters to consider taking on the fight.

"It seems to me at this stage that no one is willing to come out to promote the fight if Ve insists on his current purse," Nasaroa said.

Ramos was not reconsidering a revised purse.

"No money, no fight. That's the deal in professional boxing," Ramos said adding, "It could be promoters don't want to risk their money because Kating is challenging Ve. He only came out of the blue and has yet to prove himself."

Earlier, Kating had put forward a proposal for a winner-takes-all fight, a proposal instantly dismissed by Ramos after Kating declared, "I am certain now they are scared of losing the title" (Rabuka, 1979).

"We don't believe in any professional boxer getting nothing after a fight in the ring," Ramos said.

"Professional boxing is a sport, and most boxers earn their living from it. There is no point in having a fight, especially a title fight, with the condition of winner take all."

If the two found a promoter willing to pay Ve's purse of $7,000, Ramos said he'd happily sign the contract that very day.

"I think Ve has not fought any real middleweights in his previous fights. He is good for welterweights only," Kating said. A comment Ramos immediately disagreed with, saying that Ve had fought some of the best in the world.

Ramos added that the FBC would be writing to the boxing associations of New Caledonia, and Western and American Samoa to consider Ve as a contender for the South Seas middleweight title recently vacated by Basdeo when he retired.

Kating, dubbed the 'Tiger Shark', finally met Ve in April 1985 in a 10-round contest, losing on points. Kating ended his boxing career in 2001 because of a travel restriction after his parole for a manslaughter conviction in Vanuatu (Nasse, 2016).

Kating, aged in his early 60s, was killed in Vanuatu on January 17, 2016, (Makin, 2016).

SEPTEMBER – AGAINST APARTHEID

Chris Clarke's eleventh round TKO over fellow Canadian Clyde Gray in their Commonwealth title fight in Halifax on August 28, ended Ve's dream of a third shot against Gray. Adi Narayan, who had watched the fight, wrote to Ramos and told him that Clarke would most likely fight Ve for a purse less than paid to Gray for his last two fights in Fiji in 1978 (Sport, 1979).

The sum of US$10,000 was noted in the letter as a purse for Clarke. However, Narayan cautioned that Ve would need to first score some good wins over other Commonwealth title contenders before another approach could be made. Narayan described Clarke as a "very tough fighter" who won a Commonwealth title in only his eighteenth professional fight.

In the wings for Ve was a rematch with Thompson for the Australian's South Pacific title. The other option was former Australian welterweight champion Neil Patel.

Ve would never meet Clarke as Clarke lost the Commonwealth title to Gray in their rematch on November 13.

Thompson was asking A$6,000 while Patel was looking for A$4,500. Lautoka promoter Bala Subramani was on board for a Ve-Patel fight but was looking at Patel to reduce that amount to $4,000 flat before considering going ahead.

In a major coup for Fiji boxing and the FBC, renowned US boxing promoter Bob Arum made an approach through Edson for Ve to feature in a supporting bout for Arum's promotion of the Gerrie Coetzee versus John Tate fight for the vacant WBA heavyweight title to take place in South Africa on October 20. The title was vacated by Muhammad Ali following his retirement.

The offer was one that would afford Ve the international exposure that many past rivals and their management had called for and at the same time, give Ve the opportunity to hitch his star to Top Rank Promotions which was making huge inroads into televised boxing at the time.

The offer encountered diplomatic and political hurdles with the Fiji government's foreign policy on South Africa. South Africa at the time was governed by an oppressive apartheid regime.

When the offer was made known, it received mixed reactions from the Fiji public, with Ramos stepping in to reassure people that Ve would not in any way, "dirty Fiji's image" and would only fight in Africa if the Fiji government agreed (Madhavan, 1979).

"Ve says that the deal is all right and conditions are 100 per cent good. He will go if there are no objections," Ramos said.

Secretary of Foreign Affairs Joji Kotobalavu outlined the government's policy on South Africa: "In accordance with our constitution and the Government's policy to outlaw any discrimination, and also in light of the stand we have taken at the United Nations, the government has always tried to discourage contact with the evil practice of discrimination and apartheid in South Africa."

On the face of the offer, Ramos's clinical take on the issue was that the fight was being promoted by an American with African fighters scheduled on the programme.

"I don't know if boxing is segregated in South Africa, but I am sure Jay Edson would not advise me to do anything which was wrong," Ramos said.

"This is the biggest break in the world for Ve. He will be in the international scene, getting more money and more experience. We will put our case to the Minister of Sport and tried to explain that Ve would go as an individual in the outing, not as a Fiji representative," adding "I will support the government, that is for sure. We would not dirty Fiji's image."

The Fiji Association of Sports and National Olympic Committee (FASANOC) president Commander Stan Brown said: "This has to be a government decision. The government had not been happy about sports with South Africa in the past, for instance it rejected a request for a bowling team to play there. But it may be different with Ve because this will be a multi-racial contest. The government considers each particular case, and it will probably depend a lot on what sort of case Ve puts up.

"As for the sports people themselves, I think they will play anybody as long as it is a sporting occasion. They do not give much thought to the political aspects. I do not think Ve followers would stop supporting him if he did go."

In a formal correspondence to Ve, the government asked two questions: Who would Ve's opponent be? A representative of South Africa or a fighter outside of South Africa? And will the fight take place in front of a multi-cultural audience or a segregated one? (Rabuka, 1979).

At the time, with no emails but snail mail, international phone calling or costly telegrams being the main method of communication, Ramos decided that he would write to Edson, who negotiated the fight with Arum to provide the details.

With three weeks to go before the scheduled world title clash, Ve and Ramos ultimately decided that they would forego the opportunity.

The Coetzee-Tate fight in Pretoria was the first time since 1948 that a multi-racial audience was allowed to sit together to watch a white Afrikaner, Coetzee, go up against an African American, Tate (Sacks, 2012).

The fight before an audience of 81,000 mainly white South Africans, was televised internationally with Tate as odds-on favourite. Tate won the fight on a unanimous points decision (BoxRec, 2017).

With that issue squared away, Ve had a November fight to look forward to – a return bout against Hector Thompson following the Australian agreeing to a purse for A$4,500, down from the A$8,000 then A$6,000 that he had asked for earlier during negotiations (Rabuka, 1979).

Thompson also saw the fight against Ve as a stepping stone to putting forward a challenge for the Commonwealth welterweight title held by Dave Clarke at the time. As previous holder of the Commonwealth junior-welterweight title, Thompson was looking to add to that mantle in a different weight category. The return bout with Ve would also see Thompson put up the South Pacific welterweight title he won when he fought Ve in February.

OCTOBER – JOHNNY ABA AND THE COMMONWEALTH SUPER-FEATHERWEIGHT TITLE

Tarika left the Ramos Boxing Club after four years to pursue his own path to a Commonwealth title.

"As I had no signed contract with any of my fighters, Tarika left to pursue his ambitions for the Commonwealth super-featherweight title against Johnny Aba following an offer from another promoter," Ramos recalled.

"I was happy for him that he got a shot at the Commonwealth title because he was the product of my hard work before he fought Aba.

"Tarika was a good classic boxer with good footwork and hand speed. Although he lacked the killer punch, his wit and sensibilities are what helped him win fights. It wasn't an acrimonious parting of ways because my contract with my boxers were founded on a handshake and mutual respect. During our time together, Tarika became the Fiji featherweight champion and had the opportunity to build his professional fight record by taking on international fighters."

The October 20 fight against Aba was promoted by Andrew Miller and held at Albert Park in Suva. The usual boxing venue, the Laucala Bay Hangar, was out of commission after the South Pacific Games which were held in Suva from August 28 to September 9.

The Suva Cricket Association agreed to let Miller have Albert Park as venue on the condition that the cricket pitch was not damaged. Albert Park was normally used by Suva Rugby during the rugby season followed by Suva Cricket for the cricket season (Rabuka, 1979).

Miller offered no word on what Tarika would earn for the fight against Aba other than to say, "It will be the biggest purse ever". Tarika earned $600 in the fight against Chavez, his biggest to date. Miller also accommodated Tarika in a Suva hotel before the Aba fight.

Tarika's exit gave Ramos more time with his other boxers. In September, he wrote to the Commonwealth Boxing Championships Committee asking them to recognise Dawai in their rankings after his win against Gattling in Deuba.

The written response from the CBC secretary Ray Clarke was not what he expected (Rabuka, 1979).

Asking Ramos to make the contents of his letter public, Clarke said that the CBC did not recognise either of the Fiji boxing bodies (PBWAF and the FBC) to listen to their recommendations and would most likely make their own decisions on records.

Clarke had suggested Dawai fight Tony Mundine of Australia or Bunny Johnson of England first. Ramos said that he would seek to get Johnson for Dawai.

FBC president Jo Tokaibai said that he would send the CBC a copy of their constitution while it waited for its membership to the World Boxing Council to come through as the CBC was an affiliate of the WBC.

In the same letter, Clarke also referred to the Aba-Tarika fight in which he said that if Aba wanted to make a voluntary defence, then provided the opponent was a reasonable one, the match would appear reasonable.

However, Clarke said that at the committee's last meeting it had been decided that Aba must defend his title against Kazeem Armah of Nigeria or David Kotey of Ghana by October 31.

"Aba's manager will have to explain why he did not do so, otherwise he will probably lose his title. I suggest that you make this public in Fiji," Clarke said in his correspondence.

Miller in response to the notification, said: "As far as I know it is a title fight and it's 100 per cent on."

With Tarika's exit, a spot for a featherweight opened up at the club and former PBWAF Fiji featherweight champion Kaminieli Vunimasi joined Ramos (Sport, 1979). Ramos said that as a former Fiji champion, Vunimasi would automatically be eligible to fight for the FBC featherweight title should it be vacated by Tarika.

The excitement of another Commonwealth title fight in Fiji saw fans turn out in the hundreds to watch Aba spar at the United Club in Suva (Sport, 1979). Among the fans was PBWAF secretary Mumtaz Ali who was impressed with Aba's form.

"He certainly knows how and when to punch," Ali said after watching Aba spar against former SPG bantamweight gold medallist Pita Cama.

Tarika lost the 10-round contest on points. But the loss opened another door of opportunity for Tarika who signed a two-year contract with Aba's manager Bernie Hall and left with his family for Australia on October 24.

Tarika fought Aba twice, the second challenge for the Commonwealth title again in March 1980, which he also lost on points.

He lost his third attempt at a Commonwealth title, when beaten for the lightweight title by tough Australian Barry Michael when he was knocked out in the tenth round.

The initial November 10 date for the Ve-Thompson fight had to be put back to November 24 because several boxing programmes were scheduled too close together (Rabuka, 1979).

The shift in the date would also permit Ramos to travel with Dawai to Noumea for a fight promoted by Jack Rennie against former French amateur heavyweight champion Vincent Kafoa. The delay in this programme was due to a request from Rennie for an amateur heavyweight from Fiji to feature on the programme.

NOVEMBER – HECTOR THOMPSON AND THE SOUTH PACIFIC WELTERWEIGHT TITLE

Vincent Kafoa, originally from Wallis and Futuna but based in France, was trained by former French champion François Anéwy to become the New Caledonia amateur heavyweight champion in 1971, the amateur heavyweight champion of Oceania in 1973 and gold medallist at the SPG in Guam in 1975 (Dhie, 2013).

Having spent his amateur years fighting in New Zealand, Jo Dawai was confident that he would have little trouble with southpaw Kafoa having watched him beat Fiji's Salusalu Viavia to win the Oceania title in 1973 (Rabuka, 1979).

"He is a slugger and a southpaw. He was then representing Wallis and Futuna," Dawai said.

The extra two weeks given by the fight delay he said, gave him the extra time he needed to improve his fitness, adding he had the ability to outsmart a slugger having fought many southpaws in Fiji.

At the time Dawai said that he wouldn't fight for the FBC light heavyweight title as it would be too easy to beat contenders. Instead, he would focus on the South Seas heavyweight title held by Fossie Schmidt. Dawai was also interested in a shot at the Commonwealth heavyweight title and was willing to meet Bunny Johnson of England or Garry Summerhays of Canada first.

The Noumea outing was a disappointment for Dawai and Ramos as Kafoa knocked Dawai to the canvas in three rounds (Rabuka, 1979). This was the first international fight for a Ramos fighter held outside of Fiji.

Ramos's take on the fight was that Dawai could easily beat Kafoa when they met next in a return bout planned for December 22. Although he lost so spectacularly, Dawai was not disappointed in his performance. He said Kafoa was a true slugger and a left he caught in the first round did the damage.

"It took Dawai by surprise on the chin and I was surprised that he got up to become the first fighter to put Kafoa on the canvas," Ramos said adding that it was just fortunate that Kafoa was saved by the bell.

Kafoa died in a car accident on February 28, 1981, at the age of 30. In New Caledonia his name is on the Vincent Kafoa Municipal Boxing Hall in Dumbéa.

Upon his return from Noumea, Ramos had to get Ve ready for his fight against Thompson at the Ba Sports Stadium (now called Govind Park) in Ba.

Speaking to *The Fiji Times* from Newcastle in Australia, Thompson said that he liked Fiji so much, he was considering a fight against Chris Clarke in Fiji, but first he would have to beat Ve (Rabuka, 1979). Thompson admitted in the same interview that he had underestimated Ve's boxing ability when they met back in February.

"Now that I know what Ve is up to and what I expect from him this time, I have trained myself to be 100 per cent fit. Honestly, I have gone through a tough schedule just as I used to do in most of my world-class fights," Thompson said adding, he expected a repeat of the same result as in February.

Ve maintained a low profile this time around, concentrating on building his stamina, working the punching bag and speedball.

The FBC also announced that Ramos club member Setareki Bolatawa who was now the FBC middleweight champion, would go up against Mark

Junior (Apakuki Saukuru) for the vacant FBC light heavyweight title on December 8.

The 19-year-old Bolatawa was confident that he would be a dual title holder by the end of his sixth professional fight. Three weeks earlier, Bolatawa had watched Junior demolish Joe Fabiano in one round in Albert Park, on the Tarika-Aba card.

Ramos said that after Junior, he would try to secure Australian middleweight champion Wally Carr for Bolatawa who was receiving $500 for the title fight against Junior.

On November 13, Gray met Clarke in a return bout, three months after losing his Commonwealth crown to the Nova Scotia native in an eleventh round TKO. In the second encounter, Clarke relinquished the title in a tenth round TKO after Gray dropped him three times in that round. Gray fought four rounds with a cut over his right eye (BoxRec, 2016) to become the Commonwealth welterweight champion again.

Thompson arrived in Fiji with his wife Lynette a week before the November 24 fight. Trainer Wal Bentley followed a few days later after supervising two of his other fighters on the Johnny Aba-Eusebio Pedroza fight for the WBA world featherweight title undercard in Port Moresby, Papua New Guinea on November 17.

Thompson had this to say about his preparations: "I have had the heaviest training of my whole boxing career. I have done 20 rounds of sparring apart from heavy road running. I time my running, and I have done tremendous preparation and am a lot fitter this time (Daunabuna, 1979).

"I have to win this one," he said of his plans to take on Clarke. "I love the country, and I really want to fight for the title here."

Thompson wasn't going to be a walkover by any measure, so Ve took five days off work from the bank to prepare for the fight (Rabuka, 1979).

"This will give him the last five days to work out his fight plans and get a good rest after daily training," Ramos said.

"Ve has learnt a lot from the defeats against Gray and Thompson, and if Ve wants that third shot at the Commonwealth title, he has to win this fight or that chance slips away for good."

Promoter Bala Subramani, having watched Thompson at training at the Sugar City Hotel, said Ve would have to stay back and box if he wanted to beat the former Commonwealth champion.

"Thompson is in great form – even fitter than the last time they fought. Ve must not try and mix it, especially at close quarters, because Thompson is fast with both hands and even better at close range," he said.

Confident that he had the fight in hand, Thompson predicted a knockout win over the 'Ve-Bomb' (Rabuka & Duanabuna, 1979).

"I have never seen him in better form," said Thompson's wife Lynette.

Ramos said the last time the two met, Ve wasn't prepared for Thompson's hard body punches.

"This time Thompson could find himself hitting a body that feels like a rock," adding that Ve's preparations included a seven-mile run, sparring 10 rounds with Setareki Bolatawa, Isikeli Veitala and Tevita Ravuravu as well as an hour-and-a-half of swimming daily.

Ramos had supported Ve's decision to quit in the seventh round in their last encounter.

"He is not a coward as some people said after the fight. Ve will be at his peak on Saturday and will give everything to win."

Ba-based boxing trainer Liakat Ali also had his money on Thompson to beat Ve (Sport, 1979).

"I have never seen anyone so fit and relaxed. I am sure he will knock Ve out on Saturday. There is no way that Ve can beat him," Ali said after observing Thompson breathe normally after 15 vigorous rounds of training.

"That proved he is fit, and I cannot see how Ve can beat him."

Should Ve lose to Thompson, Ali was keen to have Ve defend his FBC welterweight title against his fighter Peni Rauga (Sport, 1979). Rauga was scheduled to meet Bolatawa in one of the supporting bouts of the Ve-Thompson fight.

Ramos said Ali knew only one side of the story.

"He has not seen Ve preparing for the fight and doesn't have a single clue of how the challenger will shape up on Saturday" (Sport, 1979).

"Watch for Ve's left jabs and his counterpunches. Ve has had three warm-up fights while Thompson's last fight was when they met here in February."

The Ve-Thompson fight was to be refereed by Kevin Conlan, A Fiji-based Australian diplomat who also happened to be the former Malaysian amateur heavyweight champion (1969-1972). Conlan was also the chair of the FBC's committee of referees (Rabuka, 1979).

The weigh-in on the eve of the fight was not without drama as Thompson demanded an extra $500 for being kept waiting 105 minutes for Ve to show up (Daunabuna, 1979). The arrival mix-up was put down to Ve being told the weigh-in was at 3pm, and Thompson, 1.30pm. Thompson arrived before 1.30pm and Ve at 2.55pm.

"It happens all over the world that boxers demand money if they are held up at official weigh-ins because of the late arrival of an opponent," said Thompson's manager Wal Bentley, adding that he would be lodging his demand when he met officials to discuss the rules to be applied during the fight.

Accompanying Ve to the weigh-in was Father Brian Wilson, who was also in Ve's corner for both his Commonwealth title fights. Fr Wilson told Bentley that his demand was best addressed with promoter Rajendra Bali. Ramos was not at the weigh-in as he had work commitments in Suva.

"That is your deal with the promoter because we were told to be here at 3pm," Fr Wilson said. When approached, promoter Bali did not want to comment on the incident. Ve weighed in at 142lbs (64.4kg), two pounds (0.9kg) heavier than Thompson.

The importance of this fight for Ve could not be underscored.

"It's now or never. We either do it tomorrow or we miss out altogether," said Ramos when asked of Ve's chances against Thompson for the South Pacific welterweight title (Rabuka, 1979).

Ramos had taken Ve from a talented amateur to be the highest paid professional boxer in Fiji at the time. The number of overseas opponents travelling to Fiji to fight the 'Golden Boy' has never since been matched. The two losses to Gray the year before followed closely by that to Thompson in February, and a questionable decision against Davies in August, had taken some of the lustre off Ve's brilliant record thus far.

Keeping his fight plan close to his chest, Ve was determined to provide a performance to restate his dominance and put paid to criticism that he was on a downward spiral.

On fight day, the stands at Ba Sports Stadium strained under the weight of fans who packed it to the rafters. The brilliant Western weather was perfect for the outdoor event.

For the first five rounds, Ve worked on Thompson's head and body. Thompson tried to get in close, but Ve worked the ring to deny him the opportunity. Thompson landed a few solid shots to Ve's body and head.

In round six, Ve responded to Thompson's hooks and jabs with a series of jabs to the head, followed by a left hook and a lightening-like combination that saw Thompson reel backwards on to the ropes with blood streaming from his mouth (Daunabuna, 1979). Sensing Thompson was in trouble, Ve leaned in and continued to work the veteran's body and head, ending the round with a caution from the referee for a foul blow. In the ninth, the crowd were on their feet as Ve rained straight shots to Thompson's head and hooks to the body.

The two champions went toe to toe until the eleventh round when a left from Ve followed by a one-two combination opened a deep cut over Thompson's right eye. Referee Conlan stopped the fight and called in the ring doctor to inspect the injury which had released a bright red rivulet down the right side of Thompson's face. It was clear to everyone present that the fight was over, and the doctor thought so too advising Conlan to stop the fight thereby awarding Ve a TKO win and the South Pacific welterweight title (Times, 1979).

"I did not want to end the fight short. I wanted to take my revenge over the distance. I would have liked to go the full fifteen rounds," Ve said after the fight.

Thompson was critical of the standard of the canvas in the ring, which he claimed offered no grip.

"I was disgusted with that ring. It was the worst ring I have fought in. I could have ended the fight in eighth round if it was a good ring," he said.

Bentley wanted a return bout with Ve saying, "It was impossible to continue with a cut like that. You can see how deep it was."

The win made Ve, holder of five titles – the South Pacific welterweight, the South Seas lightweight, South Seas junior-welterweight, FBC lightweight, and FBC welterweight championships. He has previously returned the PBWAF titles for the lightweight, welterweight and middleweight categories. Ve did not get the FBC middleweight title as part of the replacement. This title was now held by Ramos fighter, Setareki Bolatawa.

Ramos was happy that Ve fought the right style to defeat Thompson.

After the fight, Ve and Ramos were offered an $8,000 purse from Lautoka promoter Bala Subramani for Ve to fight Gray a third time. As champion, Gray would get US$15,000 tax free plus air tickets for four if he agreed (Rabuka, 1979).

The purse would be the highest so far for Ve, after four years of professional boxing, an offer that Ramos described the offer as "very attractive".

Even though Thompson and his camp had approached Ramos for a third fight, Ramos had his sights set on Gray. Again, Ramos looked to Toronto-based Adi Narayan to negotiate a third Commonwealth title fight for Ve.

"Ve proved just how good he was on Saturday. He is not a coward as some thought in the first place, but a very clever boxer who knows when to stop," Ramos said.

Joining the bid for a chance to promote Ve and a third Commonwealth championship was Ba promoter Dr Rajendra Kumar Bali, who had staged the Ve-Thompson return fight (Rabuka, 1979).

"There is no two ways about it. If I hope to take up the fight, my offer will have to be more than $8,000," Bali said.

As for the $500 inconvenience penalty demanded by Thompson following the official weigh-in mix-up, Bali said that the mix-up happened because of a misunderstanding between the two camps and as Bentley was Thompson's second and not his manager, he wasn't in a position to demand the compensation.

Ramos said that the negotiation door was still open to any FBC promoter who wanted to promote Ve's third fight against Gray. Bali expressed his disappointment that Ramos and Ve did not honour their word for him to stage the fight. Ramos responded that he and Ve were not bound legally to Dr Bali.

While on promoters, the FBC took a hard line against Nausori promoter Nur Mohammed for his continued association with the PBWAF. The long-time promoter was handed a suspension by the FBC as they awaited an explanation (Rabuka, 1979).

Mohammed, who had resigned from the PBWAF after 23 years to join the FBC, had allowed his PBWAF licence to be used to promote a PBWAF women's wrestling match scheduled for December 1. The programme was to feature female wrestlers from the United States.

Mohammed's suspension was pending a hearing before the FBC committee as the FBC preferred its promoters to totally disassociate themselves from the PBWAF.

Mohammed told *The Fiji Times* that his licence with the PBWAF had not expired and as the FBC did not have wrestling as part of its programmes, he had agreed for a Canadian promoter to use it to promote international wrestling matches.

The differences between the PBWAF and the FBC created uncertainty among boxing fans and members of the public in terms of knowing who was 'running the shop'.

The government at the time and its Minister for Youth and Sports Vivekanand Sharma appointed a committee headed by Fiji rugby stalwart and lawyer, Barry Sweetman to investigate the situation between the two (Sport, 1979).

The growing concern stemmed from both bodies running concurrent programmes on the same day in neighbouring towns and according to the minister, a committee headed by Sweetman would "look into these problems and suggest ways of solving them".

As the politicians sought a resolution to the competing professional bodies, Ramos was on to his next programme, this time for Bolatawa. In his sights was Australian middleweight champion Wally Carr for a possible South Seas middleweight title clash.

Bolatawa had also offered to put his FBC middleweight title on the line against former club member Mataiasi Tagicakibau after the latter left the club disappointed at not having had the opportunity to headline a programme or fight for a title after 18 months with the Ramos Boxing Club (Rabuka, 1979).

"This is his only chance to fight for a title. I have the promoter lined up for him. If he thinks he is good enough to become a champion, then he should take the offer to prove himself," Bolatawa said, adding that he knew Tagicakibau well and found that he was not sincere in his training.

Ramos said that the club was open to anyone looking to make it in boxing, the only condition being that the person had to exercise discipline.

"A boxer who enters the ring must be mentally and physically fit," he said. "It is the club's policy that anyone not a 100 per cent fit should not be allowed to fight."

DECEMBER – SETAREKI BOLATAWA AND THE FIJI MIDDLEWEIGHT TITLE

At just 19 years of age, Setareki Bolatawa was the FBC middleweight champion. In a week, he would be up against Mark Junior for the vacant FBC light-heavyweight title fight on December 8 at Govind Park in Ba (Rabuka, 1979).

Bolatawa won his middleweight title with a second-round KO of Viliame Naibono of Labasa in October. Junior, an eight-year veteran who had his professional boxing start in Hawaii, formed an impression on the local scene when he stopped heavyweight Joe Fabiano in the first round on October 20.

Bolatawa was calm before his big fight. "I'm not underestimating Mark Junior. I know he has had some experience fighting in Hawaii," he said.

Ramos was confident that Bolatawa, a regular sparring partner for Ve, was in peak condition to meet Junior.

Junior was keeping his fight plans close to his chest, not giving anything away going into the fight (Sport, 1979). The fight against Bolatawa was Junior's first in a 15-round contest.

"I am not the kind that boasts about his chances before the fight and I have made up my mind on the round in which to end the fight," he said.

"This is something new to me, but it will certainly be a good fight."

The fight fans who filled the stadium were not disappointed with the fight. However, the result was hard for Bolatawa and his manager to come to terms with.

Referee Paula Cokanasiga stopped the fight in the eighth round after Bolatawa copped a series of heavy blows to the body and head, awarding

Junior a TKO win and the FBC light-heavyweight championship (Daunabuna, 1979).

Ramos criticised the decision saying the stoppage was premature and the referee should have given Bolatawa a compulsory count before that. Bolatawa had earlier in the round taken two knockdowns and an eight count. The end came when Junior trapped Bolatawa in a corner and rained a series of blows to the head and body that had Bolatawa in a tucked position.

Cokanasiga told *The Fiji Times* he made the decision when he saw that Bolatawa could not defend himself from further punishment. After the fight, Bolatawa who appeared unmarked and unhurt from the encounter, staged a series of exercises behind the stands to prove that he was fine. The same could not be said of Junior who had cuts above his left eye and left cheek by the end of the third round. Despite the disappointing decision, fight fans gave Bolatawa respect for his clinical boxing.

Ramos said that the loss would not deviate him from plans for Bolatawa to fight international boxers such as Wally Carr. Bolatawa offered to meet Junior in a return bout. (Sport, 1979).

Bolatawa's stablemate, former South Seas light-heavyweight champion Jo Dawai, also issued a challenge to Vanuatu's Phil Kating after Kating's win over Anani Curebera for the South Seas light-heavyweight title on December 1 (Sport, 1979).

Kating's manager Luke Nasaroa welcomed the challenge, saying" "We will take him on anytime, anywhere."

However, Nasaroa had conditions for any fight against Dawai.

"If we are to fight for the title, it must be under the Professional Boxing and Wrestling Association of Fiji and not the Fiji Boxing Council," Nasaroa said.

"Secondly, it must be first approved by the PBWAF before we can negotiate."

Nasaroa said they were grateful to the PBWAF for the opportunity to fight for the South Seas middleweight title after they were fed up waiting for Ve to fight Kating.

Ramos felt that as a former titleholder, Dawai should be considered a contender. Dawai lost the title to Luke Sisiwa in November 1978. The title was declared vacant after Sisiwa was sentenced to a five-year jail term for rape.

Also chasing Kating was the new FBC light-heavyweight champion, Mark Junior.

Since beating Thompson in November, Ve took some time off as he waited for his next fight to be organised. At the top of Ramos's list was Neil Patel, the former Australian welterweight champion. Patel was the only top Australian welterweight at the time that Ve hadn't fought (Rabuka, 1979). Patel was coming out of a twelfth-round knockout loss to Steve Dennis in March. Ve defeated Dennis in January 1978 with a tenth round knockout.

Another contender being looked at was Australian super-lightweight, Lawrence "Baby Cassius" Austin if the Patel negotiations fell through (Rabuka, 1979). Patel's manager Frank Marwick told Ramos that Patel wanted $3,000 to fight Ve in Fiji, but Ramos told Marwick that the best offer promoter Bala Subramani could make was $1,500 plus air tickets and accommodation for two.

"If the deal should fail then we will seek Baby Cassius to give Ve a warm-up fight before taking on Clyde Gray for the third time for the Commonwealth title," Ramos said at the time.

Cassius was the logical choice because he had just outpointed Dennis earlier in the month to win the Australian welterweight title.

In a turn of events, the much-anticipated return fight between Jo Dawai and New Caledonia-based Vincent Kafoa scheduled for December 29 was cancelled. No date was rescheduled. This followed an eye injury sustained by Kafoa when he met Australian Marc Ecimovic in Noumea on December 15. Kafoa outpointed the Australian over 10 rounds to win the fight.

On the same Noumea card, New Caledonian middleweight Robert Nebayes outpointed Australian Billy Johnstone over six rounds but sustained an injury that ruled him out for four weeks. Nebayes was supposed to meet Bolatawa in the support bout to the Dawai-Kafoa fight.

As an alternative, Ramos said he would look to a Dawai-Mark Junior fight for Junior's FBC light-heavyweight title.

Junior had other plans. On December 19, he announced that he would fight Joe Fabiano in the PBWAF sanctioned East-West boxing tournament on December 22 in Lautoka despite being an FBC titleholder (Rabuka & Masi, 1979).

"I will fight even if the Fiji Boxing Council goes ahead with its threat to strip me of my title," he said. *The Fiji Times* reported that Junior changed his mind about the fight after being contacted by promoter Andrew Miller's lawyer who said he would face legal action if he went ahead.

"There are many titles in the country that I could fight for with good purses, but I would not like to put myself down by having to go to court," Junior said.

"I am glad that Mark has changed his mind because the programme is one of the most interesting fights ever to be staged with all top boxers in the country fighting," Miller said, adding that he had Aisea Ravula as a backup if Junior didn't accept the offer to fight Fabiano.

Fabiano called on the two boxing bodies to amend their constitutions to allow boxers in Fiji to fight against anyone without being sanctioned.

The East-West tournament on December 22 at Churchill Park in Lautoka featured former Ramos Boxing Club stalwart Wili Tarika in his first fight since leaving Fiji for Sydney in October. Tarika went up against the PBWAF lightweight champion Jale Fotu in a six-round contest. Fotu beat Zamal Azad for the title vacated when Ve moved across to the FBC (Thomson, 1979).

Fotu beat Tarika on points in the biggest upset of the tournament. The win prompted a call by Fotu's camp for Tarika to defend his FBC featherweight title against Fotu.

Meanwhile, negotiations for a Ve-Patel fight centred on the weight class for the bout. Ramos wanted Ve to fight at welterweight (10st, 7lbs, 66.7kg) and not as a junior middleweight at 11st (69.9kg) (Sport, 1979).

"This is because Ve will find it hard to get down to 10st 7lbs when he challenges Clyde Gray for his Commonwealth title," he said.

Promoter Bala Subramani had agreed to Patel's purse of A$2,000 plus accommodation and return tickets for two for a week in Fiji. Patel, of Australian-Aboriginal and Gujarati descent, was the first person of Gujarati heritage to win an Australian boxing title. He was also rated No.3 for the Commonwealth junior-middleweight title.

Ramos's friendship with Edson also led to another possible opportunity for Ve to fight under Bob Arum in another card he had planned for South Africa (Sport, 1979). In a letter to Ramos, Edson wrote: "Arum has told me to keep in contact because he is certain to be promoting one fight in South Africa in mid-1980 and he has promised to give Ve a fight in the programme."

Edson's earlier efforts to get Ve across to fight in South Africa in October were stopped by the Fiji government's foreign policy over apartheid in South Africa.

To conclude a great year for the club, Ramos held a prizegiving ceremony for his boxers where Ve received the Fighter of the Year award, a shield donated by Rewa Dairy. Bolatawa received the Most Promising Fighter of the Year award with a special mention to Jo Dawai for stepping in as trainer when Ramos wasn't available.

In four short years, the Ramos Boxing Club had earned itself a reputable place on the local boxing scene. In a feature article in *The Fiji Times* on the club's journey to this point, Ramos said that he knew what he was letting himself in for when he started the club on February 18, 1975, (Rabuka, 1979).

"My ambition had always been to provide the best training facility with the help of leaders in the various organisations," Ramos told the *Times*.

"From our beginnings at the Sangam Hall in Belo Street to the gym at the Nasinu Teachers College, then the Laucala Bay Hangar and now the Sport Council's Tip Top Shed, was a truly humbling journey and I will always be grateful to those in places of influence who helped us get to this place.

"Their friendship, kindness and love for boxing is what contributed to our success and allowed the members of my club to have a great place to train and become champions."

Spending time away from his family to train his boxers, negotiating for their fights or accompanying them to their fights was part of the job for anyone who wanted to take on the role of a boxing trainer or manager, Ramos said.

"The most important thing is that whoever wants to take the job must have the interests of his boxers and the sport at heart," he said.

On rumours that he received a cut of his fighters' purse, Ramos was unequivocal in his response: "I want to make one thing clear to those who have said this – I don't have any binding contract with my boxers which forces them to give me a certain percentage of their purses. I hate taking money out of boxers because I have been a professional boxer myself and I know how painful it is to be in the ring."

The only thing that Ramos asked of his boxers was that they contribute towards the upkeep of the club and if possible, help the club's amateur boxers, many of whom were unemployed.

Ramos recalled McQuillan's influence during his time in Sydney with the Australian boxing legend.

Having fought as an amateur from 1962-65 and as a professional from 1965-74, moving from the featherweight to lightweight divisions, Ramos was now trainer and manager of two fighters who held six titles between them.

Ve held five – FBC lightweight and welterweight, South Seas lightweight and junior-welterweight, and the South Pacific welterweight titles. Bolatawa held the FBC middleweight title.

Ramos said his priority was the welfare of boxers when they quit boxing, adding "I want to see that there is something for them when they retire from boxing."

Throughout the work week, Ramos admitted that he didn't have the time to spend with his three daughters and wife, Margaret, who also worked full-time at National Mutual Life Assurance in Suva. Margaret, he said, had to find her own way after work to their home in Nadera because he used the car to go training.

"I owe a lot to Margaret. She is right behind me in looking after the boxers by cooking their meals before fights," Ramos said.

With a full-time job at Carpenters Group as a costing supervisor, Ramos said it hadn't always been easy to try to juggle family with the club.

Looking ahead to the new year, Ramos laid out his plans for more international fights outside of Fiji for Ve, notably in the United States (Rabuka, 1978).

With Edson's patronage and his association with Bob Arum, Ramos was optimistic that Ve's debut on the international boxing stage would give him the added exposure needed to cement his path to world ranking.

On the cards was Pete Ranzany, the former North American Boxing Federation (NABF) welterweight champion, who beat Sammy Massias in four rounds in February. Ve took Massias out in the second round a few months later in June.

Suggested by Edson as Ve's next opponent, Ranzany, now ranked sixth for the WBC welterweight title, had fought Mexican Pipino Cuevas for his WBA welterweight title in September 1978 losing by TKO in the second round.

Cuevas also defended his WBA title against Gray in August 1977, knocking out Gray in the second round. Ranzany defended his NABF welterweight title against Gray in June, winning with a fifth-round TKO.

After Ve's win against Thompson, Edson was working on getting the Fijian a world ranking with the WBC. A win against Ranzany would lend weight to a higher ranking with the world body.

Meanwhile, finalisation of the Ve-Patel fight with promoter Bala Subramani resulted with February 2, 1980, confirmed for the much-anticipated bout in Govind Park in Ba instead of Suva.

Sakaraia Ve with the South Seas
Lightweight (1976), Fiji
Lightweight (1976), Fiji
Welterweight (1977), South
Seas Junior Welterweight
(1977), South Seas
Middleweight (1978) and the
South Pacific Welterweight
(1979) titles (John Ramos
Collection, circa 1979).

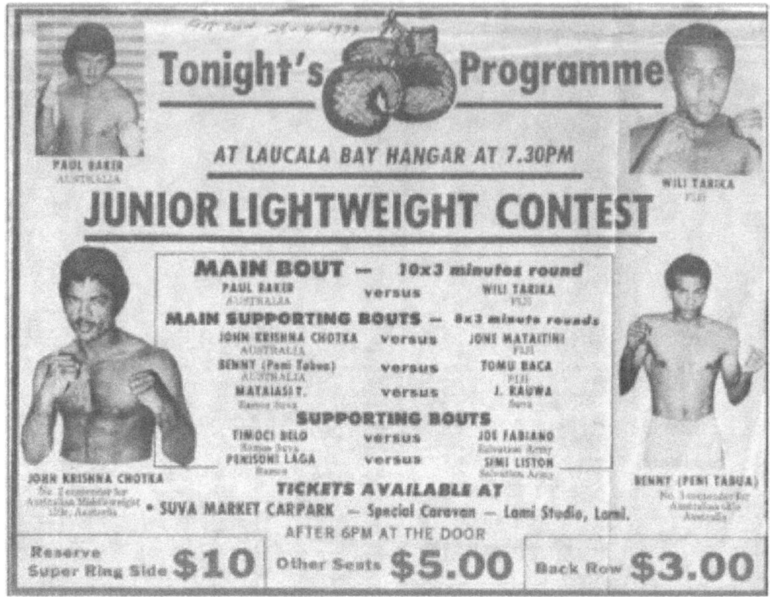

Program for the Tarika-Baker fight (Fiji Sun, April 28, 1979).

Setareki Bolatawa (John
Ramos Collection, circa
1979).

Referee Mumtaz Ali (R) raises Hector
Thompson's hand with the support of
Sakaria Ve after Thompson won the
South Pacific Welterweight
Championship title (Fiji Times, February
20, 1979).

John Ramos with his boxers and fans at their end of year Christmas party (Fiji Times, circa December 1979).

Chapter 9
1980 – End of an era

With plans for the new decade laid out, there was a lot to look forward to with the new crop of fighters Ramos had in his club.

Nearing its fifth anniversary, the fighters in the club was geared up.

JANUARY – NEGOTIATING A THIRD COMMONWEALTH TITLE FIGHT

The year started with Ramos receiving a telegram from Patel's manager Frank Marwick. It wasn't good news. The sparsely worded telegram relayed that Patel injured himself, stopping short of detailing how and when the injury happened. The February 2 fight was off (Rabuka, 1980).

"Neil Patel is scared of Ve," is how Ramos saw the cancellation, particularly as it was Patel who challenged Ve.

"The only thing I can say at this stage is that he must have read Ve's fight record back home," Ramos said.

Ramos reckoned that Patel would have been stunned by Ve's four-round demolition of Mark Barnett in October 1978. Four months later, Patel fought Barnett over 10 rounds to win the Australian welterweight title on a split points decision.

With Patel out of contention, Ramos made a quick call to Lawrence "Baby Cassius" Austin's camp to see if the Australian welterweight champion was available. Cassius had just won the title on points from Steve Dennis on December 13 the previous year (BoxRec, 1979). Dennis had taken the title off Patel earlier in March 1979 (BoxRec, 1979).

Austin also won the Commonwealth junior-welterweight, beating Hector Thompson in September 1977 (BoxRec, 1977). Ve had beaten Dennis in a tenth round knockout in January 1978 and Thompson in an eighth round TKO in November 1979 after a devastating loss to him earlier in February.

Austin had previously agreed to fight Ve if the negotiations with Patel fell through. Ramos hoped the offer still stood as Austin was a logical and reputable replacement given his fight record.

On the quiet, and not made public at the time, was another approach to Ramos by promoter Bruce Trampler of Top Rank Promotions for Ve to fight in their promotion in South Africa later in the year. The offer was for a purse of US$25,000 and three air tickets plus accommodation to fight an opponent, possibly American super lightweight Saoul Mamby on the undercard of the Gerrie Coetzee-Mike Weaver WBA world heavyweight title fight. Ve was recommended to Trampler by Edson.

Again, Ramos tried through the usual diplomatic channels to obtain government approval to travel with Ve to South Africa unfortunately, the policy on apartheid had not changed since the last request was denied.

"It was disappointing as this would have been Ve's first international fight outside of Fiji under my management. But we respected the position and decision of government at the time, so I politely declined the lucrative offer," Ramos said.

In the meantime, the FBC were preparing to host a card with three of their titles up for grabs. Scheduled for January 19 at Churchill Park in Lautoka was a contest for the bantamweight, featherweight and junior-welterweight titles (Sports, 1980). Tarika's departure to fight and live permanently in Australia, saw the FBC featherweight title vacated.

The Lautoka programme would see Tadu Chand of Sigatoka go up against Ramesh Krishna of Lautoka for the bantamweight title, Luke Sauqaqa of Lautoka up against Ilaitia Vaka of Navosa for the featherweight crown and Akuila (Krishna) Naidu of Lautoka against Ramesh Chand of Sigatoka for the junior-welterweight belt.

Chand had unsuccessfully fought Ve on three occasions for Ve's PBWAF lightweight title. In a supporting bout to the January 19 programme was South Seas featherweight champion Zamal Azad going up against Adi Narayan Reddy.

In another coup for the FBC, southpaw light-heavyweight Aisea Ravula moved across from the PBWAF after beating Joe Fabiano in December the previous year.

As the fight negotiations with Austin took shape behind the scenes, Ramos heard from Chris Dundee, Angelo's older brother. The younger Dundee was keen to match Ve with his fighter Elisha Obed (Rabuka, 1980).

Obed, a native of the Bahamas and former WBC super-welterweight champion, had an impressive 79-10-4 record during his 12-year career. The proposed Obed bout boosted plans for Ve to have more fights abroad, mainly in the United States, where the sport had a huge following and purses were better because of television broadcast rights.

Obed lost his world title to Australian Rocky Mattioli in a seventh-round knockout in Melbourne in March 1978. Now fighting at 10st 10lbs (68kg), Obed was headed into the twilight of his professional career, but his vast experience could not be underestimated.

Agreeing verbally to the offer from Dundee, Ramos needed to consult Ve about the timing of the fight, as another Gray clash was still on the cards.

"Ve certainly needs to meet a fighter of Obed's calibre, but we will not rush him too quickly," Ramos said, indicating that he would be talking to Edson about the offer.

The plans for a Ve-Austin meet moved into top gear with promoter Bala Subramani deputising Sydney-based former Ramos stablemate Peni Tabua to help facilitate the negotiations. Tabua noted that since winning the Australian title, Austin had changed management and moved from Perth to Melbourne. Tabua also felt that since Patel's withdrawal, Austin would be a better opponent for Ve than Patel because of his approach to fighting.

"He is fast with either hand and good footwork, and as tall as Gray," Tabua said. On the table was the same offer to Patel, a purse of A$2,000 and return tickets for two plus accommodations.

Two days after contacting Edson about Ve meeting Obed, Ramos revealed that Edson agreed that it would be in Ve's best interest to fight someone of Obed's calibre (Rabuka, 1980).

In a letter to Ramos, Edson said: "I'm recommending Obed because I refereed his last fight which he lost when he quit in the eighth round. I believe that Obed, with his experience and class should give Ve the standard of world-class competition that he needs."

The fight, refereed by Edson was against American Curtis Parker in Spectrum, Philadelphia in September 1979. Edson went onto say that Obed was open to fighting either in Fiji or the United States and was willing to accept a purse of US$5,000 plus expenses.

Ramos pondered the possibility of an FBC promoter taking on the programme, alternatively, make the trip to the United States if a local promoter could not be secured.

Meanwhile, the running conflict between the PBWAF and the FBC also brought into focus Ve's South Seas titles. The PBWAF had declared Ve's South Seas lightweight title vacant amid plans to hold a programme to declare a new titleholder.

Ramos and Ve reacted, saying the Tongan, New Caledonian and Western Samoan boxing associations recognised Ve as the true title holder and the plans by PBWAF to host a championship bout were null and void.

Two weeks after negotiations started with the Austin camp, a breakthrough was made when the Australian welterweight champion agreed to meet Ve on February 16 (Rabuka, 1980).

In a phone call to Ramos, Austin's manager Ray Gale accepted the offer of a fight purse of A$2,000 plus air tickets and accommodation for three to include Gale and a trainer. Promoter Subramani when informed by Ramos of the proposal, immediately agreed.

The 10-round clash now set to be held at the National Gymnasium in Suva, would see Austin, described by Gale as "the most scientific welterweight in Australia today", in peak form to fight the 'Ve-Bomb' after taking time off to recover from a nagging ankle injury.

Austin would be Ve's fifteenth international fight opponent since turning professional in November 1975.

Buoyed by the confirmation of the fight, Subramani was still chasing Gray's camp for a possible third fight with Ve.

"I'm willing to go all the way to Toronto to put the cash down before Gray and Ungerman to agree to fight Ve again for the Commonwealth welterweight title fight," Subramani said (Sport, 1980).

In the meantime, Subramani said that he would await the outcome of the Ve-Austin fight before pursuing the Commonwealth champion further with his offer.

The offer was a purse of US$15,000 plus return tickets and accommodation for five.

Since winning the Commonwealth title back from Clarke in November 1979, Gray had until May 1980 to defend his title as mandated by the six-months rule of the CBC. Ramos was in no rush to pressure the champion at this point.

The FBC's January 19 programme hit a snag when Zamal Azad pulled out of his undercard fight against Adi Narayan Reddy the day before (Masi, 1980). Azad's manager Tomasi Sivo said that Azad was not on contract to the FBC and therefore did not know how his name came to be on the FBC programme. He said Azad was signed to the PBWAF.

"I was surprised to see my name on the Fiji Boxing Council programme in Nadi," Azad told *The Fiji Times*.

"I cannot fight two programmes in one day," he said about his scheduled PBWAF bout against Aisea Aroi for the vacant PBWAF South Seas lightweight title scheduled to be held in Sigatoka Valley. Yes, the same title Ramos said Ve still held.

"How can they do this when they know that I still have the title?" an incredulous Ve demanded.

"Anyone can make a new title and call it whatever they want, but I have the official South Seas lightweight title and if anyone wants it, they have to fight me for it."

Aroi proved to be no match for Azad in a one-sided contest at the Nadubalevu Square Garden in Sigatoka (Dean, 1980).

The Fiji Times described the fight as a mismatch and Aroi never looked like winning. Aroi took a ten count in the sixth round after a punch that looked more of a push. When asked, Azad couldn't say for certain which of his punches brought about the result.

"His style of fighting did not match mine," was all Azad would say on the matter.

Ve was adamant that the title was still his and did not accept or recognise the PBWAF's authority to strip him of his South Seas titles.

"They can stage all the fights they like, but I'm still the recognised champion and the belt is in my possession," Ve said after the Azad-Aroi spectacle (Naulivou, 1980).

"If they want the belt, they can get it off me from inside the ring – not outside. I'm interested only in the sport and not the politics like some people."

Ramos was puzzled and irate by the handling of the South Seas title saga. Ramos said the PBWAF was not the controlling body for the South Seas titles. He challenged them to provide evidence to the contrary as there were five countries eligible to fight for those titles and therefore five boxing associations that had a say in its administration. The five countries eligible to fight for the South Seas championship at the time were Fiji, Tonga, Western Samoa, New Caledonia and Tahiti.

Meanwhile, the FBC's Lautoka programme on January 19 saw Tadu Chand of Sigatoka go up against Ramesh Krishna of Lautoka for the FBC bantamweight title, and Luke Sauqaqa of Lautoka up against Ilaitia Vaka of Navosa for the featherweight title.

Ramesh Chand in his junior-welterweight challenge, faced possible disciplinary action after he attempted to kick Akuila Naidu who had slipped on the canvas. This after Naidu knocked Chand out of the ring – literally – in their 10-round encounter. Referee Kolaia Buli awarded the fight and the FBC junior-welterweight title to Naidu (Sport, 1980).

In keeping with plans to continuously build on recent successes, the Ramos Boxing Club found itself a new clubhouse at the Tip Top Shed next to the National Stadium after lengthy negotiations with the Fiji Sports Council (Sport, 1980).

"For the first time we will be able to provide our boxers with real first-class training facilities," Ramos said of the venue that would now cost the club $200 a month in rental. The new facility also had a permanent ring, a heavy and a light punching bag, speed ball and proper exercise benches.

"Ve's handicap when he fought Gray for the Commonwealth titles was the non-availability of a proper gym for training," Ramos said. "Now that Ve has some important fights ahead of him, we will not be faced with similar problems."

With the new facilities providing a bigger space and a better range of equipment, the maker of champions was hard at work, planning the Josaia Dawai-Phillip Kating preamble before deciding if Kating should meet Ve.

The non-title contest was mooted to Kating and manager Luke Nasaroi with a purse of $1,500 on offer for the ni-Vanuatu fighter (Sport, 1980). This followed Kating's recent string of successes including a win over Anani Curebera for the South Seas light-heavyweight championship on December 1 the previous year.

While Kating now held a South Seas title, he still hadn't fought and beaten boxers the calibre of which Dawai had like Fossie Schmidt of New Zealand and Al Gattling of Australia, Ramos said.

Again, the issue of a possible South Seas title fight brought the PBWAF into the mix with Nasaroi saying that a non-title fight did not require Kating to get a clearance from the PBWAF to fight a boxer from the FBC roster.

Ramos discounted this saying that even if it was a South Seas title fight, the PBWAF did not have the authority to, nor should approval be sought from it, for boxers from either body to contest the title.

"The South Seas championship title should be fought for by a worthy challenger from any affiliated body in the South Seas region," Ramos said, adding that the championship did not belong to the PBWAF or the FBC.

Dawai, fancying his chances against Kating, was interested in going for the South Seas title (Sport, 1980). In an all-or-nothing challenge, the former South Seas light-heavyweight champion said that as a former title holder, a non-title fight would be a waste of his time.

While Kating had accepted the $1,500 purse for a non-title fight, Ramos soon found that no promoter was willing to put up that amount for a non-title fight between Dawai and Kating. A title fight was an entirely different matter.

"They are prepared to stage it with the title at stake for the same purse," Ramos said.

Ramos was also hopeful for a Dawai-Kafoa return bout and had plans to write to Noumea to see if Kafoa was still interested in fighting in Fiji.

News of the club's new digs brought Mataiasi Tagicakibau back into the spotlight as he sought to rejoin the club after leaving in November the previous year. Tagicakibau had claimed then that he wasn't given the opportunity to have important fights as his reason for leaving (Sport, 1980).

Tagicakibau said that it was difficult for him to improve on his boxing because of the lack of facilities.

"This is why I want to rejoin the Ramos Club," he said but Ramos denied his request given the very public nature of Tagicakibau's exit from the club.

Tarika returned to Sydney after a short break in Fiji following his loss to Jale Fotu in the East-West tournament in December 1979. Tarika was determined to have return match with Fotu (Masi, 1980).

"I wanted to show the public and Fiji the experience I have got from Australia, but Fotu was too serious about the fight," Tarika said.

"I want to make it clear that I can fight Fotu at any time, and if he wants to have a shot at me, I am willing to come back and show him I am worth more in the ring than he is."

After returning to Australia, Tarika began preparations for his fight against the Tahitian featherweight champion Maurice Apeang in Tahiti before looking at taking another crack at the New South Wales featherweight championship.

FEBRUARY – LAWRENCE "BABY CASSIUS" AUSTIN

Aged just 28, Tevita Tui had his ring career cut short because of failing eyesight thought to have been exacerbated through boxing. Now married to Laveti, 22, Tui was living with his brother and no longer able to box or work as a plumber at the Public Works Department.

Before losing his eyesight, Tui was a threat in the middleweight and light-heavyweight divisions, according to Ramos who trained the slugger on and off over the past three years.

Tui told *The Fiji Times* that his eye problems started after his fight against Australian middleweight champion Semi Bula in 1977 which Tui lost in a tenth round knockout.

After Bula, Tui went to New Zealand where he fought Fiji's light-heavyweight champion Luke Sisiwa, winning in eight rounds. It was after the Sisiwa fight that Tui found he had vision problems in his left eye (Masi, 1980).

While Tui maintained regular check-ups, his vision did not improve and a few months later was completely blind in the left eye. Despite several operations in 1979, Tui also lost vision in his right eye, leaving him dependent on his family for his welfare and survival.

Dr Champak Rathod, an ophthalmology specialist and medical superintendent of the Colonial War Memorial Hospital at the time, recommended Tui travel to New Zealand for further treatment in the hopes that his vision could be restored.

Ramos always advocated for boxers such as Tui and the late Waisea Tavusa, saying it was the responsibility of those who oversaw boxing in Fiji to care for fighters.

In his prime, Tui fought under the Ramos banner since the club opened in August 1975. As Ramos did not bind his fighters under contract, Tui was free to travel and box as he wished which saw him take a stab at making it internationally when he went to New Zealand to fight in 1977.

Tui regretted his current fortunes; however, he remained optimistic that treatment in New Zealand would help restore him to full sight.

"I cannot work for my own living now, but with the help of Ramos and my brother who have been looking after me and have been working hard to take me somewhere where I can get my eyesight back," Tui said.

A few days after Tui's story appeared in *The Fiji Times*, his overseas medical treatment plan received a boost with The Fiji Sixes Charity Chest, a lottery game run by *The Fiji Times*, stepping in to present him a cheque for $2,500 (Sport, 1980).

"I was happy when I heard that an eye operation in New Zealand could give me my sight back. But that was short lived as I have not been working for the past year and did not have the money to go to New Zealand for the operation," Tui said at the handover of the cheque.

However, Ramos and the FBC worked to find the funds for Tui and when Ramos told him that Fiji Sixes would assist with paying for the treatment, Tui was in disbelief.

"I found it hard to believe that at last I can go to New Zealand for the operation. I feel really happy and am truly grateful to the Fiji Sixes. I had started to believe that I would remain blind forever, but now I have hope," he said.

Lautoka promoter Bala Subramani stepped in to pay for Laveti's return airfare to New Zealand so she could accompany her husband. The pair left for treatment in early March (Sports, 1980).

With Tui's medical treatment costs taken care of, Ramos turned his attention to getting Ve prepared for his fight with Lawrence Austin. Peni Tabua had a word of caution for the 'Ve-Bomb' – watch out!

"Watch out, Ve. Austin is physically very fit and very fast. If Ve is 100 per cent fit this will be a very exciting fight," Tabua said after watching Austin train in Melbourne (Rabuka, 1980).

"I'm very impressed. He is fast with his hands as well as his feet. So, Ve has to keep him within his reach."

The Australian champ would be training in the club's new gym in the Tip Top Shed with two hours each allotted for Austin and Ve each day at the gym.

"If Ve wins, he is going to be in big demand. If he loses it could be the end of the road," Ramos said in quiet reference to a possible third Commonwealth title attempt.

"But judging by the way Ve has been preparing for the fight, there is no way Austin will have his way."

Ramos also had Australian triple champion Wally Carr in his sights for Dawai in a middleweight contest on March 1. Carr was the NSW State welterweight, Australian super-welterweight and Australian middleweight champion at the time.

As the Australian-based go-between for fight negotiations, Tabua said that Carr felt that Dawai would be too heavy for him to fight as a light-heavyweight. Tabua said that Carr also wanted a purse of A$2,000, which was more than the A$1,500 on offer from Lautoka promoter Bala Subramani. Instead Tabua discussed with Ramos the option of NSW heavyweight champion Fatei Namoa as an option for Dawai.

Austin arrived for the fight a week prior, and Ve took the opportunity before his arrival to get away to his home village of Lovoni for the weekend (Sports, 1980).

When Ve returned to Suva, he picked up right where he left off. Ve knew that a lot was resting on the results of this fight, and he needed to get into the right headspace for that.

"I will take the fight to him. I'm easy, I'm cool and I'm fit to take Austin all the way," Ve said upon his return to training.

After Ve sparred with Bolatawa and Dawai, Dawai said Ve's punches were heavier and getting faster. Ramos said the proper ring facility was helping Ve improve his footwork and speed, which he needed to go up against a fighter like Austin. All that was left was to get Ve used to fighting close up to an opponent who moved around the ring.

"We expect Austin to do this, and Ve will be prepared," Ramos said.

Subramani, who had doggedly pursued Gray and Ungerman to promote the third title fight, found himself with competition. Eric Emberson and Raghunath Singh of Shore Promotions threw their hats into the ring.

Using the sparring sessions to stay in shape for his fight against Joe Fabiano in a supporting bout on the Ve-Austin card, Dawai had not lost sight of a fight against Phil Kating. The response to Dawai's earlier challenge left the former champ less than impressed.

"I think they are out of their minds," is how Dawai described Kating's demand for a purse of $3,000 to defend his South Seas light heavyweight title against Dawai. Kating claimed the title from Ananai Curubera the previous December (Sport, 1980).

"Kating is not a drawcard in Fiji and no promoter would risk staging a fight for that amount of money. When I fought Aisea Ravula for the title, I got a purse of $1,000 and when I defended it against Luke Sisiwa it was for $1,500," Dawai said, "which is what Kating should be defending it for."

He said that Kating had not fought experienced boxers to have really tested his ability and was therefore, not in a position to make such a demand.

Before arriving in Suva, Austin had completed more than 200 rounds of sparring to prepare for Ve, according to his manager Raymond Giles (Daunabuna, 1980).

With a 23-7-2 record with four by KO, Austin who was only a year younger than Ve, had fought and lost against Jeff Malcolm twice for the Australian and Commonwealth super-lightweight titles in 1978. Following those back-to-back losses, Austin took a year off from the ring, returning to draw with Frank Ropis in November 1979. His next fight against Steve Dennis a month later, saw Austin wrest the Australian welterweight title on points in a fifteen rounds battle.

"Cassius used to be a sluggish fighter before we teamed up. But he is a different man now. He is a sort of a reflex fighter – cool and calm and nothing worries him," Giles said.

"But we have to be very careful against a man of Ve's calibre. If he can stop Hector Thompson, he has to be good."

On the lay-off, Giles said, "He just got sick of boxing, so he had a layoff. If there is a chance, we will take it, but we have the right plan to beat Ve comfortably on points."

Arriving with Austin and Giles was Tabua who was matched to meet Pita Domoni in a supporting bout.

Ramos watched Austin train at the Tip Top Shed and was impressed with his form (Sport, 1980).

"He is a very classy fighter. Just the right opponent for Ve when he is on his way to take on Clyde Gray again for his Commonwealth welterweight title," he said.

Giles was also complimentary about Ve, having watched him at training describing him as "a very powerful puncher" (Rabuka, 1980).

Two days before the fight, Ve revealed that he was battling a boil under his arm.

"It seems that whenever Ve is in great shape, these things appear," Ramos said.

Joining Ramos in Ve's corner for the fight was Father Brian Wilson, who was also part of Ve's team for both his Commonwealth title challenges (Sport, 1980).

The official weigh-in at the Outrigger Motel in Suva saw Austin tipping the scale at 10st 4lbs (65.3kg) and Ve at 10st 2lbs (64.4kg) (Sports, 1980).

Checked into a Suva hotel the night before the fight, Ve shot a few rounds of pool before calling it a night.

The National Gymnasium in Suva was at capacity as fans turned out to support Ve. Fans who travelled from Tavua and Rakiraki had to be turned away at the gate as tickets had sold out.

For Ve, this fight was to be a show of brilliance to mark a turning point after the string of recent losses. He won the epic ten rounder on points, never looking in trouble.

Ve boxed coolly and placed his punches more confidently as the fight went on. Austin never gave Ve any real problems and the Fiji and South Pacific welterweight champion was the heavier puncher. Ve hit Austin almost at will through his counterpunches and his weaving style upset Austin (Rabuka, 1980).

The two fight judges and referee Joe Campbell awarded the fight 99-98, 92-83 and 98.5-94 respectively to Ve. There was no argument from Giles on the decision in a fight where there were no knockdowns.

In the supporting bouts, Tabua upset Pita Domoni with a cut above Domoni's left eye in the first round which saw the fight stopped. And in an upset, Dawai was knocked out by Joe Fabiano in the fourth round.

Immediately after the win, Ve challenged Gray for a third defence. This was met with an outright refusal from Gray's camp to Subramani's offer of US$15,000, asking instead for US$20,000 (Rabuka, 1980).

Ramos said that no promoter would be willing to put up such a purse, adding, "It is one way to stop Ve from taking the title from Gray."

In the interim, Ramos was confident Ve could make the junior-welterweight division and fight at 140lbs (63.5kg). This shifted the focus from Canada to Nigeria, where the Commonwealth junior-welterweight champion Obisia Nwankpa was based. Nwankpa won the title from Jeff Malcolm in March 1979.

Subramani told *The Fiji Times* that while his offer to Gray for a purse of US$15,000 purse was still open, he would now focus on getting the Nigerian to defend his title against Ve for US$8,000.

"I think it would be cheaper to bring Nwankpa to defend his title in Fiji than Gray at this stage," said the Lautoka promoter, who was determined to see Ve win a Commonwealth title.

"Our plan now is to get the title from Nwankpa, then challenge Gray if he is still the champion for the heavier division," Ramos said.

With the Nwankpa plan in the pipeline, Ramos wrote to the CBC secretary Ray Clarke to extend an invitation on behalf of promoter Subramani for Clarke to visit Fiji (Rabuka, 1980).

The invitation was extended on the basis that negotiations with Nwankpa had started. If it did, Subramani was willing to pay half of Clarke's fare and accommodation for him to come to Fiji to watch a Ve-Nwankpa fight.

"We would like him to become one of the officials," Subramani said at the time. Ramos had proposed and Subramani agreed, that Jay Edson would officiate the fight should it happen.

Ramos also had questions for Clarke on how the Commonwealth rankings were being collated after Ve's wins over former junior-welterweight champions, Hector Thompson and 'Baby Cassius' Austin.

"If anything, Ve should be rated in the top four in the division after his points win over Austin," Ramos said.

Ungerman agreed with Ramos about the ranking after hearing about Ve's win over Austin (Rabuka, 1980).

Ungerman also agreed to give Ve a third chance to fight for the title on May 3 after protracted negotiations over the purse which had risen to US$30,000 for Gray at one point. Ungerman had made it known that Gray was being offered US$40,000 to fight Chris Clarke in a return bout. Ungerman was also reported as saying that Gray earned US$30,000 to fight Clarke the first time.

With Edson's mediation and report to Ungerman on how well Ve performed against Hector Thompson, Ungerman agreed to a purse of US$20,000 plus four first-class airfares and accommodation for the third fight.

Ungerman said: "Ve should be rated in the first four in the division." He also supported Ve improving his international ranking and agreeing to the third fight was a way in helping the Fijian achieve that.

The fight was locked in with Bala Subramani as promoter, Jay Edson as the main fight official and the National Stadium sought as the fight venue. The decision as to which boxing body would host the programme was not of concern to Ungerman provided the fight was held in accordance with international rules.

"I'm happy that Gray has given me another chance," Ve said.

"In fact, I'd like to fight Gray better than anyone else, because of the fact that he's beaten me twice. This coming fight will be a different story altogether. I am well geared up now, especially after the wins over Thompson and Austin."

MARCH – WBC MEMBERSHIP

A week after Ungerman agreed to the third fight, the proposed venue was shifted from Suva to Churchill Park in Lautoka by Subramani who said it was the "public demand of boxing fans in the west" that had led to the change of venue (Singh & Daunabuna, 1980). The May 3 date remained unchanged.

With about 2,000 fans missing out on seeing the Ve-Austin fight, Subramani was mindful of the need to maintain the interest of paying fans by ensuring his top draws were shared between boxers from the east and the west.

With less than two months before the big day, Subramani was also in negotiations with a local builder to put in temporary stands at Churchill Park for the fans similar to that put in for the Ve-Gray fight in 1978. The change of venue raised debate among boxing fans as to which division had the bigger fan following for Ve.

The Fiji Times interviewed ardent fan Sami Nair, who was more pragmatic in his views on the venue change.

"The Fiji Sports Council price for the National Stadium is high and the promoter may have found it easier to stage the fight in Lautoka," he said.

Another fan, Mosese Kama, said that the demand from the west would seem to be bigger because fans were more vocal than southern fans who did not complain because of the many bouts that were held in Suva.

"If I was a promoter, I would want to stage the fight in Suva because that's where the greater demand is," he said.

"People from outside Suva have spent a lot of money over the years coming for major sports which are normally held in Suva. It is time someone realised that these same events can be staged in other centres because the demand is throughout in a sporting country like Fiji," said another fan, Salend Kumar, of Suva.

A week after the move was announced, Subramani informed *The Fiji Times* that the change was advised by the Fiji Sports Council manager, Brian Wightman who said that a fight at the National Stadium would damage the running track (Sports, 1980).

Subramani was grateful for the advice as he would be liable for costs to any damage if the fight was staged at the stadium.

"It's a pity that I have to deprive the Suva fans from watching Ve in his own town. But at the same time, I thought it was time that the west people have a chance to watch Ve in action," he said.

The final hurdle in getting the fight off the ground was the approval of the CBC in accepting Ve as a suitable challenger for the Commonwealth title. This came in a letter to Ramos from the CBC's Clarke who gave the green light for Ve to challenge either Nwankpa or Gray for their titles (Sport, 1980).

Clarke also noted that although Ve was not in their last ratings, the board had considered that he had just beaten two former Commonwealth junior-welterweight champions, Thompson and Austin. He told Ramos that Ve's rating would come before the board at its next meeting.

"I'm happy that we have been given the green light to go ahead from the board," Ramos said.

Ramos also received further good news at a personal and professional level when he was accepted by the World Boxing Council as a member (Sport, 1980).

As the first from Fiji to be made a WBC official, Ramos said: "It is an honour indeed to become an official of the WBC not only to me and my family, (but also) to the sport in Fiji and the South Pacific region."

Ramos's membership followed recommendation by Edson who had been associated with the world body for 18 years. Ramos said he would use his position to get more boxers from the Pacific region on to the world boxing rankings. By Pacific he meant countries in the region other than Australia and New Zealand.

"WBC has never been represented in Fiji and this could be the one reason why our boxers have not been given ratings among the top contenders," he said.

"I don't care whether they are members of the Fiji Boxing Council or Professional Boxing and Wrestling Association of Fiji, as long as they are worthy of a rating, I will do my duty."

Ramos said that at the time only Ve was worthy of a WBC rating given the number of internationally recognised fighters he had fought. He said he would recommend that the FBC become an affiliate of the WBC.

In the meantime, former Ramos fighter Wili Tarika was also getting ready to meet Commonwealth junior-lightweight champion Johnny Aba in PNG for a second attempt for title on March 21 (Sport, 1980). Tarika's first attempt for the title the previous October ended with an Aba points win.

However, Tarika lost his second attempt on points for Aba's title over fifteen rounds.

With Tarika's previous foe Kaminieli Vunimasi in training with Ramos, Ramos was looking at Aba as a possible opponent for Vunimasi who comfortably beat Sonny Kumar of Ba on March 22 (Sport, 1980).

Ramos was confident that with a few international fights, Vunimasi would be ready to take on Aba for the title.

Vunimasi appeared on the undercard of a Bala Subramani promotion in Lautoka featuring FBC heavyweight champion Luke Tui and Samoan Fossie Schmidt.

Tui was knocked out in the second round after a short right to the chin followed by a series of lefts and rights to the head. Also appearing on the card was Silio Tiko, a former lightweight now fighting as a junior middleweight. Tiko lost on points to the South Seas junior-middleweight champion George Tanoa in a non-title fight. Tanoa, impressed with Tiko's showing, offered to put his title on the line in June.

APRIL – ERIC KING

At the end of March, after much debate and hand wringing, Ve resigned from the Bank of New Zealand to fight fulltime as a professional (Naulivou, 1980). With his focus and energy now channelled to becoming a fulltime professional boxer, his next decision was what to do to develop as a fighter on the international stage. After discussions with Ramos, Ve planned to move to Miami to train under the watchful gaze of Edson, who, with links to the Dundee brothers, Angelo and Chris, would give him an opportunity that other fighters from the Pacific could only dream of having.

Ve told *The Fiji Times* that his move to the United States would not affect his partnership with Ramos and his decision to resign his fulltime position as a bank officer came after Edson's offer for Ve to train under Chris Dundee in Florida.

"You see, America has the world's greatest fighters, and I plan to take up Edson's invitation and see the best boxers and also observe their training style," Ve said.

"I just might get into the action myself, and if the trip does come off, I plan to spend enough time there, so I can grasp all I can for my young fighters. But my going to America does not mean that will be breaking off my association with John."

While still with Ramos, Ve and fellow boxer Sakiusa Vaka formed an amateur boxing club out of a Suva garage as a means of providing guidance and support to future boxers looking to make a living in the professional ranks. Ve's plans to go to the US was intended to follow his third fight against Gray.

While the US travel plans were in the works, Edson was in contact with Ramos about the possibility of Ve fighting former WBC super-welterweight champion Elisha Obed from the Bahamas (Rabuka, 1980).

Obed was in the Dundee stable and had won the WBC title from Miguel de Oliveira in November 1975. Obed defended the title twice, successfully against American Tony Gardner in February 1976 and Ivorian Sea Robinson in April the same year before relinquishing it to German Eckhard Dagge in June.

In March 1978, Obed had another attempt at regaining the WBC title, this time against Australian Rocky Mattioli, but was counted out in the seventh round (BoxRec, n.d.).

The Ve-Obed fight was planned for May 31 in Suva as a warm-up before Ve took on Gray on the now-revised July 12 date. Obed was willing to fight Ve for US$5,000 plus air travel and accommodation but a promoter was still to be found.

"This will be best for Ve before a tough fight – he'll be facing a former world champion," Ramos said.

With a fight record of 79-10-4 against Ve's 28-4-1 at age 24, the 28-year-old Obed's pro record stretched back to 1967. Born Everette Ferguson in New Providence in Nassau, Bahamas, Obed started fighting in his home island at age 12, racking up an impressive 46-0-0 record before turning pro at age 14. Between February 1968 and April 1976, Obed was undefeated in 63 consecutive fights.

Standing at 5ft 11in to Ve's 5ft 7in, Obed's height and reach advantage as well as his experience would be a great preparation for Ve before his anticipated third attempt at the Commonwealth title. Ramos wanted the fight, billed for 10 three-minute rounds, at the 10st 10lb (68kg) limit.

But before Obed, Ramos quietly organised a fight for Ve against Australian super-welterweight Eric King in Subrail Park, Labasa on April 5. King, with a record of 23-53-10, looked to be no more than a sparring bout for the 'Golden Boy'. This would be the first time that the people of Labasa would see an international fight card with Ve as the headliner.

The bad weather delayed Ve's departure from Suva and the fight by two days to April 7 (Sport, 1980). About 2,000 eager fans turned up on the day and waited for more than three hours in the pouring rain before promoter Bala Subramani made the announcement that the fight was cancelled.

Back in Suva, Ramos tried feverishly to organise a helicopter to fly them to Labasa, but none were available and attempts to get a seaplane to take them across were also futile as no pilot in his right mind wanted to chance the bad weather to risk an hour-long flight across the Koro Sea.

Subramani refunded fans who asked for it and rescheduled the fight for the following Monday, April 7 starting at 11am.

King and his manager John McColl were confident of a win by knockout (Rabuka, 1980).

McColl, who had also brought former Commonwealth champion, Jeff Malcolm to fight Ve in 1978, told *The Fiji Times*, "It could go either way, but it will be a knockout fight".

McColl was confident that if King beat Ve, "He could make plenty of money because there would be a great demand to fight him."

With the weather improving by Monday, close to 1,000 fans turned up early looking for tickets but many had to be turned away disappointed.

King's bluster did not match his bite, which according to Ramos, "forced Ve to knock him out early" (Madhavan, 1980). If people were still trying to get to their seats, they would have missed the bout altogether. The fight ended in the second round.

Both fighters started out somewhat cautiously. In the first minute of the second round, Ve came at King forcing the Australian to take a standing eight count. In the second minute, Ve again took the fight to King again, putting him on the ropes to deliver a barrage of jabs and hooks that sent King to the floor for the full count.

Ramos was disappointed that the fight didn't go at least six rounds so that Ve could get a good workout. Ve on the other hand reflected after the fight that he hadn't meant to knock King out so early.

"I was going to take it easy and fight longer for the sake of the crowd, but King was forcing the fight in two rounds," Ve said.

"I think my punch that knocked him out was pretty heavy and I got him just right. I didn't feel many of his punches because I was weaving and guarding well."

McColl, who last watched Ve take out Jeff Malcolm in April 1978, said Ve had improved "100 per cent since the last time I saw him fight. He's got too much class, and he punches too hard."

After the fight all King had to say was that Ve was "the best puncher I have fought in my 122 fights. If I lost another eight pounds and was fitter, I'd like to come back for a rematch."

The ankle-deep mud and poor facilities did not stop the 3,000 strong Ve fans in the north from packing the stands and the grounds to capacity. In the main supporting bout, Ramos fighter Sikeli Veitala knocked out Iliesa Camaitai in the third round.

In another FBC programme following the Ve-King fight, promoter Bala Subramani was having problems finding a challenger for former Australian middleweight champion Wally Carr, whom he had lined up to fight Aisea Ravula. Ravula pulled out of the fight three days before the April 12 programme because of boils (Sport, 1980). Carr, McColl and Ramos had met to discuss alternative fighters should Ravula's condition not improve. In the mix were Phil Kating or Jo Dawai as possible last-minute challengers.

Carr, having had a bad experience with getting paid when he fought Apimeleki Rainima in Suva in December 1978, made known his reservations about the current situation.

"I was given only $650 of the $1,000 purse promised to me for fighting Rainima," Carr told *The Fiji Times*.

"I ended up paying my fare back home and now I'm getting this deal," he said of the Ravula confusion and the promised $1,000 to meet him, "Give me $2,500 and I will fight anybody."

McColl was clear that Carr would fight only FBC light-heavyweight champion Mark Junior or Ravula as scheduled.

After further discussions with McColl and Carr, it was confirmed that Ravula could not fight. Carr and McColl agreed to South Seas light-heavyweight champion Fossie Schmidt as a suitable replacement for Ravula.

Despite travelling from Lautoka to Suva to show Carr the boils on his hands, the Australian was not letting the Fijian go that easily, saying that he was scared to fight him. Ravula was undeterred, "I am not scared of him and can beat him, but with my left hand in this condition I simply cannot fight."

McColl, who drove a hard bargain, managed to get promoter Subramani to agree to a renegotiated purse of $2,500 for Carr given the programme change. Schmidt, the Samoan slugger, promised to have Carr on the canvas by the fifth round (Sport, 1980).

"I will be representing not only the South Pacific, but Fiji and I want everyone to come and see me knock the 'jumping kangaroo' out," Schmidt said.

Still recovering from a cut brow, he received when he fought Luke Tui in Suva in late March, Schmidt said he maintained his training schedule after that fight and was confident he could beat Carr. Stepping on the scale at 184lbs (83.5kg), the Samoan was four pounds lighter than Carr.

Schmidt's confidence was short lived. Cyclone Wally flattened him by TKO in the third round at the National Gymnasium when they met. While the South Seas champion had predicted that the fight wouldn't last five rounds, he was right as Carr displayed class and cunning that proved all too much for the Samoan (Rabuka, 1980).

While Schmidt didn't hesitate to take the fight to Carr, a bit more caution wouldn't have gone amiss as the crafty Australian exploited Schmidt's healing cut to draw first blood. Schmidt's solid punches seem to deflect off Carr and his solid lefts to Schmidt's body and head left Schmidt bleeding from the nose in the second round, a bleed that his team could not stop.

After a second knockdown in the fifth round, referee Joe Campbell decided Schmidt had had enough and stopped the fight. Carr took that one on a fifth round TKO.

In supporting bouts, Ramos fighters Sikeli Veitala and Jo Dawai did well to dispose of Felipe Tuivuna and J. Malimali both by knockout respectively.

A week after the Carr-Schmidt fight, Ramos received an invitation in the mail to participate as a delegate at the World Boxing Council's annual convention in Mexico later in the year (Singh, 1980).

Ramos was excited by the prospect of joining affiliates from 96 other countries and introducing Fiji boxing on the global stage. It was also timely as it came in the wake of Ramos's ongoing request to the WBC to recognise Ve in their top 20 rankings.

"Ve has had 18 international fights and losing three. Among those, he has beaten Australian Jeff Malcolm, who is rated fifteenth in the super-lightweight division of the WBC. This is why I asked for Ve's rating in the Top 20. I have also sent a letter to Jay Edson who knows how Ve fights and will be able to recommend him," Ramos said.

The WBC at the time required boxers to have at least 15 professional fights to be considered for a Top 10 ranking.

As the July date approached for the Ve-Gray return-return fight, Gray had still not signed the contract. Ramos was optimistic that Gray would by June 4 when he received a part payment of the US$10,000 purse to guarantee the fight which was now planned for July 12 at Churchill Park in Lautoka.

MAY – THE BREAK-UP, ELISHA OBED

At the beginning of May, the negotiations for Ve and Obed were finalised, and the ten rounds junior-middleweight contest was set for May 31 at the National Gymnasium in Suva (Sport, 1980). On board was Lautoka promoter Bala Subramani who had agreed to pay the former world champion a purse of US$6,500 and the cost of return travel for three people.

The go-ahead followed a telegram from Chris Dundee to Ramos agreeing to the fight and informing him that he would be travelling with Obed. The arrangement was to be a first for Fiji in terms of a former world champion coming to fight a local champion. Edson was expected to referee the fight.

The transfer of Kaminieli Vunimasi to the Ramos camp after Tarika's departure the previous October, gave Ramos an opportunity to build another champion for his club. Vunimasi was scheduled to meet Iqbal Azad of Lautoka for the FBC junior-lightweight title fight on May 4 and Ramos was confident that the former PBWAF featherweight champion had what it took to be the next FBC junior-lightweight champion (Rabuka, 1980).

Behind the scenes, Ve and Ramos's struggles to maintain a successful partnership since the beginning of the year finally became public. Ve's breakdown in discipline in terms of maintaining sobriety and attending training when scheduled, was cause for many conversations between Ramos and the champion with little success. It seemed Ve was outgrowing the patronage of Ramos and wanted a greater say in his fight negotiations as well as management. This was the beginning of the end of this once-successful relationship.

As manager and trainer for undeniably the most financially successful professional boxer Fiji had ever seen, Ramos was in it for the passion of the sport. For his fighters to realise their potential they had to follow his directions to the letter. Discipline, humility and respect were all Ramos ever asked of those who wanted to join the club. The formation of Ve's own amateur boxing club in March was just the first indication of the separation that had started between the two.

The public spillover of the camp struggles wasn't what Ramos wanted but he was left with little choice when Ve refused to sign the third fight contract against Gray. That was further compounded by Ve pulling out of the fight against Obed, a short time after the fight was confirmed. To describe Ramos's disposition at the time as unhappy or disappointed would be an understatement. Ramos operated on the premise that his word was his bond and the change in the relationship had caused damage to his reputation as a manager and negotiator, or so he felt.

Closer to home, Ramos had always seen Ve as an older brother to his three young daughters. The welcoming of Ve's wife Una into the family fold and the respect they showed to Margaret was acknowledged.

"The club was like a big family. We always cared, respected and looked out for one another. If ever there was one thing, I always told my fighters, was that to be a champion you never give up on the good things and always be kind to others," Ramos said.

Having shared so much personally and professionally with Ve over the past five years, the exodus by the man that he considered a son was devastating especially when the split became public.

The Fiji Times reported on Ve's exodus with the opening line reading: "Sakaraia Ve's chances to have a shot at Clyde Gray's Commonwealth welterweight title for the third time slipped away yesterday. And Ve's clash with former world junior-middleweight champion Elisha Obed on May 31 is off" (Rabuka, 1980).

The culmination of the behind-the-scenes drama came about when Ve asked Ramos to intercede in negotiations, he (Ve) had started with promoter Bala Subramani on behalf of former South Pacific Games gold medallist Kaminieli Vaubula.

Ve wanted Subramani to pay Vaubula $200 for an eight-round fight in Subramani's Ve-Obed programme. Subramani turned down the proposal, offering a six-rounder instead for $80. Ve's position was that Vaubula was a better fighter than others that Subramani had planned to put on the card. Ve had informed Ramos that he wouldn't fight Obed unless Subramani agreed to the proposal. The demand placed Ramos in an awkward position as a third-party negotiator and he did his best to find some middle ground with Subramani, however the issue resulted in a rift between Subramani and Ramos which led Ramos to contemplate ending the relationship with Ve.

At this point, while there was anticipation that a third Ve-Gray was going to happen, Ve had still not signed his contract for the fight, something that Subramani was feverishly trying to accomplish before pushing Gray to do the same. The contract had a proviso that should Ve win, he would defend the title against Gray within 90 days in an Apollo Promotions programme in Canada. Those were the conditions Gray's manager Irvin Ungerman insisted on for the third fight.

Ve told Subramani that he would only sign after the fight against Obed as a win would put him in a better position to renegotiate the purse – or so Ve thought.

According to *The Fiji Times*, "Ve told Subramani he did not want to be caught on the wrong side of the fence because he knew he would not be able to get a higher purse should he beat Obed."

Incidentally, Gray had his last fight in August 1980 against Allen Clarke, the older brother of Chris Clarke, for the Canadian welterweight title. Gray beat Clarke in a tenth round knockout. Gray retired as Commonwealth and Canadian welterweight champion after that fight to take on a position with the Ontario Athletic Commission where he remained for nine years, serving the last seven as the commissioner of the province (Hanley, 2006).

The demands from Ve had Subramani on the ropes and he quit the fight – calling off both the programmes. This left May 31 and July 12 dates open for other cards and Subramani was looking to schedule Neil Patel, the former Australian welterweight champion now fighting as a middleweight, to meet the FBC light-heavyweight champion Mark Junior on May 31 and Papua New Guinea's Commonwealth junior-lightweight champion Johnny Aba against either Jale Fotu or Kaminieli Vunimasi for July 12.

Ve was not shaken by Subramani's decision. He was confident that there were other promoters available to take on the Obed and Gray programmes.

"I'm very disappointed because I wanted to help Ve win a world title," Subramani said.

Ramos's thoughts on parting ways with Ve was being weighed. He pondered where they were at the present time in their relationship and Ve having started his own gym with boxer Ilaitia Vaka was a key consideration.

"As a manager and trainer, I expect my fighter to train in my gymnasium and to also have respect for me. If he thinks he can negotiate for himself, it's time that I concentrate on my other boys," Ramos said.

"I don't lose anything at all if we split because I'm not a paid manager."

It came out later that the conversation Ve and Ramos had on the phone regarding Vaubula ended with Ve slamming the phone on Ramos when Ramos "told him that I could not arrange anything because it's up to the promoter" (Singh, 1980).

"When someone does this to his old-time trainer/manager who brought him so far, all it means is that he has no more respect for the manager and I have my own principles, so I took that as a slap in the face and it has broken my heart," Ramos said at the time.

"I brought Ve from nothing to be the highest paid boxer in the country and also the most successful but what he did was a slap in the face for me."

Since October 1975, Ve had acquired three national titles, two South Seas titles and one South Pacific championship title under Ramos's guidance. Added to that were two unsuccessful Commonwealth title challenges among the 36 fights under Ramos, of which 16 were against international opponents, many of whom were of world-class calibre.

"When Ve lost to Clyde Gray and Hector Thompson promoters would not look at him and there was one case where he was only offered $1,000 but I had confidence and I stuck to him," Ramos said.

"Ve himself knows that when he was in the mud, I cleaned him up and brought him up again and at all those times I never took a cent from his purses which any another professional trainer and manager would have done."

As Ve was running his own boxing club, Ramos felt that he probably wanted to manage his own training schedule and arrange his own fights. It was the manner that Ve responded when Ramos declined to assist him with Vaubula that rankled.

"He was trying to dictate terms to me when he has no right to do so. I'm not being paid to be his trainer/manager, I'm doing all that at my own expense," Ramos said.

With Ramos's international connections with boxing, the rift was going to end with lost opportunities for Ve, and Ramos knew that.

"I have my own pride and respect and know that I am a dedicated trainer and I'm also proud that we have spilt while Ve is still at the top and not on the floor, because if he was down people would say that I left him on the floor."

Ramos resigned as Ve's trainer/manager immediately afterwards and informed the Fiji Boxing Council of the decision.

"I have three daughters, and Ve was like a brother to them and I treated him more like my own son than a fighter. I don't know what made him threaten to pull out of the fight if his fighter did not get in or why he slammed the phone."

At the time, Ve could not be reached for comment by *The Fiji Times*.

With Ve now off the card for the Obed fight, Ramos stepped in to help Subramani make up for the loss of Fiji's most prized fighter from the programme. A former world boxing champion had agreed to come and fight in Fiji. It would be a lost opportunity if a replacement could not be found quickly.

The first fighter in the line-up for consideration was FBC light-heavyweight champion Mark Junior to fight Obed as a middleweight (Rabuka, 1980). Subramani had contacted Chris Dundee with the replacement suggestion, and it was agreed. Junior did not hesitate to sign the contract.

While Ve-Obed was to be a junior-middleweight contest, Junior, as a light-heavyweight stood a better chance of making fight weight as a middleweight than a junior-middleweight on such short notice. As a junior middleweight, making weight as a middleweight would not be an issue for Obed.

"If he wins this fight, I will give him another overseas opponent," Subramani said of Junior's chances.

"Another reason why I want Obed to come is because the people of Fiji want to see a former world champion fight here."

The rather acrimonious parting of ways between Ramos and Ve required a meeting of the club and its members to decide on its future. At the meeting, the amateur and professional fighters stood behind their mentor despite the departure of the club's marquee fighter.

"While we are very disappointed at the attitude taken by Ve, we have confidence in you," were the words spoken by Viliame Tabualevu to Ramos on behalf of everyone in the club.

Tabualevu, the former amateur heavyweight champion, was supported by aspiring junior-middleweight Isikeli Veitala, Tarika's younger brother Vilitati Gonewai, veteran light-heavyweight Jo Dawai and FBC middleweight champion Setareki Bolatawa.

Tabualevu told *The Fiji Times* that they were not happy with what had happened.

"If Ve has to fight for some boxers, it must be us who have helped him in his training for his previous fights," he said after the team held a lengthy discussion on the issue before deciding that the club would move on without Ve.

Ramos was honest with his club members about the mental strain that the split had caused him and informed them that he would be taking some time off to regroup.

In his absence Father Brian Wilson, who was helping Ramos train the amateur fighters, would run the club while he was away. Fr Wilson was also Ve's second for both his fights against Gray.

With Ramos taking some time away, Fr Wilson took Ramos fighters Bolatawa, Dawai and Veitala to their respective bouts on the Obed-Junior undercard on May 31. Fr. Wilson would also prepare Viliame Tabualevu for his scheduled heavyweight clash with Seva Tuwai in the main supporting bout to the Neil Patel-Silio Tiko encounter in Ba on June 14.

Junior, who had built his professional career fighting in Sydney, had beaten Bolatawa for the FBC light-heavyweight title and Subramani was keen to give him further international fights if he did well against Obed (Rabuka, 1980). Junior was confident that he could take the former world champion by a knockout.

Subramani, undeterred by the loss of a drawcard like Ve, looked forward to building his programmes around other local fighters among whom was the former PBWAF lightweight champion, Jale Fotu, whom he signed on a three-year contract (Sport, 1980).

Obed's arrival into the country with Dundee a week before the fight was akin to the arrival of boxing royalty with a former world boxing champion and the brother of Angelo, trainer of 'The Greatest' Muhammad Ali.

Obed took no time to fit in, enjoying the Suva weather and the people who made him feel at home.

"This is so much like my hometown Nassau in the Bahamas," he said. "The people here are so much like my people. You even drive on the side we drive at home" (Dean, 1980).

Taking a day to acclimatise, Obed started his light workouts to round out his fight preparations at the Ramos Boxing Club gym (Sport, 1980).

Dundee, who has trained several world champions, warned Junior of Obed's powerful left – demonstrated for the media with a bag workout that, "flew from one side to another", as reported by *The Fiji Times*.

"Obed's left jabs are straight and fast and his timing for a one-two combination is first class," according to *The Fiji Times*.

"It would be a good idea for Junior to tighten his defence if he has any hope of a win."

For Dundee, the fight was important for Obed as they both sought another crack at the world title.

Junior tipped the scales at 156lbs (70.8kg) by official weight time. He was 160lbs (72.6kg) when he weighed himself earlier and worried that he would not make the weight limit (Rabuka, 1980).

"I'm just right for the fight," Junior said, "It's my biggest chance and I'll do my best."

Obed stepped on the scales at 154lbs (69.9kg). On the tale of the tape, Junior had the advantage standing at 6ft 0in (1.8m) with a reach of 32in (0.8m) and a fist of 9in (0.2m) to Obed's 5ft 9in (1.7m) with a reach of 28in (0.7m) and a fist of 7in (0.17m).

The fight was another story with Obed outpointing Junior over 10 rounds. Fans were left disappointed as both Junior and Obed failed to thrill the crowd as expected (Rabuka, 1980).

Obed described Junior as a very "awkward fighter".

"He is the most awkward fighter I have ever fought in my career," Obed said adding that it would have been a good fight had Junior gone toe-to-toe but, "He either kept moving away or grabbed me in clinches."

All credit to Junior, there were no knockdowns and Obed paid him the compliment of saying that Junior was one of the toughest fighters that he has ever met. Obed was cautioned twice by referee Joe Campbell for his low blows.

In the main supporting bout, Ramos fighter Mataiasi Tagicakibau scored a shock first round knockout over top-ranking light-heavyweight, southpaw Aisea Ravula. The fight ended 55 seconds into the first round with a Tagicakibau haymaker, a solid right to Ravula's chin, putting the Lautoka fighter on to the canvas.

Tarika's younger brother, Vilitati Gonewai of the Ramos Club also did well in his fight against Orisi Fotu with a fifth round knockout. Fellow club members Isikeli Veitala also had a fifth round knockout over Tomasi Qilia and Setareki Bolatawa knocked out Aisea Nama in the third round. Club member Tevita Ravuravu did not fare as well against Jeremaia Tadu who beat him in a second round knockout.

Dundee was impressed with the fights and spoke to Ramos about the possibility of taking a few boxers back with him to train at his gym. In particular, Dundee was keen on Ramos boxers Veitala and Gonewai (Rabuka, 1980).

"Veitala has the punching powers but needs a bit more moulding," Dundee told *The Fiji Times*. "He is a beautiful counterpuncher."

"Gonewai has got style and with further development of how to throw his punches, he could be a force to be reckoned with."

Promoter Subramani lost heavily in promoting the Junior-Obed fight, with only 400 people turning up on the day. Despite the small crowd, he was proud to have brought a former world champion to fight in Fiji. Subramani even contemplated the possibility of bringing three-time world champion Muhammad Ali to Fiji for an exhibition match.

But boxers like Ali are in a different class altogether.

JUNE – CHRIS DUNDEE

For a boxer like Muhammed Ali to come to Fiji, costs would involve first-class air travel and accommodation for up to 12 people, according to Chris Dundee (Sport, 1980).

Dundee said the travel party would include Ali's long-time sparring partner Jimmy Ellis.

"The other top fighter in the party would be former European and Commonwealth heavyweight champion and one-time title contender Joe Bugner of Britain," Dundee told *The Fiji Times* on the eve of his departure home.

Dundee was overwhelmed with the warmth and friendliness of the Fijian people and said that he would recommend a trip to Fiji to Ali upon his return. Ali, he said, would often take his recommendations for places to visit.

Before Dundee's departure, Ramos discussed with him the possibility of attending the WBC five-day annual convention in Mexico City on November 2 (Singh, 1980). Dundee said Ramos should attend in the interests of boxing in Fiji.

"The most important thing in boxing is to get close contact with people from the other side of the world for the simple fact that he will be able to meet people who will be willing to help promote Fiji boxing abroad," Dundee said.

In an interesting aside, at the time of the report on Dundee and Obed's departure from Fiji, another Fijian was making a name for himself in amateur boxing in England. *The Fiji Times* reported that Ross Ligairi, a trainee diplomat, had been awarded an Oxford University Blue for his outstanding contribution to the prestigious university's sporting achievement in boxing (Grimshaw, 1980).

Grimshaw reported in *The Oxford Mail* that Ligairi, a postgraduate student in International Law and Diplomacy, represented Oxford nine times as a middleweight against competitors from the Royal Navy, the Sandhurst Military Academy and first Battalion the Queen's Regiment as well as Kent, Glasgow and York universities.

"Ligairi's only loss came at the hand of Frank Bruno who had been the middleweight champion of the British Universities since 1978," the report said.

Bruno turned professional in 1982 and went on to have a colourful boxing career as a heavyweight which saw him attempt a string of unsuccessful world title attempts: against Tim Witherspoon in 1986 for the WBA title, Mike Tyson in 1989 for the undisputed world heavyweight title and in 1993 against Lennox Lewis for the WBC title.

It wasn't until September 1995 that Bruno finally became the WBC world heavyweight champion after he despatched Oliver McColl on points over 12 rounds. That reign was short lived as Bruno had to stage his first title defence against "Iron" Mike Tyson who was undefeated at the time. Tyson stopped Bruno in three rounds in March 1996. That was to have been Bruno's last professional fight.

Ligairi on the other hand, ended his impressive amateur boxing career, which started in the early 1970s, with a record 79 fights with only three losses by the time he finished at Oxford. Ligairi went on to become a career diplomat serving Fiji's interests at the United Nations, European Union and throughout the Pacific. He passed away at the Colonial War Memorial Hospital in Suva on May 21, 2009, (Uncensored, 2009).

Ramos boxer Tevita Tui, who had left for New Zealand with his wife Laveti in March for treatment with hope that his vision would be restored, was rocked by failure (Rabuka, 1980).

While in NZ, Tui learned how to read and write with Braille, and walk with the assistance of specialised cane.

"This cane has given me great independence," Tui told *The Fiji Times*. While optimistic of also learning a new trade that would help him find employment with his disability, The Royal New Zealand Foundation of the Blind had offered to train him as a darkroom technician.

"Unfortunately, there was no point in my learning to do this work as there is no possibility of me being allowed to obtain employment at the CWM Hospital in Suva, which was my intention."

After a two month lay-off following the Eric King fight and a very public split from Ramos, Ve announced his return to the ring for July 12 through Bala Subramani (Sport, 1980). Lined up for Ve was South Seas middleweight champion George Tanoa of Western Samoa. If he won the junior-middleweight fight, Ve could challenge the Samoan for his South Seas title in that weight division. Many felt that had Ve fought Obed, he would have easily beaten the former world champion.

Subramani was also planning to bring Commonwealth champion Johnny Aba to defend his title against Jale Fotu on August 31. The 15-round fight was listed for Churchill Park in Lautoka.

A day after the Ve-Tanoa fight was made public, Subramani announced that the fight was off after negotiations broke down with Ve over boxers Ve wanted featured on the undercard (Sport, 1980). It was a replay of the Obed programme.

Subramani told *The Fiji Times* that Ve wanted six of his boxers including Kaminieli Vaubula on the card. Subramani didn't agree and negotiations fell apart resulting in Ve withdrawing from the fight. Subramani did not miss a beat, looking immediately to FBC middleweight champion Silio Tiko as Ve's replacement.

Subramani always had a few irons in the fire as far as his promotions went. He was savvy and knew that he could not rely solely on those that he did negotiations with, so he decided the time was right to feature other up-and-coming fighters on his programmes.

Planned for July was a lightweight fight featuring Cook Islander Tevita Vakarima, 23, and Isikeli Veitala, 22. Vakarima denied Ve a gold medal at the 1975 South Pacific Games in Guam (Rabuka, 1980). Subramani had plans to bring the undefeated Vakarima to Fiji for several fights over a three-month period. His plans for the Vakarima-Veitala battle would follow a planned promotion he had for Veitala and Tiko on July 27.

Accompanying Vakarima would be his compatriot, light-heavyweight Leota Fomai, who had a 11-3-0 record, 10 by knockout. The possible opponents for Fomai were Jo Dawai, Viliame Tabualevu or Mark Junior.

JULY – SIKELI VEITALA AND THE FIJI JUNIOR MIDDLEWEIGHT TITLE

Having come through an emotional rollercoaster with Ve, Ramos decided to do things differently with his boxers this time. He bonded Veitala to a five-year contract as his trainer/manager (Rabuka, 1980). Ramos knew he had a future champion on his hands with Veitala unbeaten as a junior middleweight in eight professional fights, all by knockout.

"Give me eight months and I will make him a champion," Ramos said following the contract signing.

Lined up for Veitala was a fight on July 26 against the FBC junior-middleweight champion Silio Tiko in Wairiki, Taveuni for the Vanua Levu title and a fight against Vakarima on August 23 in Suva. The two fights were part of a warm-up strategy Ramos had before sending Veitala to Dundee in Florida for a training camp once the American confirmed the plan.

The fight against Tiko was expected to be a good one following Tiko's outpointing of former Australian welterweight champion Neil Patel on June 15 in Ba.

The news of Ve and Ramos's separation was yet to reach abroad as Ramos was approached by Australian promoter Reg Layton for Ve to fight on one of his cards. Ramos politely informed Layton that Ve was under new management and redirected his enquiries.

In the meantime, Subramani and Ramos had lined up a Fomai-Dawai charity exhibition match to raise money for a Ra Provincial Youth Council

Project on August 2 with Vakarima also on the programme with an opponent who was yet to be identified.

Veitala's fight against Tiko was to be his biggest to date. Unemployed and boxing fulltime as a professional, Veitala knew the fight against the current FBC middleweight champion was not to be taken lightly as many looked to Veitala as the next Ve for the Ramos Boxing Club (Rabuka, 1980).

Originally from Tacilevu Village in Savusavu, Veitala's road to boxing was mapped by his difficulty in finding suitable employment. His decision to turn professional came a year after starting out as an amateur.

"I want boxing to be my career, and I believe I can make it to the top," Veitala said.

"But I don't want to rush experienced opponents at this stage because I want to improve my ability as I go along."

Ramos was confident of Veitala's chances against Tiko, describing him as being good with either hand, and a brilliant counterpuncher. Ramos figured the fight would not last more than 10 of the scheduled 15 rounds.

Ramos guided Veitala to a fifth round TKO win in front of Tiko's home crowd from Vuna (Rabuka, 1980). The win gave Veitala the junior-middleweight championship.

The fight was entertaining with Tiko and Veitala going toe-to-toe in the first two rounds. In the fourth round, Veitala unleashed a series of brilliant one-two combinations that sent Tiko to the canvas for a compulsory standing eight count. Veitala continued the assault in the fifth and referee Ilisoni Nate had to stop the fight. On the same card, another Ramos boxer Viliame Tabualevu kept his unbeaten record by stopping Akuila of Nawakawau in two rounds.

The next fight targeted by Ramos for Veitala was against former New Zealand and Australasian welterweight champion Ali Afakasi. Ramos called Maurice Payne in New Zealand right after the Tiko fight to gauge Afakasi's availability.

Meanwhile the planned Veitala-Vakarima fight for August was cancelled after Vakarima signed a contract to fight in Hawaii that same month.

AUGUST – RETURN TO THE PBWAF

The media proposition that Veitala may be the next new golden boy did not sit well with Ve.

"I'm still Fiji's golden boy and I'm ready to fight the world," was Ve's response in an in-depth interview with Stan Ritova in *The Fiji Times* after Veitala's win over Tiko (Ritova, 1980).

The interview laid bare Ve's side of the story and his reasons for leaving Ramos's management. It was an exposé that lifted the lid on how he viewed his time with the man who chaperoned him to two Commonwealth title challenges. This is a condensed version of the interview:

"I am now independent of all those people who used to boss me around," Ve said.

"My boys and I are going to do our own thing, and no one is going to dictate to us."

Ve, puffing away on a big cigar made from Fiji-grown tobacco leaf, said he has good reason for going ahead to win a Commonwealth and world title.

"I now have my wife Una and one-year-old daughter Akesa staying with me. And my future fighting career will revolve around them," Ve said as he cuddled Akesa.

Mrs Ve and Akesa moved to Suva a month ago from Levuka where she resigned her steady job with the Pacific Fishing Company. She became the 'mystery wife' because she was rarely seen with her boxer husband.

"Now I eat well, and I am ready any time to take on the world," he said with a smile.

Ve is scheduled to fight Australian middleweight No.3 contender Ritchie Roberts in Suva on August 16. And promoting the fight will be Raj Kumar Singh who will handle all Ve's future fights.

"I have complete faith in Mr. Singh because he is dedicated to the sport of boxing," Ve said.

"He is not a fly-by-night promoter who is only after the money."

Singh, who has been promoting fights in Fiji for over 22 years said that he was happy to be associated with Ve. Their relationship would be built purely on business lines, he said.

"I will have no hold over Ve whatsoever," Singh added.

Ve poo-hooed rumours that he was "all washed up" and was not going to fight anymore.

"People in Fiji like talking – specially about other people because they haven't anything better to do," he said.

"I will have the last laugh because I am going to strive to go further with my boxing career – and alone.

"I am going after class now and it has to be someone that's either Commonwealth or world rated after my Roberts' encounter.

"After all, the Australians in my division can't say very much because I have thrashed them all. This fighter Roberts, whom I am going to meet soon, is only one of two Australians left worth fighting."

One thing that has become Ve's pet hate is dictatorship.

"I just hate all reference to the word because I was subjected to it for many years under the John Marimuttu Ramos regime," he said.

Everything was hard for him at the time because he could not make decisions concerning himself, Ve said.

"I couldn't do anything because I had no power." Ve said his former trainer and manager "did not respect what I wanted."

"He manipulated and dominated me, and I had to do what he wanted. But I am now free as a bird."

Ve has recruited the services of Suva lawyer Bob Lateef as his adviser.

"I am the manager of myself, and my boys and Mr. Lateef will see we are doing the right thing administration and financial wise," he said.

Ve's most promising fighter is Kamisese Vaubula who won the South Pacific Games light-heavyweight gold medal last year (1979).

"This is a future Fiji champion, and I am going to make him one. This is the boy that promoter Bala Subramani and Marimuttu did not want to put on the programme when I was supposed to fight former world champion Elisha Obed in Suva."

Ve said this was the reason that he withdrew from the fight and finally from the Marimuttu camp. Ve said he had planned to fight in Hawaii, but he decided to fight Roberts first before looking to America.

Ve has taken up singing and skylarking with the Gaunavou Dance Band in Suva night clubs and dance halls to occupy his leisure hours.

"It makes me feel very happy to be up on that stage. It reminds me of being in the ring and giving an opponent the hiding of his life with my fans screaming their heads off with joy ... a lovely, lovely reward ... a lovely, lovely feeling of victory," he added.

"Definitely no alcoholic booze but some yaqona and my cigar, of course," Ve answered when asked whether it was true that he was on the beer.

"If I was drinking booze, I would be overweight but as you can see I am around 11st. When I'm in training my weight drops."

As for the cigar? *"The cigar is necessary because it helps preserve my teeth. And of course, I don't inhale the smoke. I don't think anyone who smokes Fiji-made cigars inhales the smoke. The cigars are very strong and if they did inhale, they would end up on their back on the floor like I would if I don't keep training."*

The decision by Ve to go with Singh as his preferred promoter was his own to make, but the decision by the Fiji Boxing Council to issue Singh with an FBC licence did not sit well with Ramos. Ramos resigned as member of the FBC and returned to the PBWAF (Singh, 1980).

Ramos's reasons went back to Singh's pressure on the PBWAF to strip Ve of his titles, which Ramos viewed as a promoter "dictating" terms to the association.

Ramos recalled also disparaging remarks Singh made about the FBC when it was formed and the rival contests that he would schedule at the same time as the infant council's programmes.

"Yet he applies to join them (FBC) and although they know about him, they just let him come in on the excuse that Ve only fights under him," Ramos said.

Exiting with Ramos was promoter Bala Subramani who was described as a stalwart of FBC. Subramani had suffered significant financial losses staging FBC programmes.

"I'm surprised that Ve went back to Singh after all the damage that Singh did to him and I think Singh used him to gain entry into the council," Ramos said.

"Personally, I have nothing against Singh but in the boxing world, I just can't stand him. How can the council be so sure of themselves because many of them don't even know the correct weight for the various divisions?"

Ramos gave credit to referees Joe Campbell and Ilisoni Nate as the only ones having the correct knowledge to control fights.

"Boxing is in my blood, and I know what Singh is like because I have fought under his promotions as far back as 1966 in Sigatoka until 1970," Ramos said.

He said Singh offered Ve only $3,000 to fight Kating, but Ve the drawcard demanded $5,000 and was turned down.

"After being kicked in the back the way Ve did, it is no more free help from me and all my boxers will have to sign a contract with me like my new golden boy Isikeli Veitala has done."

Under the terms of their contract, Veitala would not give Ramos a percentage of his purse but would have to give Ramos 50% of his earnings if he left before the end of five years. All expenses for preparing Veitala would be covered in an arrangement Ramos would make with promoters.

The switch back to the PBWAF followed talks with his club members who were given the option to stay and fight for the FBC. The consensus was to go with Ramos and return to the PBWAF fold.

The Ramos-FBC fallout was felt across the boxing fraternity prompting a statement from the PBWAF secretary Muntaz Ali who said, "The standard of boxing has dropped dramatically and it is now a dying sport facing the danger of fading away in the years to come" (Singh, 1980).

"The only thing that can bring Fiji boxing back to its glamour of old is to just have one boxing body in Fiji. But no-one, not even government has done anything about this," Ali said.

With 23 years as a boxing administrator, Ali's credentials included membership of the Commonwealth Boxing Council, an honorary member of the Australian Boxing Federation and a founding member of the Tongan Boxing Association.

It was Ali's view that the formation of the FBC was detrimental to boxing in Fiji leading to a decline in the standard of boxing and promotions. He said the same also happened in countries such as New Zealand, Tonga and Samoa where the appearance of rival boxing bodies had caused a drop-off in the quality and standard of boxing.

"This is where in Fiji, the government, especially the Ministry of Sport, has failed the boxing world badly," he said. Ali added that he had corresponded several times with the ministry to have something done but was always given a "flimsy excuse" of being busy.

With Ramos and Ali reconciled, at least professionally, it seemed that a return to the PBWAF fold for the man who made boxing in Fiji a viable commercial enterprise was the most logical thing to do.

Amid the break-up and make-up, Ramos did not lose sight of the social enterprise that he made part of his club. Continuing with his community initiatives, the Ramos Boxing Club had an entrant in the inaugural three-day Miss Nasinu Festival in Valelevu. Twenty-one-year-old indent clerk Roslyn Raju would carry the Miss Ramos Boxing Club banner into the festival.

Roslyn was a lovely, soft-spoken and well-presented young lady who did well as an ambassador for the club. She articulately presented the club mission, which was for young people to be good citizens and leaders for their communities.

The festival preparations and fundraising were a welcome distraction from the drama of the past few months and gave club members something else to focus on while the issues ironed themselves out. The end of the weeklong pageant also gave everyone in the club something to celebrate because Roslyn was crowned the inaugural Miss Nasinu at the end of the festival on August 9 (Times, 1980).

On August 16, Ve returned to ring for the first time since his forgettable fight against Eric King in February. His first fight since leaving the Ramos camp was against Ritchie Roberts, the southpaw ranked third for the Australian middleweight title who was coming into the ring with a 11-6-2 record, two by knockout.

A respectable crowd of around 3,000 turned up at the National Gymnasium in Suva to watch the 10-rounder promoted by Raj Kumar Singh under the FBC banner. Ve put Ritchie to the canvas at least four times by the sixth round before referee Ilisoni Nate stopped the fight.

When asked by *The Fiji Times* after the fight if he still thought of himself as Fiji boxing's 'golden boy', Ve responded: "All I can say is that I am sure to give most fighters a run for their money" (Dean, 1980).

After the Roberts fight, Kumar said that this was the last fight that Ve would have against an Australian, instead he would look elsewhere for suitable overseas opponents (Ritova, 1980).

The first non-Australian floated to fight Ve was welterweight Juan Antonia Merlo, whom FBC assistant secretary Ilisoni Nate claimed was ranked eighth in the world. The fight was to be promoted by Singh (Sports, 1980).

That claim was soon disputed by Hawaiian trainer Peter Jhun who pointed out that the true world eighth-ranked welterweight according to *Ring* magazine was Adolfo Viruet of New Jersey, who he was happy to arrange for Ve to fight (Sport, 1980).

To say that the credibility of the FBC in making such an untrue statement was affected, was an understatement.

Laurence "Baby Cassius" Austin (L)
and Sakaraia Ve after their weigh-in
(Fiji Times, circa Feb 1980).

Middleweight boxer Isikeli
Veitala of Ramos Boxing Club
(n.d.).

John Ramos at Tip Top Shed club (Fiji
Times, January 24, 1980).

John Marimuttu Ramos shows off the World Boxing Council's monthly Bulletin. He could be attending the world body's convention in Mexico in November.

Fiji Times, April 18, 1980.

The World Boxing Council membership patch sent to John Ramos following acceptance of his membership, a first for Fiji. Ramos was nominated to the august body by Jay Edson.

Epilogue
Final words by John Ramos

The reason I was so successful in boxing was because of my commitment. It was from the heart and wasn't an easy path to take with a full-time job, a wife and three young daughters to raise. Margaret was my rock and gave me the foundations to achieve the level of success that I had with the club.

To manage and train fighters, then find the right opponents for them so that they could benefit and make progress from a support bout to main event fighter is, and should be, the goal for every good trainer/manager. That was the path that I took for all my boxers.

I continued to manage my club until early 1981, focusing on building the group of talented fighters I still had like Veitala, Boletawa, Tabualevu and Dawai. My marriage, however, did not survive and by December 1980, Margaret and I separated for the last time. The support she provided to me, and the boys was invaluable, but regrettably our marriage became irretrievably broken in large part to my absence and partiality to alcohol at the time. It would be two decades later when I came to the realisation that alcohol was a contributing factor to many of my shortcomings. I decided in 2001 to stop drinking alcohol altogether.

I left Fiji for Australia not long after my marriage ended. I resigned my job at Carpenters, a job I had had for almost 20 years and closed the doors to my club. It was a very difficult decision, but I needed to get away from everything and process the changes in my personal life and this included stepping away from the public light and from boxing.

My time in Australia was spent working odd jobs and moving between residences. I was adrift and needed to find an anchor. After almost two years away, I returned to Fiji hoping to get back into that one thing that was familiar and like home to me – boxing.

Upon my brief return, I got back into boxing and engineered a fight between Silio Tiko of Ba and Inoke Qarau of the Salvation Army Club in Raiwaqa. This was held at the Isa Lei Hotel in Lami where people came to a

Las Vegas-style live boxing event where you could wine and dine and watch boxing. This was no different to the Gattling-Dawai fight held in Deuba in August 1979.

In January 1985, I moved to Vancouver, Canada permanently. My mother and brothers Adi and Vincent now lived in Vancouver with their families and my family presented an opportunity for me to regroup and make a fresh start.

I never forgot Ve even though we parted under difficult circumstances. In October 1985, I arranged a fight for him against Michael "The Silk" Olajide at the National Stadium in Suva. Olajide was an up-and-coming middleweight in Vancouver, and I thought he would be a great stepping stone for Ve as this was a fight for the World Athletics Association middleweight title.

I felt an international title added to his collection would have boosted Ve and Fiji boxing. However, at eight years younger and with a height and reach advantage, Olajide proved to be the better fighter with a ninth-round knockout.

Ve was an extraordinary talent and whether he would have been better off taking up the many international training opportunities he was offered, maybe? We will never know. He was and still is an extraordinary man and fighter to me and there will be no other like him.

In our time together, Ve's highest ranking was at No.2 for the Commonwealth welterweight ranking with Clyde Gray the champion and in the top 15 of the interim welterweight rankings by the WBC. This was 1979. Ve, ever respectful of his fans and opponents, was to also become the highest paid local fighter at the time.

In its time, the club held 11 titles and championships with six belonging to Ve. Wili Tarika, Anthony Naidu, Kaminieli Vunimasi, Isikeli Veitala and Setareki Bolatawa were our other champions.

All this was inspired by the 'Maker of Champions' sign I saw at Ern McQuillan's gym in Newtown, Sydney in 1974. It was what inspired me to never give up and to keep fighting for the love of boxing.

As a trainer/manager the challenge was always to prepare your fighter 110 per cent for the main event. It is not only stressful when you have a family and a full-time job to contend with, but it occupies your every waking thought from the date you sign that contract to the fight and every day in between. The trick was to work through each challenge at a time and be patient. Most importantly, you had to enjoy it.

Through boxing I met some great people who were world-class managers, trainers, referees, fight coordinators and boxers from the South Pacific, France and North America. Wherever Ve went to fight, the economy in that town would be stimulated because he drew the fight fans from all over the country.

Without the support and interest of the sports writers for *The Fiji Times* and the original *Fiji Sun*, people like Eliki Rabuka, Torika Tora, Gabriel Singh, Peter Lomas and Harris Choy, the public profile of boxing would not have been what it became at the time. They did some great reports.

My only regret is that we did not have television in Fiji in those days. If we did, it would have changed boxing completely in terms of the profits today from pay-per-view. We would have been able to draw a larger, more international audience with our boxers.

I had my share of adversaries in the business, but I always did my best to be fair in how I dealt with them. It served no useful purpose to hold grudges or animosity towards them because of our small community.

I can hold my head high and say proudly that I never profited financially from the boxers who fought under my management. Whatever I did was purely out of my love for the sport of boxing and to see it grow.

I had received numerous offers from promoters in Australia, New Zealand and Hawaii, asking me to take my best fighters across to fight on their programmes. These offers came with flights and accommodation but always a purse lower than what I thought my boxers deserved. If it wasn't in the best interest of my fighters, it wasn't worth considering. I could easily have taken those offers and enjoyed a free overseas trip, but that went against everything I stood for.

When I visited Fiji in July 2010, only the third time since leaving Fiji in 1985, I made it a point to see Ve again and to present him with his runner-up title for the fight against Olajide. I was saddened to see the hardship that he was going through, having lost his hard-earned wealth because of tax avoidance, or so it was deemed. I can say that in our time as a team I ensured that his purses were tax-free with the tax paid for by the promoter.

In retrospect, it probably would have been in his best interest to have an accountant advise on these matters. But that was a time when professionalism was still in its budding stages and having a professional management team in that regard was not a consideration. We were about the passion and the love of boxing, sadly, the tax department didn't see it in that light.

When Ve and I spoke during my visit then, we were quite sad to see the decline in boxing in Fiji. The formation of the Boxing Commission of Fiji (BCF) while honourable in its intentions was short in its understanding of the governance surrounding amateur and professional boxing. The two are mutually exclusive and do not have a servant-master relationship.

I have always believed the amateur ranks form the core to professional boxing. Without a strong amateur development programme, the fundamentals and the ringcraft of boxing are lost in the professional ranks.

The interference of the commission in the affairs of amateur boxing at the time did not do it any great favours, causing the sport to further languish. This was an anomaly that my daughter, Sylvia, tried time and again as the secretary of the Fiji Amateur Boxing Association (FABA, 2011-12) to explain to the commission with the support of FASANOC but to no avail. Amateur boxing worldwide is governed through AIBA, the Amateur International Boxing Association, with delegated powers through the national amateur body in this case FABA. Unlike professional boxing, there is only one recognised amateur boxing body in any one country, and they are independent of any professional association. As the commission was tasked with oversight of both amateur and professional boxing in Fiji, this presented a conflict with the AIBA rules.

While I was there, I also presented the commission with two titles in memory of former Fiji boxing greats, Sunia Cama and Marika Naivalu, which were accepted.

I was happy to see Ve again as I hadn't seen him since 1985. We reminisced about our time together and we both agreed that we did achieve a lot in that short time, and I really wanted to continue that reconnection, so I decided that with the support of my brother Raymond as club manager, Ramos Boxing Club would reopen its doors with Ve as the trainer.

We both wanted to help the sport, and this was how we thought we could achieve that. We wanted to bring back those memories of the old Ve style of boxing and that appeal to boxing fans. Ve had a lot of experience and the skills that he could pass on, so it was the perfect combination.

The club had a small number of local and Nauruan boxers who formed its core team. They had several outings, facing stiff competition from the Police and Army boxers. With each programme, the boys got progressively better.

The club produced one outstanding fighter in the 64kg category, 17-year-old Mel Halsted, who took out the Best Scientific Boxer accolade at the 2011 FABA championship when he beat the Army's top fighter, veteran Sepeti Qio, in the 64kg to take gold. This was the same title Ve won in his last fight as an amateur in 1975. Mel's ringcraft had not been seen in a long, long while. His use of the ring space, agility and timing of counterpunches took one back to the golden age of boxing. This is what boxing needed. This is what Fiji needs if it is to have a thriving professional programme.

Sadly, the club had to close in 2012 following Raymond's untimely passing and the infrequency of organised amateur competitions. Raymond was the backbone of the revival, and he gave of his time freely because like me he wanted to offer young men an opportunity beyond the dark landscape of unemployment and the unsavoury influences of drugs and crime.

In my opinion, to get boxing back on its feet we need to go back to the very basics, the amateur code. The first step would be for the amateur body, FABA, to elect a dedicated and knowledgeable team of volunteers to serve on its executive team. FABA is to also have its headquarters in Suva, so it is close to the decision makers and major sponsors.

The next step is to find a home for amateur boxing contests where weekly competitions can be held. The venue should be able to seat about 300 people, so revenue can be generated through the door. Approaches to sponsors should also be made to support the weekly competitions.

FABA will need to have each boxing club register with it and nominate a member of their team for referee, judge or timekeeper who will be given the proper training on how to manage these responsibilities. If you're not registered, you cannot enter a fighter on the programme.

Once a regular cycle of weekly competitions has been established, a Fiji championship can be held again to find the top amateur in each weight category. An active amateur scene will provide an avenue to select Fiji's national representatives.

Within two years, the programme can be taken to Western and Northern Viti Levu with Suva catering for the Eastern and Southern divisions. To ensure there is continuity, FABA can provide guidance to sub-committees formed in the west and north on how to organise the weekly competitions and manage sponsorship arrangements. Certainly, every nominated referee, judge and ringside official from these regions would undergo training of AIBA rules.

Fiji fighters have never been successful at the Olympic Games level but that is not to say that we can't in the future. We have had successes at the Commonwealth Games with boxing. Winston Hill's bronze medal win at the GC2018 ended a 36-year medal drought for the sport since light-heavyweight Sani Fine won gold at the 1982 Brisbane games. The only other time that Fiji boxing won medals at the games was back in 1962 when middleweight Moses Evans and heavyweight Holgar Johansen won bronze in Perth, Australia.

For the professional code, an association much like the former PBWAF governed by a constitution and affiliated with one or two recognised world boxing bodies would do well for a start. It would be a bonus if it had a paid administrator and a team of elected volunteers with the wherewithal of professional boxing.

The role of the boxing commission should be reviewed to provide oversight of the professional association or any other professional boxing body that may subsequently be formed to ensure that these bodies govern in accordance with their constitution (approved by the commission) and that proper licences are issued, and rules are followed. The commission could mediate and adjudicate matters that are referred to it when internal mechanisms of the association are exhausted, but they do not interfere or direct how an association is run. The members of the association are the ones to hold its executives accountable and may refer matters requiring an independent review to the commission for its attention.

The value of having local boxing associations linked to world bodies helps build knowledge of the technical aspects of boxing. This is invaluable. It also provides a gateway for local fighters seeking international exposure through a sister-association network and sets up professional boxing as a legitimate career choice for a professional athlete in Fiji.

It is my sincere hope that the powers that be, can see the value of the amateur code and how best the professional code can be best directed for the next generation of boxers after Winston Hill, so they can restore the glory of boxing in Fiji.

Ramos Boxing Club 2011 – medal haul from the 2011 Fiji Amateur Boxing Association Championship. (L-R) Simi (cornerman), Fulton Amram (Bronze 75kg), Mel Halsted (Gold 64kg and Most Scientific Boxer Award), Jonathan Prasad (Bronze 56kg), Vincent Nair (Silver 52 kg) and trainer/manager, the late Raymond Nair (Sylvia Low Tiffany Collection).

Acknowledgement

This book is an acknowledgement to the great journalism that existed in Fiji in the 1970s and '80s. Without the great follow-up by these hard-nosed journalists, this book would not have been possible as the best of memories fade over time. I am forever grateful to the men and women that provided a timeline and report of events that helped contribute to the chronological sequence of this book.

Sincere gratitude to the editor of The Fiji Times, Fred Wesley, for giving me access to their archive – a treasure trove of information that holds a great chunk of Fiji's history since 1874 in its repository. To the Fiji Times librarian Reapi Mataniniu, thank you for the countless hours spent searching and scanning the many pages of boxing related news story that I sent, across to you. Being responsive to my many emails and being such a great help. I cannot thank you both enough.

To my brother Jordan Ramos and daughter, Laryssa Fiu, the help with research and scanning of archival material is very appreciated.

To Lyndall Fisher and Lorraine Mar (FASANOC), the work that you do and have done to support and encourage amateur sports in Fiji is phenomenal, thank you both for the archival material provided.

To Margaret Hatch, thank you for Hector's boxing records. Hector was the cornerstone for amateur boxing in Fiji and will always be remembered for his tireless effort in bringing amateur boxing in the national consciousness during his administration. He is greatly missed.

To my cousin Margaret Joseph, thank you for sharing family photos for this book and to my aunt Surya Khan, the ancestry lesson was very welcome – thank you so much for that.

Kevin McDonald and Martin Tiffany, thank you for casting your keen eye over this freshman effort, your notes, pickups and edits are appreciated.

Greg Madhavan, *arigato gozaimasu* for your feedback and review.

To my father, John, your stories are what inspired this effort. Your legacy is a blueprint for Fiji's boxing future. Writing this book was an onerous task, one that I took on not knowing how to start or end it, but once I started, I felt myself being transported back in time, following you around, listening and recalling the events as they transpired. The smell of sweat on the ring canvas and the thud of a gloved fist on the body formed a huge part of the first 12 years of my life. I wouldn't change that for the world.

This book is written to the best of memories and the records as published.

Always, Sylvia.

Bibliography

AAP, 1976. Boxer near death. *The Fiji Times,* Issue April 3, p. 24.

AAP, 1979. Boxers to give up titles. *The Fiji Times,* Issue January 18, p. 19.

Ashenden, M., 2016. *Sky Sports.* [Online]
Available at: http://www.skysports.com/football/news/11686/10558444/hull-city-in-talks-to-sign-former-watford-and-crystal-palace-man-adrian-mariappa
[Accessed 23 October 2016].

Berwick, S., 1978. I am staying here, says Ve. *The Fiji Times,* Issue December 6, p. n.p..

Berwick, S., 1978. It's up to Ve - Ramos. *The Fiji Time,* Issue December 5, p. 20.

Berwick, S., 1979. "It's just a hobby" Ve talks abot what boxing means to him. *The Fiji Times,* Issue February 20, p. n.p..

Box Rec, 2015. *Weight Divisions.* s.l.:s.n.

BoxRec, 1977. *Lawrence Austin vs Hector Thompson.* [Online]
Available at: http://boxrec.com/en/event/62631/103344
[Accessed 25 March 2018].

BoxRec, 1979. *Eusebio Pedroza vs Johnny Aba.* [Online]
Available at: http://boxrec.com/en/event/14588/20909
[Accessed 2 April 2018].

BoxRec, 1979. *Greg Stevens vs Neil Pattell.* [Online]
Available at: http://boxrec.com/en/event/274761/602763
[Accessed 25 March 2018].

BoxRec, 1979. *Lawrence Austin vs Steve Dennis.* [Online]
Available at: http://boxrec.com/en/event/62633/103346
[Accessed 25 March 2018].

BoxRec, 1979. *Steve Dennis vs Neil Pattell.* [Online]
Available at: http://boxrec.com/en/event/152841/480411
[Accessed 25 March 2018].

BoxRec, 2016. *Artie Dixon.* [Online]
Available at: http://boxrec.com/boxer/35798

[Accessed 01 May 2016].

BoxRec, 2016. *Billy Hester.* 2016: s.n.

BoxRec, 2016. *Bobby Sands.* [Online]
Available at: http://boxrec.com/boxer/26322
[Accessed 1 May 2016].

BoxRec, 2016. *Clyde Gray vs. Chris Clarke (2nd meeting).* [Online]
Available at: http://boxrec.com/media/index.php/Clyde_Gray_vs._Chris_Clarke_(2nd_meeting)
[Accessed 11 March 2018].

BoxRec, 2017. *BoxRec.* [Online]
Available at: http://boxrec.com/media/index.php/John_Tate_vs._Gerrie_Coetzee
[Accessed 4 March 2018].

BoxRec, 2017. *Jay Edson.* [Online]
Available at: http://boxrec.com/media/index.php/Jay_Edson
[Accessed 4 February 2018].

BoxRec, n.d. *BoxRec.* [Online]
Available at: http://boxrec.com/en/event/85654/144861
[Accessed 28 February 2018].

BoxRec, n.d. *BoxRec.* [Online]
Available at: http://boxrec.com/media/index.php/Majority_draw
[Accessed 28 February 2018].

BoxRec, n.d. *Elisha Obed.* [Online]
Available at: http://boxrec.com/en/boxer/2379
[Accessed 8 April 2018].

BoxRec, n.d. *Jimmy Carruthers.* [Online]
Available at: http://boxrec.com/en/boxer/16365
[Accessed 13 May 2018].

Cashman, R. I., 2012. *McQuillan, Ernest Edward (Ern) (1905–1988).* [Online]
Available at: http://adb.anu.edu.au/biography/mcquillan-ernest-edward-ern-14219
[Accessed 13 May 2018].

Daunabuna, V., 1976. Sisiwa grabs crown, KO in 50 seconds. *The Fiji Times,* Issue November 15, p. 16.

Daunabuna, V., 1977. Champ gets offer - Catarogo puts both titles on the line. *The Fiji Times,* Issue February 7, p. 16.

Daunabuna, V., 1977. Wili Tarika is still the champ. *The Fiji Times,* Issue April 4, p. 19.

Daunabuna, V., 1978. Azad ready to fight Tarika. *The Fiji Times,* Issue January 26, p. 19.

Daunabuna, V., 1978. Edson will be the ref. *The Fiji Times,* Issue December 2, p. n.p..

Daunabuna, V., 1978. I have no favourite says Edson. *The Fiji Times,* Issue November 30, p. 26.

Daunabuna, V., 1978. Jone after Ve return fight. *The Fiji Times,* Issue May 30, p. 16.

Daunabuna, V., 1978. Ve can expect toughest bout yet-Jone. *The Fiji Times,* Issue January 23, p. 23.

Daunabuna, V., 1978. 'Ve not to last eight'. *The Fiji Times,* Issue January 12, p. 20.

Daunabuna, V., 1978. Ve urged to go overseas - offer to train with Angelo Dundee. *The Fiji Times,* Issue December 4, p. 24.

Daunabuna, V., 1979. Bring on Clyde Gray - Winner Ve throws out the challenge. *The Fiji Times,* Issue November 25, p. 28.

Daunabuna, V., 1979. Hector's fitter than ever. *The Fiji Times,* Issue November 18, p. 28.

Daunabuna, V., 1979. Junior takes title - Bolatawa too beaten to go on - referee. *The Fiji TIMes,* Issue December 9, p. 28.

Daunabuna, V., 1979. Kating is after Ve's title. *The Fiji Times,* Issue July 15, p. 26.

Daunabuna, V., 1979. Ve aims for Gray again - Fight may be held in Suva in October. *The Fiji Times,* Issue April 9, p. 11.

Daunabuna, V., 1979. Weigh-in shock- Mix-up so Thompson wants $500. *The Fiji Times,* Issue November 24, p. 32.

Daunabuna, V., 1980. Austin's in top shape. *The Fiji Times,* Issue February 10, p. 28.

Daunibuna, V., 1977. New-look Basdeo out to get Ve. *The Fiji Times,* Issue February 3, p. 24.

Dean, A., 1977. I can't lose says Ayerst. *The Fiji Times,* Issue December 3, p. 28.

Dean, A., 1978. Peni Bout Plan. *The Fiji Times,* Issue February 20, p. n.p..

Dean, A., 1979. Boxers mean business - confident of wins over Ve and Tarika. *The Fiji Times,* Issue June 22, p. 24.

Dean, A., 1979. Down and out!. *The Fiji Times,* Issue July 1, p. 32.

Dean, A., 1979. New boxer for Tarika. *The Fiji Times,* Issue March 30, p. 32.

Dean, A., 1979. Ramos hits at FPBWA. *The Fiji Times,* Issue July 8, p. 26.

Dean, A., 1979. Tarika is the champ again - Vunimasi given a boxing lesson. *The Fiji Times,* Issue March 19, pp. 10, 11.

Dean, A., 1980. A mismatch - 6th round KO gives Azad the title. *The Fiji Times,* Issue January 21, p. 20.

Dean, A., 1980. It's just like home. *The Fiji Times,* Issue May 24, p. 36.

Dean, A., 1980. Sakaraia still the greatest - Roberts no match for local champ. *The Fiji Times,* Issue August 17, p. 28.

Dhie, F., 2013. *NC Presse - New Caledonie.* [Online]
Available at: https://www.ncpresse.nc/Riviere-Salee-bapteme-de-la-salle-de-boxe-Vincent-Kafoa_a468.html
[Accessed 4 March 2018].

Editorial, 1977. Sunia's barred. *The Fiji Times,* Issue August 9, p. 1.

Editorial, 1977. The Sun says. *The Fiji Sun,* Issue September 22, p. 7.

Edwards, P., 1979. The Fiji Sun. *Give "Ramos" The MBE,* Issue July 27, p. 9.

FASANOC, 1986. *1986 Olympic Handbook.* Suva: FASANOC.

FASANOC, 2016. *2005 Hector Hatch - Boxing.* s.l.:s.n.

Fiji Development Bank, 2012. Jasper's drive to succeed. *Bulakin,* Issue 9, Issue 9, p. 3.

Grimshaw, R., 1980. Oxford Blue for Fiji. *Oxford Mail in The Fiji Times,* Issue June 3, p. 20.

Hanley, D., 2006. *Touching gloves with...Clyde Gray.* [Online]
Available at: http://www.cyberboxingzone.com/boxing/0106-hanley.html
[Accessed 15 April 2018].

Madhavan, V., 1979. Ve won't 'do the dirty'. *The Fiji Times,* Issue September 23, p. 24.

Madhavan, V., 1980. Easy for Ve - King is KO'd in the second round. *The Fiji Times,* Issue April 8, p. 20.

Makin, B., 2016. *Vanuatu Digest.* [Online]
Available at: https://vanuatudigest.com/2016/01/18/three-vanuatu-personalities-dead-heather-lini-leo-philip-kating-mavis-salt/
[Accessed 28 February 2018].

Masi, M., 1980. Hope for blind boxer. *The Fiji Times,* Issue February 5, p. 24.

Masi, M., 1980. Tarika: I don't fear Fotu. *The Fiji Times,* Issue January 10, p. 24.

Masi, M., 1980. Zamal pulls out of fight. *The Fiji Times,* Issue January 19, p. 28.

Naidu, J., 1978. Ramos, Ungerman clash. *The Fiji Sun,* Issue December 1, p. n.p..

Nasse, R., 2016. *Vanuatu Daily Post.* [Online]
Available at: http://dailypost.vu/vanuatu_sports/vanuatu-boxing-family-mourns-the-loss-of-a-hero/article_fdd46bdc-ff45-56f6-acde-08365e1281fc.html
[Accessed 28 February 2018].

Naulivou, S., 1980. It's my belt - Ve says he won't give up the title. *The Fiji Times,* Issue January 22, p. 20.

Naulivou, S., 1980. Sakaraia hopes to fight in the US. *The Fiji Times,* Issue April 1, p. 20.

Rabuka, E., 1975. Catarogo tipped to keep his title. *The Fiji Times,* Issue August 16, p. 24.

Rabuka, E., 1975. Champ makes short work of Vucago. *The Fiji Times,* Issue August 19, p. 16.

Rabuka, E., 1975. Sakaraia to quit amateur ranks. *The Fiji Times,* Issue Wednesday, Octber 15, p. 16.

Rabuka, E., 1975. Singh pulls out of Ve contest. *The Fiji Times,* Issue December 16, p. 28.

Rabuka, E., 1975. Ve fighting fit, ready for Singh. *The Fiji Times,* Issue December 2, p. 28.

Rabuka, E., 1975. Ve fighting fit, ready for Singh. *The Fiji Times,* Issue December 2, p. 28.

Rabuka, E., 1976. *Battered Basdeo nearly gave it up.* Suva: Fiji Times.

Rabuka, E., 1976. Battered Basdeo nearly gave it up. *The Fiji Times,* Issue October 25, p. 15.

Rabuka, E., 1976. Bose to give Dawai crack at his title. *The Fiji Times,* Volume Wednesday, February 15, p. 15.

Rabuka, E., 1976. Ramos predicts early victory for Sakaraia Ve. *The Fiji Times,* Volume Tuesday, January 27, p. 15.

Rabuka, E., 1976. Ve may take on Catarogo if he downs Basdeo. *The Fiji Times,* Issue December 14, p. 16.

Rabuka, E., 1976. Ve wins as Singh hits blow the belt. *The Fiji Times,* 27 April, Issue April 27, p. 16.

Rabuka, E., 1977. Afakasi will be back...as Ve eyes a C'wealth title. *The Fiji Times,* Issue November 7, p. 20.

Rabuka, E., 1977. Ayerst fight with Ve still on. *The Fiji Times,* Issue November 23, p. 23.

Rabuka, E., 1977. Bula punches Tui to defeat in 9th - Champ too good for Fiji fighter. *The Fiji Times,* Issue January 18, p. 16.

Rabuka, E., 1977. End for Ve, says Ayerst. *The Fiji Times,* Issue December 2, p. 12.

Rabuka, E., 1977. Flat-footed Waqabaca not fighter he used to be. *The Fiji Times,* Issue May 4, p. 27.

Rabuka, E., 1977. I'll make it brief says Ve. *The Fiji Times,* Issue November 30, p. 24.

Rabuka, E., 1977. PBWA lifts Ramos ban. *The Fiji Times,* Issue February 15, p. 16.

Rabuka, E., 1977. Ramos in Ve's corner. *The Fiji Times,* Issue November 3, p. 28.

Rabuka, E., 1977. Referee question for title clash. *The Fiji Times,* Issue February 4, p. 24.

Rabuka, E., 1977. Sakaraia looks in top form. *The Fiji Times,* Issue October 26, p. 24.

Rabuka, E., 1977. Southpaw to test Ve. *The Fiji Times,* Issue December 8, p. 28.

Rabuka, E., 1977. Ve does it in eight - according to plan. *The Fiji Times,* Issue July 12, p. 9.

Rabuka, E., 1977. Ve seen as hope for major title in world fight game. *The Fiji Times,* Issue April 7, p. 24.

Rabuka, E., 1977. Ve still not happy about the referee. *The Fiji Times,* Issue February 5, p. 24.

Rabuka, E., 1977. Ve to win inside 10 round: trainer. *The Fiji Times,* Issue July 5, p. 23.

Rabuka, E., 1977. 'What a mismatch' Ve chases Ayerst for 10 rounds. *The Fiji Times,* Issue December 5, p. 23.

Rabuka, E., 1977. You must be fit, warns Ali. *The Fiji Times,* Issue December 23, p. 26.

Rabuka, E., 1978. 7000 sat stunned. *The Fiji Times,* Issue August 20, pp. 12-13.

Rabuka, E., 1978. All over in 10 - Jone. *The Fiji Times,* Issue February 22, p. 28.

Rabuka, E., 1978. 'Bachelor' Gray in great shape. *The Fiji Times,* Issue November 21, p. 24.

Rabuka, E., 1978. Basdeo is a champ...at last!. *The Fiji Times,* Issue May 23, p. 16.

Rabuka, E., 1978. C'mon Ve, let's mix it: Namosi - Ve agrees to fight if purse is right. *The Fiji Times,* Issue September 6, p. 23.

Rabuka, E., 1978. Excuses out for Ve today. *The Fiji Times,* Issue October 14, p. 32.

Rabuka, E., 1978. Gray here 10 days before th fight. *The Fiji Times,* Issue June 20, p. 16.

Rabuka, E., 1978. Gray okays return bout. *The Fiji Times,* Issue September 30, p. 32.

Rabuka, E., 1978. Gray praises Ve 'It was tough...he is a damn good fighter'. *The Fiji Times,* Issue December 4, p. n.p..

Rabuka, E., 1978. Gray wants more money - higher stakes or no return bout, Ungerman. *The Fiji Times,* Issue August 21, p. 20.

Rabuka, E., 1978. Green bout is on - Ramos. *The Fiji Times,* Issue January 2, p. 16.

Rabuka, E., 1978. I won't take pay cut - Ve. *The Fiji Times*, Issue August 22, p. 20.

Rabuka, E., 1978. I'm no Muhammed Ali. *The Fiji Times*, Issue February 15, p. 48.

Rabuka, E., 1978. Is Ve's fight legal?. *The Fiji Times*, Issue November 9, p. 32.

Rabuka, E., 1978. Kaminieli tips upset in title bout. *The Fiji Times*, Issue April 12, p. 31.

Rabuka, E., 1978. No home decisions here - Ali. *The Fiji Times*, Issue August 20, p. n.p..

Rabuka, E., 1978. Our bet - Ve by a knockout. *The Fiji Times*, Issue November n.d., p. n.p..

Rabuka, E., 1978. Painful end - false tooth ends Ve's title hopes. *The Fiji Times*, Issue August 20, p. 24.

Rabuka, E., 1978. PBWA to decide fight - ref. *The Fiji Times*, Issue December 1, p. 32.

Rabuka, E., 1978. PBWAF to discuss promoter. *The Fiji Times*, Issue December 15, p. 35.

Rabuka, E., 1978. Ramos is waiting for answer. *The Fiji Times*, Issue January 10, p. 23.

Rabuka, E., 1978. Ramos offers to put up money to stage Ve's title fight in Fiji. *The Fiji Times*, Issue January 2, p. 15.

Rabuka, E., 1978. Ramos seeks third crack at title. *The Fiji Times*, Issue December 4, p. n.p..

Rabuka, E., 1978. Ramos tips KO in sixth. *The Fiji Times*, Issue June 17, p. 32.

Rabuka, E., 1978. Return bout is possible. *The Fiji Times*, Issue August 20, p. 24.

Rabuka, E., 1978. Round by round. *The Fiji TImes*, Issue December 4, p. n.p..

Rabuka, E., 1978. Sakaraia confident of title victory. *The Fiji Times*, Issue August 11, p. 36.

Rabuka, E., 1978. Science test! Ve's opponent a good mover. *The Fiji Times*, Issue April 5, p. 32.

Rabuka, E., 1978. Tarika promises excitement. *The Fiji TImes,* Issue February 15, p. 48.

Rabuka, E., 1978. The fight is on - Ve gets a shot at Commonwealth title. *The Fiji Times,* Issue June 9, p. 24.

Rabuka, E., 1978. Title fight is OK. *The Fiji Time,* Issue November 10, p. 32.

Rabuka, E., 1978. Tough one for Ve. *The Fiji Times,* Issue October 11, p. 22.

Rabuka, E., 1978. Trainer was not impressed. *The Fiji Times,* Issue December 4, p. 22.

Rabuka, E., 1978. Ungerman brings world-rated ref. *The Fiji Times,* Issue November 29, p. 31.

Rabuka, E., 1978. 'Ve can win on a KO'. *The Fiji Times,* Issue January 7, p. 24.

Rabuka, E., 1978. Ve ranked No.4 contender. *The Fiji Times,* Issue February 7, p. 20.

Rabuka, E., 1978. Ve says no to Kumar. *The Fiji Times,* Issue September 20, p. 28.

Rabuka, E., 1978. Ve should vacate two titles - Vula. *The Fiji Times,* Issue September 29, p. 32.

Rabuka, E., 1978. Ve urged to defend titles. *The Fiji Times,* Issue December 4, p. 22.

Rabuka, E., 1978. Ve wanted to quit in the 11th. *The Fiji Times,* Issue February 27, p. n.p..

Rabuka, E., 1978. Ve will take on the world. *The Fiji Times,* Issue December 29, p. 32.

Rabuka, E., 1978. Ve willing to help Tongans' games effort. *The Fiji Times,* Issue November 27, p. 20.

Rabuka, E., 1978. Ve-Barnett date set. *The Fiji Times,* Issue September 23, p. 32.

Rabuka, E., 1978. West to give Ve a tough fight - Ramos. *The Fiji Times,* Issue February 2, p. 19.

Rabuka, E., 1978. West to give Ve a tough fight - Ramos. *The Fiji Times,* Issue 2 February, p. 19.

Rabuka, E., 1978. What Sakaraia Ve did to Dennis. *The Fiji Times,* Issue January 16, p. 15.

Rabuka, E., 1979. A few hints from a top ref. *The Fiji Times,* Issue June 28, p. 43.

Rabuka, E., 1979. A hard road to the top...but for Ramos, its been worth it. *The Fiji Times,* Issue December 26, p. 20.

Rabuka, E., 1979. Ali is not worried by pressure group. *The Fiji Times,* Issue March 22, p. 31.

Rabuka, E., 1979. And then there were none?. *The Fiji Times,* Issue October 11, p. 24.

Rabuka, E., 1979. Another change for Dawai. *The Fiji Times,* Issue November 13, p. 16.

Rabuka, E., 1979. Baker is due on Saturday. *The Fiji Times,* Issue April 18, p. 28.

Rabuka, E., 1979. Bolatawa looking for another belt. *The Fiji Times,* Issue December 5, p. 31.

Rabuka, E., 1979. Boxing official calls fro changes. *The Fiji TImes,* Issue June 6, p. 21.

Rabuka, E., 1979. Cassius in stand-by to fight Ve. *The Fiji Times,* Issue December 19, p. 35.

Rabuka, E., 1979. Cassius is next in line to fight Sakaraia Ve. *The Fiji TImes,* Issue June 8, p. 22.

Rabuka, E., 1979. Close, but It's a victory to Ve. *The Fiji Times,* Issue August 26, p. 28.

Rabuka, E., 1979. Dawai can move up the list. *The Fiji Times,* Issue August 13, p. 18.

Rabuka, E., 1979. Dundee to visit Fiji - Ali's trainer will be big boost to boxing. *The Fiji Times,* Issue March 21, p. 27.

Rabuka, E., 1979. Fight offer by Bolatawa. *The Fiji Times,* Issue November 21, p. 31.

Rabuka, E., 1979. Gattling warns Ve about Davies. *The Fiji Times,* Issue August 20, p. 19.

Rabuka, E., 1979. Govt asks about Ve bout. *The Fiji Times,* Issue September 29, p. 40.

Rabuka, E., 1979. Hector back in November. *The Fiji Times,* Issue September 25, p. 20.

Rabuka, E., 1979. Hector wants a shot at Clarke here. *The Fiji Times,* Issue November 8, p. 31.

Rabuka, E., 1979. I want a KO, says Thompson. *The Fiji Times,* Issue February 12, p. 24.

Rabuka, E., 1979. It's Dawai on points. *The Fiji Times,* Issue August 19, p. 28.

Rabuka, E., 1979. Kating hits Ve with a challenge. *The Fiji Times,* Issue August 17, p. 24.

Rabuka, E., 1979. Make or break for Ve - Ramos. *The Fiji Times,* Issue November 24, p. 32.

Rabuka, E., 1979. Mataitini after Ve bout. *The Fiji Times,* Issue April 7, p. 43.

Rabuka, E., 1979. Mumtaz invited to UK meeting. *The Fiji Times,* Issue July 4, p. 22.

Rabuka, E., 1979. New date for Ve bout. *The Fiji Times,* Issue November 17, p. 36.

Rabuka, E., 1979. New group offers boxers a $10 rise. *The Fiji Times,* Issue July 23, p. 18.

Rabuka, E., 1979. Nitiva too powerful for Vai. *The Fiji Times,* Issue June 3, p. 27.

Rabuka, E., 1979. Of course I'll go on fighting, says Sakaraia. *The Fiji Times,* Issue February 19, p. 20.

Rabuka, E., 1979. Promoter suspended. *The Fiji Times,* Issue November 28, p. 30.

Rabuka, E., 1979. Promoters bid for Ve. *The Fiji Times,* Issue November 27, p. 20.

Rabuka, E., 1979. Promoter's won't pay Ve's price. *The Fiji Times,* Issue August 22, p. 47.

Rabuka, E., 1979. Ramos, Ve to invite Angelo Dundee here. *The Fiji Times,* Issue January 11, p. 28.

Rabuka, E., 1979. Rebel boxers will get new titles. *The Fiji Times,* Issue July 25, p. 27.

Rabuka, E., 1979. Sakaraia strikes it rich. *The Fiji Times,* Issue November 26, p. 20.

Rabuka, E., 1979. Southpaws no worry for me, says Dawai. *The Fiji Times,* Issue November 2, p. 32.

Rabuka, E., 1979. Tarika at the park?. *The Fiji Times,* Issue October 3, p. 32.

Rabuka, E., 1979. Tarika gets Aba contest. *The Fiji Times,* Issue March 15, p. 28.

Rabuka, E., 1979. Tarika looking for a KO. *The Fiji Times,* Issue April 28, p. 32.

Rabuka, E., 1979. Tarika wins on points. *The Fiji Times,* Issue April 30, p. 19.

Rabuka, E., 1979. Tarikato win by a knock-out - Ramos. *The Fiji Times,* Issue March 17, p. 32.

Rabuka, E., 1979. The man in the middle - Conlan will control the big fight. *The Fiji Times,* Issue November 23, p. 32.

Rabuka, E., 1979. They have what it takes - Edson. *The Fiji Times,* Issue July 2, p. 15.

Rabuka, E., 1979. Thompson may give Ve another chance. *The Fiji Times,* Issue July 11, p. 27.

Rabuka, E., 1979. Thompson's advice to Ve. *The Fiji Times,* Issue February 19, p. 11.

Rabuka, E., 1979. Thomson one of the best, says Tapp. *The Fiji Times,* Issue February 16, p. 24.

Rabuka, E., 1979. US boxer for Wili. *The Fiji Times,* Issue April 26, p. 32.

Rabuka, E., 1979. US boxer pulls out of Suva contest. *The Fiji Times,* Issue March 29, p. 28.

Rabuka, E., 1979. Ve gets new challenger. *The Fiji Times,* Issue December n.d., p. np.

Rabuka, E., 1979. Ve is after a fast KO. *The Fiji Times,* Issue June 15, p. 23.

Rabuka, E., 1979. Ve should not have won - Ali. *The Fiji Times,* Issue August 27, p. 19.

Rabuka, E., 1979. Ve's only work will be boxing. *The Fiji Times,* Issue November 20, p. 18.

Rabuka, E., 1980. A boost to Ve's career. *The Fiji Times*, Issue January 9, p. 24.

Rabuka, E., 1980. Bg fight tonight. *The Fiji Times*, Issue May 31, p. 28.

Rabuka, E., 1980. Bring on Gray - Winner Ve throws out a challenge. *The Fiji Times*, Issue February 17, p. 28.

Rabuka, E., 1980. Dundee wants Fiji fighters. *The Fiji Times*, Issue June 2, p. 23.

Rabuka, E., 1980. I'll fight Ve, says Austin. *The Fiji Times*, Issue January 14, p. 18.

Rabuka, E., 1980. I'll knock Obed cold - Junior. *The Fiji Times*, Issue May 22, p. 31.

Rabuka, E., 1980. Is Veitala new golden boy of Fiji boxing?. *The Fiji Times*, Issue July 28, p. 19.

Rabuka, E., 1980. 'It won't go the distance' Big-puncher King predicts and early finish. *The Fii Times*, Issue April 7, p. 16.

Rabuka, E., 1980. It's 'Cyclone Wally'. *The Fiji Times*, Issue April 13, p. 28.

Rabuka, E., 1980. Man who beat Ve is coming. *The Fiji Times*, Issue June 26, p. 30.

Rabuka, E., 1980. Now Ve chases junior title. *The Fiji Times*, Issue February 19, p. 24.

Rabuka, E., 1980. Obed will fight Junior now. *The Fiji Times*, Issue May 13, p. 20.

Rabuka, E., 1980. Pattel scared to fight Ve, says Ramos. *The Fiji Times*, Issue January 6, p. 26.

Rabuka, E., 1980. Ramos confident his man will win. *The Fiji Times*, Issue May 3, p. 32.

Rabuka, E., 1980. Sakaraia is at his peak...even Austin's trainer says so. *The Fiji Times*, Issue February 14, p. 24.

Rabuka, E., 1980. Tevita Tui making progress in NZ. *The Fiji Times*, Issue June 19, p. 23.

Rabuka, E., 1980. UK boxing chief may watch Ve fight. *The Fiji Times*, Issue February 22, p. 22.

Rabuka, E., 1980. Ve gets third chance at Gray's title. *The Fiji Times*, Issue February 28, p. 24.

Rabuka, E., 1980. Ve receives a top offer. *The Fiji Times,* Issue January 8, p. 16.

Rabuka, E., 1980. Ve will take on ex-champ. *The Fiji Times,* Issue April 2, p. 40.

Rabuka, E., 1980. Veitala's big break comes. *The Fiji Times,* Issue July 25, p. 34.

Rabuka, E., 1980. Ve-Ramos spilt - Obed clash off. *The Fiji Times,* Issue May 9, p. 40.

Rabuka, E., 1980. Watch out Ve - Tabua warns that Austin's in top form. *The Fiji Times,* Issue February 7, p. 24.

Rabuka, E., 1980. Winning combination. *The Fiji Times,* Issue July 4, p. 30.

Rabuka, E., 1980. Yawns as Obed scores. *The Fiji Times,* Issue June 1, p. 28.

Rabuka, E. & Duanabuna, V., 1979. Hector tips an early KO. *The Fiji Times,* Issue November 21, p. n.p..

Rabuka, E. & Masi, M., 1979. Junior will fight Fabiano. *The Fiji Times,* Issue December 20, p. 38.

Rabuka, E., n.d.

Radrodro, F., 1978. For the record. *The Fiji Times,* Issue March 13, p. n.p..

Ritova, S., 1978. A quiet chat boosts my hopes. *The Fiji TImes,* Issue November 24, p. 28.

Ritova, S., 1978. From the sidelines. *The Fiji Times,* Issue December 2, p. n.p..

Ritova, S., 1978. How much is a boxer worth?. *The Fiji Times,* Issue November 17, p. n.p..

Ritova, S., 1978. Sakaraia got me to the church on time. *The Fiji Times,* Issue October 16, p. 24.

Ritova, S., 1978. Ve is learning the hard way. *The Fiji TImes,* Issue December 4, p. 24.

Ritova, S., 1978. Ve must be a certainty to win return fight. *The Fiji Times,* Issue August 21, p. 19.

Ritova, S., 1979. From the sidelines. *The Fiji Times,* Issue February 19, p. 11.

Ritova, S., 1980. I'm golden boy still - Ve. *The Fiji Times,* Issue August 1, p. 44.

Ritova, S., 1980. On Sakaraia, you nearly boobed. *The Fiji Times,* Issue August 18, p. 20.

Sacks, T., 2012. *A Hollow Sporting Footnote in Apartheid-Era South Africa.* [Online]

Available at: http://www.nytimes.com/2012/10/21/sports/gerrie-coetzee-vs-john-tate-in-apartheid-era-south-africa.html

[Accessed 4 March 2018].

Simpson, D., 1977. Setareki a boxer to watch. *The Fiji Times,* Issue June 1, p. 24.

Simpson, D., 1977. Tarika is now after Azad's South Seas title. *The Fiji Times,* Issue December 21, p. 23.

Simpson, D., 1978. Tarika ready for title bout. *The Fiji Times,* Issue January 24, p. 15.

Simpson, D., 1978. Title fight move for Ve. *The Fiji Times,* Issue January 17, p. 16.

Simpson, D., 1978. Ve faces a tough double. *The Fiji Times,* Issue April 29, p. 24.

Simpson, D., 1978. Ve shows his class - NSW's Eadie just not good enough. *The Fiji Times,* Issue June 18, pp. 8-9.

Singh, G., 1980. Boxing in deep trouble. *The Fiji Times,* Issue August 8, p. 32.

Singh, G., 1980. Ramos for Mexico?. *The Fiji Times,* Issue June 4, p. 26.

Singh, G., 1980. Ramos for WBC? Trip may mean big step for Fiji boxing. *The Fiji Times,* Issue April 18, p. 28.

Singh, G., 1980. Ramos to throw in the towel. *The Fiji Times,* Issue May 10, p. n.p..

Singh, G., 1980. Why I resigned from FBC. *The Fiji Times,* Issue August 13, p. 31.

Singh, G. & Daunabuna, V., 1980. Ve fight switch. *The Fiji Times,* Issue March 7, p. 24.

Sport, F. T., 1975. Ve, Tui fighting fit for Monday. *The Fiji Times,* Issue December 12, p. 24.

Sport, F. T., 1976. 6 weeks grace for Singh to defend title. *The Fiji Times,* Issue February 7, p. 24.

Sport, F. T., 1976. Afakasi stripped off his crown. *The Fiji Times,* Issue June 3, p. 24.

Sport, F. T., 1976. Apeang-Ve fight put off due to injury. *The Fiji Times,* Issue June 9, p. 20.

Sport, F. T., 1976. Catarogo to see Ve-Basdeo clash. *The Fiji Times,* Issue December 2, p. 23.

Sport, F. T., 1976. Esala Vula is after lightweight title. *The Fiji Times,* Issue February 6, p. 20.

Sport, F. T., 1976. Ex-champ Shankar will be in Ve's corner. *The Fiji Times,* Issue December 15, p. 19.

Sport, F. T., 1976. I'll dance him silly. *The Fiji Times,* Issue November 11, p. 20.

Sport, F. T., 1976. It's mine till I retire, says Tarika. *The Fiji Times,* Volume October 26, p. 16.

Sport, F. T., 1976. Medallist Basdeo is eager to battle Ve. *The Fiji Times,* Issue August 17, p. 16.

Sport, F. T., 1976. Offer to Ve. *The Fiji Times,* Issue October 7, p. 21.

Sport, F. T., 1976. Put up or shut up, says Tarika. *The Fiji Times,* Issue April 13, p. 20.

Sport, F. T., 1976. Qoro says no to fight with Tarika. *The Fiji Times,* Issue April 22, p. 27.

Sport, F. T., 1976. Row erupts on title battle. *The Fiji Times,* 12 November, Issue November 12, p. 20.

Sport, F. T., 1976. Sakaraia Qoro eye's Ve's title. *The Fiji Times,* Issue April 10, p. 32.

Sport, F. T., 1976. Sakaraia Ve to meet clubmate Tabua tonight. 7 April, Issue April 17, p. 34.

Sport, F. T., 1976. Singh-Ve battle due to take place April 29. *The Fiji Times,* Issue March 11, p. 24.

Sport, F. T., 1976. Sisiwa to face the toughest fight of his career. *The Fiji Times,* Issue November 26, p. 28.

Sport, F. T., 1976. Talks on for Ve to battle Catarogo. *The Fiji Times,* 30 October, Issue October 30, p. 24.

Sport, F. T., 1976. Tarika may bring title back after 20 years. *The Fiji Times,* Issue October 20, p. 23.

Sport, F. T., 1976. Tarika t meet Rabi's Ratu for new title. *The Fiji Times,* Issue December 9, p. 30.

Sport, F. T., 1976. Title fight talks off do Ve-Basdeo return match. *The Fiji Times,* Issue November 2, p. 18.

Sport, F. T., 1976. Title fight talks off for Ve-BAsdeo return match. *The Fiji Times,* Issue November 2, p. 18.

Sport, F. T., 1976. Vakacegu keen to get back into the ring. *The Fiji Times,* 21 October, Issue October 21, p. 16.

Sport, F. T., 1976. Ve and Singh to fight for title. *The Fiji Times,* Issue July 22, p. 22.

Sport, F. T., 1976. Ve pledges to beat Basdeo for Christmas. *The Fiji Times,* Issue December 8, p. 23.

Sport, F. T., 1976. Ve waits patiently for Singh. *The Fiji Times,* Issue February 3, p. 18.

Sport, F. T., 1976. Ve wins as singh hits below belt. *The Fiji Times,* Issue April 27, p. 16.

Sport, F. T., 1976. Ve-Basdeo clash now set up for December 11 - backers fix date. *The Fiji Times,* Issue November 11, p. 24.

Sport, F. T., 1976. Waka and Tevita Tui to clash. *The Fiji Times,* Issue November 16, p. 16.

Sport, F. T., 1976. Weight limit no trouble for Sakaraia. *The Fiji Times,* Issue April 21, p. 15.

Sport, F. T., 1976. Wili Tarika spurns 'unknown' Azad. *The Fiji Times,* Issue November 25, p. 23.

Sport, F. T., 1977 . It's a fine comeback by Vakacegu. *The Fiji Times,* Volume February 7, p. 8.

Sport, F. T., 1977. Angry trainer hits out after loss - Tarika has it wn all the way - Ramos. *The Fiji Times,* Issue June 13, p. 14.

Sport, F. T., 1977. Azad second rate - Ramos. *The Fiji Times,* Issue July 7, p. 19.

Sport, F. T., 1977. Basdeo, Ve both predict title battle knockouts. *The Fiji Times,* Issue January 6, p. 23.

Sport, F. T., 1977. Catarogo banned for life for blow at ref. *The Fiji TImes,* Issue April 22, p. 24.

Sport, F. T., 1977. Catarogo to get first go at title. *The Fiji Times,* Issue August 9, p. 15.

Sport, F. T., 1977. Catarogo to get first go at title. *The Fiji Times,* Issue August 9, p. 15.

Sport, F. T., 1977. Catarogo will fight Rauga on July 22. *The Fiji Times,* Issue July 14, p. 28.

Sport, F. T., 1977. Champ at peak fitness for Ve fight. *The Fiji Times,* Issue March 23, p. 20.

Sport, F. T., 1977. Champ at peak fitness for Ve fight. *The Fiji Times,* Issue March 23, p. 20.

Sport, F. T., 1977. Dead boxer's family will get help from champ. *The Fiji Times,* Issue February 12, p. 20.

Sport, F. T., 1977. Decision today on Ramos. *The Fiji Times,* Issue November 2, p. 23.

Sport, F. T., 1977. Everyone wants Ve. *The Fiji Times,* Issue November 9, p. 24.

Sport, F. T., 1977. Eye injury puts Ve out for 4 weeks. *The Fiji Times,* Issue February 8, p. 15.

Sport, F. T., 1977. Fight purse row. *The Fiji Times,* Issue April 4, p. 20.

Sport, F. T., 1977. Gallant Basdeo slugs it out until he 13th. *The Fiji Times,* Issue February 7, p. 16.

Sport, F. T., 1977. I'll finish Azad, says Tarika. *The Fiji Times,* Issue February 18, p. 19.

Sport, F. T., 1977. I'm not sorry: Ramos. *The Fiji Times,* Issue September 9, p. 19.

Sport, F. T., 1977. I'm ready for Ve, says Rauga. *The Fiji Times,* Issue December 19, p. 19.

Sport, F. T., 1977. Just a 'brief encounter'...and not a test of skill. *The Fiji Times,* Issue December 5, p. 24.

Sport, F. T., 1977. Lautoka man aims to form rival boxing body. *The Fiji Times,* Issue July 21, p. 23.

Sport, F. T., 1977. New pro boxer aids family. *The Fiji Times,* Issue May 23, p. 23.

Sport, F. T., 1977. PBWA bars Ramos for 'outbursts'. *The Fiji TImes*, Issue September 22, p. 24.

Sport, F. T., 1977. PBWA lifts Catarogo's life ban. *The Fiji Times*, Issue July 6, p. 19.

Sport, F. T., 1977. Prasad wants to take on Ve. *The Fiji Times*, Issue August 9, p. 15.

Sport, F. T., 1977. Promoter gives way for Ve. *The Fiji Times*, Issue October 12, p. 20.

Sport, F. T., 1977. Ramos says no to PBWA election. *The Fiji Times*, Issue February 17, p. 14.

Sport, F. T., 1977. Ramos will still train his boxers. *The Fiji Times*, Issue February 8, p. 15.

Sport, F. T., 1977. Switch by Cama to Ramos club. *The Fiji Times*, Issue July 14, p. 26.

Sport, F. T., 1977. Tahitian Champ will have his eye on Ve. *The Fiji Times*, Issue January 20, p. 23.

Sport, F. T., 1977. Tarika will fight only 'a fit Singh'. *The Fiji Times*, Issue August 12, p. 23.

Sport, F. T., 1977. Tui lost because he ignored plan - manager. *The Fiji Times*, Volume January 19, p. 19.

Sport, F. T., 1977. Ve is urged: Quit titles. *The Fiji Times*, Issue September 24, p. 28.

Sport, F. T., 1977. Ve looks for bout with PNG man. *The Fiji Times*, Issue April 6, p. 28.

Sport, F. T., 1977. Ve now ready to fight Prasad for title. *The Fiji Times*, Issue July 13, p. 22.

Sport, F. T., 1977. Ve out after fourth title - He'll meet Catarogo in Suva on April 4. *The Fiji Times*, Issue February 23, p. 24.

Sport, F. T., 1977. Ve pleads: Lift ban on Inia Catarogo - Life sentence under fire. *The Fiji Times*, Issue May 14, p. 28.

Sport, F. T., 1977. Ve sends another $20 to boxer's daughter. *The Fiji Times*, Issue April 6, p. 28.

Sport, F. T., 1977. Ve to meet Aust champ next year. *The Fiji Times*, Issue November 26, p. 28.

Sport, F. T., 1977. Ve wants a title fight every month. *The Fiji Times,* Volume April 22, p. 23.

Sport, F. T., 1977. Ve wants quick end to Rauga bout. *The Fiji Times,* Issue December 16, p. 24.

Sport, F. T., 1977. Ve warned: don't try and mix it. *The Fiji Times,* Issue March 30, p. 24.

Sport, F. T., 1977. Ve warned: don't try to mix it. *The Fiji Times,* Issue March 30, p. 24.

Sport, F. T., 1977. Waka offers to fight for title. *The Fiji Times,* Issue July 6, p. 23.

Sport, F. T., 1978. "Ve making a mistake"... *The Fiji Times,* Issue February 23, p. 24.

Sport, F. T., 1978. A whole new slate for Ve. *The Fiji Times,* Issue February 6, p. 16.

Sport, F. T., 1978. Basdeo now wants shot at Ve's title. *The Fiji Times,* Issue November 24, p. 28.

Sport, F. T., 1978. Boxers warned - 14-day layoff is the rule - PBWA man. *The Fiji Times,* Issue December 7, p. 16.

Sport, F. T., 1978. Gray says: 'I've fought harder hotters than Ve'. *The Fiji Times,* Issue December 1, p. 31.

Sport, F. T., 1978. I dont wan't this man - challenger. *The Fiji Times,* Issue November 30, p. 28.

Sport, F. T., 1978. Mocesui hangs up gloves. *The Fiji Times,* Issue December 22, p. 41.

Sport, F. T., 1978. PBWA looks at neutral official. *The Fiji Times,* Issue November 27, p. 20.

Sport, F. T., 1978. Ramos asks PBWA to strip Azad of his title. *The Fiji Times,* Issue October 13, p. 30.

Sport, F. T., 1978. Ramos' trainer here for bout. *The Fiji Times,* Issue November 21, p. 24.

Sport, F. T., 1978. Ruling may upset Ve fight. *The Fiji Times,* Issue November 4, p. 32.

Sport, F. T., 1978. Sugar Ray is interested in Ve: Sain. *The Fiji Times,* Issue November 1, p. 24.

Sport, F. T., 1978. Tarika told to meet Fotu first. *The Fiji Times,* Issue April 18, p. 20.

Sport, F. T., 1978. Tarika wants title fight: Ramos. *The Fiji Times,* Issue November 1, p. 22.

Sport, F. T., 1978. Top US man to help Ve. *The Fiji Times,* Issue November 18, p. 32.

Sport, F. T., 1978. Tui tells Dawai 'I'll fight you'. *The Fiji Times,* Issue May 6, p. 30.

Sport, F. T., 1978. Ve can have next crack - Gray. *The Fiji Times,* Issue May 9, p. 16.

Sport, F. T., 1978. Ve ready for 'busy' fight with Barnett. *The Fiji Tmes,* Issue October 12, p. 28.

Sport, F. T., 1978. Ve takes two weeks leave. *The Fiji Times,* Issue November 23, p. 30.

Sport, F. T., 1978. Vunimasi, Tarika fight on. *The Fiji TImes,* Issue November 21, p. 24.

Sport, F. T., 1979. Ali tips a win for Thompson. *The Fiji Times,* Issue November 22, p. 26.

Sport, F. T., 1979. Bolatawa wants anothr chance. *The Fiji Times,* Issue December 12, p. 24.

Sport, F. T., 1979. Boxing dates clash. *The Fiji Times,* Issue January 12, p. 28.

Sport, F. T., 1979. Champ Tarika is fighting fit. *The Fij Times,* Issue June 21, p. 20.

Sport, F. T., 1979. Dawai fight gets a permit. *The Fiji Times,* Issue August 18, p. 28.

Sport, F. T., 1979. Dawai fight gets permit. *The Fiji Times,* Issue August 18, p. 28.

Sport, F. T., 1979. Dawai fight in doubt. *The Fiji Times,* Issue August 10, p. 22.

Sport, F. T., 1979. Dawai issues challenge to Kating. *The Fiji Times,* Issue December 5, p. 31.

Sport, F. T., 1979. Defeat? No way, says Ramos. *The Fiji Times,* Issue November 23, p. 32.

Sport, F. T., 1979. Fight weight limit set. *The Fiji Times,* Issue December 20, p. 38.

Sport, F. T., 1979. Hundreds watch Aba spar. *The Fiji Times,* Issue October 17, p. 36.

Sport, F. T., 1979. I'm not going to settle in Aust: Ve. *The Fiji Times,* Issue April 10, p. 24.

Sport, F. T., 1979. Junior knows but won't say. *The Fiji Times,* Issue December 6, p. 39.

Sport, F. T., 1979. PBWA is biased - Dawai. *The Fiji Times,* Issue July 12, p. 24.

Sport, F. T., 1979. Probe into boxing. *The Fiji Times,* Issue November 30, p. 36.

Sport, F. T., 1979. Semesa can earn a title chance. *The Fiji Times,* Issue November 22, p. 28.

Sport, F. T., 1979. South African fight lined up for Ve. *The Fiji Times,* Issue December 24, p. 28.

Sport, F. T., 1979. Take Dundee offer, pro tells Ve. *The Fiji TImes,* Issue January 11, p. 28.

Sport, F. T., 1979. Tarika is offered NZ fight. *The Fiji Times,* Issue March 7, p. 24.

Sport, F. T., 1979. Tarika to rest at hotel before fight. *The Fiji Times,* Issue April 20, p. 32.

Sport, F. T., 1979. Tarika to rest at hotel before fight. *The Fiji Times,* Issue April 20, p. 32.

Sport, F. T., 1979. Thompson happy with date change. *The Fiji Times,* Issue January 18, p. 19.

Sport, F. T., 1979. Ve and Ramos are willing to negotiate. *The Fiji Times,* Issue November 28, p. 30.

Sport, F. T., 1979. Ve finished training for his title defence. *The Fiji Times,* Issue April 6, p. 23.

Sport, F. T., 1979. Ve has a price on his head. *The Fiji Times,* Issue July 17, p. 14.

Sport, F. T., 1979. Ve is willing to meet Azad...for $3000. *The Fiji TImes,* Issue July 3, p. 14.

Sport, F. T., 1979. Ve seeks another shot. *The Fiji Times,* Issue September 12, p. 24.

Sport, F. T., 1979. Ve to finish Paula in 4, says Ramos. *The Fiji TImes,* Issue April 3, p. 19.

Sport, F. T., 1979. Ve's next bout is in Suva on August 25. *The Fiji Times,* Issue August 9, p. 22.

Sport, F. T., 1979. Ve's U.S. oppoent named. *The Fiji Times,* Issue April 14, p. 28.

Sport, F. T., 1979. Ve-Thompson fight gets ABF approval. *The Fiji Times,* Issue January 23, p. 20.

Sport, F. T., 1979. Vunimasi joins Ramos. *The Fiji Times,* Issue October 16, p. 19.

Sport, F. T., 1980 . Fossie fighting fit - 'I will win in five' - Schmidt. *The Fiji Times,* Issue April 12, p. 36.

Sport, F. T., 1980. A gift of hope for Tevita Tui. *The Fiji Times,* Issue February 22, p. 22.

Sport, F. T., 1980. A great fight, promises Ramos. *The Fiji Times,* Issue February 15, p. 28.

Sport, F. T., 1980. Aba gets a new Fiji challenge. *The Fiji Times,* Issue March 24, p. 23.

Sport, F. T., 1980. Austin's style impresses Ramos. *The Fiji Times,* Issue February 13, p. 22.

Sport, F. T., 1980. Bad news and good news for fight followers. *The Fiji Times,* Issue August 30, p. 29.

Sport, F. T., 1980. Big fight finalised. *The Fiji Times,* Issue May 3, p. 32.

Sport, F. T., 1980. Canada trip may bring Gray to Fiji. *The Fiji Times,* Issue January 14, p. 18.

Sport, F. T., 1980. Dawai to take on Kating. *The Fiji Times,* Issue January 25, p. 24.

Sport, F. T., 1980. For boxers, a home away from home. *The Fiji Times,* Issue January 24, p. n.p..

Sport, F. T., 1980. Fotu signs with Bala. *The Fiji Times,* Issue May 22, p. 31.

Sport, F. T., 1980. Green light for Ve to fight Gray. *The Fiji Times,* Issue March 10, p. 19.

Sport, F. T., 1980. Kating wants too much, says Dawai. *The Fiji Times,* Issue February 9, p. 27.

Sport, F. T., 1980. Obed looking good. *The Fiji Times,* Issue May 27, p. 19.

Sport, F. T., 1980. Ramesh goes out...then boot goes in. *The Fiji Times,* Issue January 21, p. 19.

Sport, F. T., 1980. Ramos is WBC official. *The Fiji Times,* Issue March 20, p. 20.

Sport, F. T., 1980. Ravula fight in doubt - Fiji boxer hurt, but Ramos says he'll recover. *The Fiji Times,* Issue April 10, p. 28.

Sport, F. T., 1980. Some bad news for Tagicakibau. *The Fiji Times,* Issue January 26, p. 35.

Sport, F. T., 1980. Tarika takes on Aba in PNG. *The Fiji Times,* Issue March 20, p. 20.

Sport, F. T., 1980. The cost of bringing Ali. *The Fiji Times,* Issue June 3, p. 20.

Sport, F. T., 1980. Title or nothing - Dawai. *The Fiji Times,* Issue January 27, p. 15.

Sport, F. T., 1980. Ve fight is on tomorrow. *The Fiji Times,* Issue April 6, p. 28.

Sport, F. T., 1980. Ve pulls out of fight with Tanoa. *The Fiji Times,* Issue June 25, p. 32.

Sport, F. T., 1980. Welcome back chanp - Ve returning to the ring. *The Fiji Times,* Issue June 24, p. 20.

Sport, S., 1977. Ban on boxing man doesn't stop talk. *The Fiji Sun,* Issue September 24.

Sport, S., 1977. 'Dear John' Letter gets W.P.B. Treatment. *The Fiji Sun,* Issue September 14.

Sports, F. T., 1976. Basdeo to fall - champ Ve predicts. *The Fiji Times,* Issue October 23, p. 24.

Sports, F. T., 1976. Boxers to help children. *The Fiji Times,* Issue June 16, p. 16.

Sports, F. T., 1976. Tui wants to floor Tongan middleweight. *The Fiji Times,* Issue November 10, p. 19.

Sports, F. T., 1977. I'm not sorry: Ramos. *The Fiji Times,* Issue September 9, p. 19.

Sports, F. T., 1980. FBC titles up for grabs. *The Fiji Times,* Issue January 7, p. 19.

Sports, F. T., 1980. Reports dont worry our boy. *The Fiji Times,* Issue February 8, p. 24.

Sports, F. T., 1980. Set for a great battle. *The Fiji Times,* Issue February 16, p. 32.

Sports, F. T., 1980. Top ranked fight arranged for Ve. *The Fiji Times,* Issue August 29, p. 33.

Sports, F. T., 1980. Tui's off to NZ. *The Fiji Times,* Issue March 7, p. 22.

Sports, F. T., 1980. Why the Ve fight will be in Lautoka. *The Fiji Times,* Issue March 13, p. 26.

Sports, S., 2000-2016. *Jimmy Carruthers.* [Online]
Available at: http://www.sports-reference.com/olympics/athletes/ca/jimmy-carruthers-1.html
[Accessed 29 May 2016].

Sports, T., 1975. Tarika to turn professional after Monday. *The Fiji Times,* Issue 25 November, p. 16.

Sport, T., 1975. Champ says he can beat Ve. *The Fiji Times,* Issue November 12, p. 19.

Sport, T., 1975. Champion Catarogo to fight Radaniva. *The Fiji Times,* Issue August 30, p. 43.

Sport, T., 1978. Jone confident he can beat Ve. *The Fiji Times,* Issue February 4, p. n.p..

Sport, T., 1978. Ve still has not mad up mind on title. *The Fiji Times,* Issue March 3, p. 26.

Sport, T., 1979. Tarika to fight Robert?. *The Fiji Times,* Issue February 19, p. n.p..

Thompson, R., 1979. Ve-ry distressing. *The Fiji Times,* Issue February 19, p. n.p..

Thomson, R., 1979. Gray may be back in June. *The Fiji Times,* Issue February 6, p. 20.

Thomson, R., 1979. The end for Ve, says Hector. *The Fiji Times,* Issue February 6, p. 20.

Thomson, R., 1979. Title is Fotu's traget. *The Fiji Times,* Issue December 12, p. 28.

Thomson, R., 1979. Ve can't afford to lose!. *The Fiji Times,* Issue January 18, p. 28.

Times, F., 1980. Nasinu queen. *The Fiji Times,* Issue August 11, p. n.p..

Times, T. S., 1979. Sokeraia -Ve gets gloves on new title. *The Sunday Times,* Issue November 25, p. 1.

Uncensored, F., 2009. *Roving ambassador Ross Ligairi passes away.* [Online]

Available at: https://fijiuncensored.wordpress.com/2009/05/21/roving-ambassador-ross-ligairi-passes-away/

[Accessed 22 April 2018].

Up, F., 1977. Critises boxing group's secretary. *The Fiji Sun,* Volume September 30.

Veisamasama, J., 1979. Boxing Council. *The Fiji Sun,* Issue July 27, p. 9.

Volavola, E., 1976. *Its mine till I retire says Tarika.* Suva: The Fiji Times.

Volavola, E., 1976. Lautoka fights will show young talent. *The Fiji Times,* 21 January, Issue January 21, p. 19.

Volavola, E., 1976. Lautoka fights will show young talent. *The Fiji Times,* Issue January 21, p. 19.

Volavola, E., 1976. Ve, Basdeo in return bout. *The Fiji Times,* Issue October 26, p. 16.

Volavola, E., 1976. Ve, the ko king, may do it again. *The Fiji Times,* Issue October 21, p. 16.

Volavola, E., 1977. Catarogo in Suva for tough battle tonight. *The Fiji Times,* Issue April 1, p. 24.

Volavola, E., 1977. Ramos won't be in Ve's corner - Manager steps down for 'vital' fight. *The Fiji Times,* Issue October 6, p. 20.

Volavola, E., 1977. Ve faces big test against tough ring veteran. *The Fiji Times,* Issue June 4, p. 28.

[1] *Kati* is a like a raffle but with playing cards. A suit or the entire card park are sold for a nominal amount per card to win a prize. The winning card is drawn from another deck of cards that either matches the suit in play or the whole pack with the winner taking home the prize at stake. This is repeated with each prize.